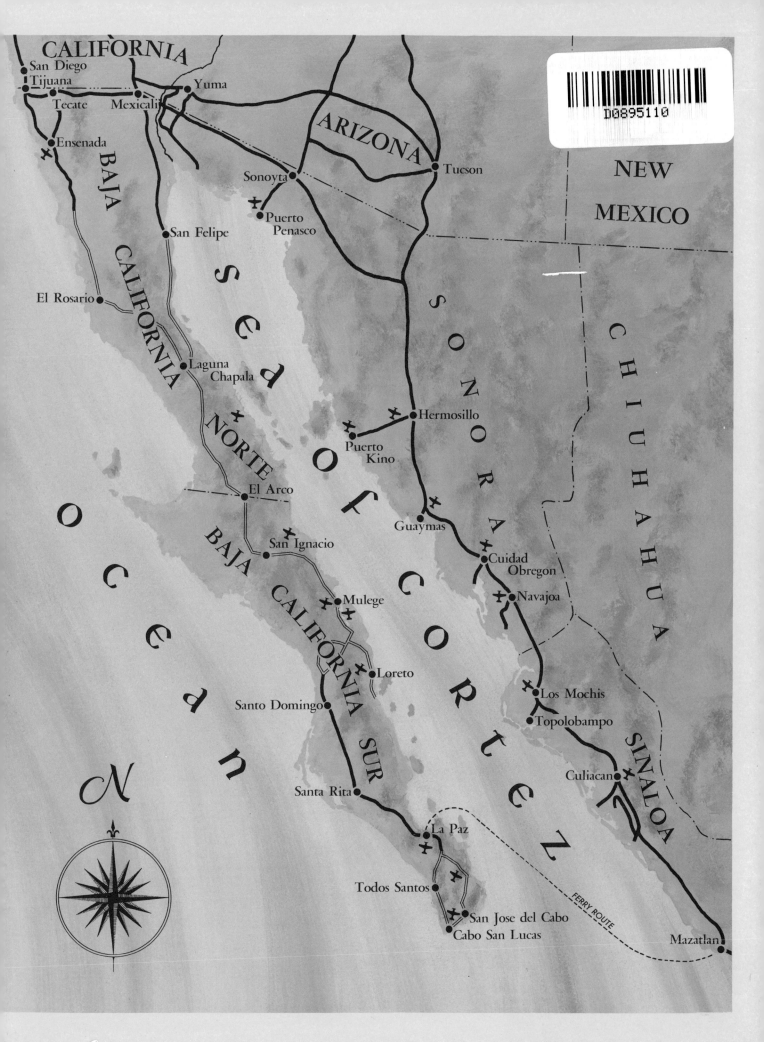

The SEA of CORTEZ

A Sunset Book

THE SEA of

Travel Editor of Sunset Magazine: Martin Litton

Supervising Editor: Jack McDowell

Contributing Editors: Dorothy Krell, Frederic M. Rea, Mary Smith

Book Design and Layout: William Gibson, Joe Seney

Maps: Michael Fahay, William Burke, Peter Slavinskis

Botanical Illustrations: Thomas Creath Watson

Marine Life Illustrations: Michael Fahay

Marine Life Consultant: Dr. Boyd Walker
HEAD OF FISHERIES STUDIES, UNIVERSITY OF CALIFORNIA AT LOS ANGELES

Lane Magazine & Book Company • Menlo Park, California

CORTEZ

by **RAY CANNON** and the Sunset Editors

This book was printed and bound in San Francisco, California. Color and duotone pages were printed by Stecher-Traung Schmidt Corp., using lithograph film made by Balzer-Shopes. Jacket and cover were lithographed by Stecher-Traung Schmidt, and the binding was by Cardoza Bookbinding Company. Body type is Caledonia, composed by Holmes Typography, Inc., San Jose, California. Type for heads is Garamond. Paper for body pages is Mountie Enamel; paper for the single-color signature is Mountie Offset Antique — both furnished by Northwest Paper Company, Cloquet, Minnesota.

FRONT COVER: *Sunrise at Loreto by Martin Litton.* BACK COVER: *Ranch in the Cape Region by Harry Merrick.* TITLE PAGE: *Black Marlin by Al Tetzlaff. Endsheet design by Joe Seney.*

FOREWORD

It comes as a surprise to most Americans — particularly those in the
Western United States — to learn that an undiscovered world of natural
beauty lies only a few miles below the U.S.-Mexican border. A calm,
peaceful body of water for most of the year, the Sea of Cortez is bounded
on the east by the Mexican Mainland, on the west by Baja California.
Little of this region of primitive contrasts has been seen, and little of a
general nature has been published to tell of it.

The editors of *Sunset Magazine* have for years traveled into both the
Mainland and Baja. They have logged many miles along the coasts of the
Cortez. Their findings, appearing from time to time in *Sunset*, have
stimulated those vacationers who have a yen to seek out new and
interesting places.

Of all explorers of the Sea of Cortez, none is more knowledgeable than
Ray Cannon. Few other people have his understanding and sympathy
for this place of fresh beauty — none has his vision and know-how of the
waters and of the fish that exist in primeval abundance. He has explored
the islands; he has charted the shores and measured the depths; he has
hunted the game of the land and caught the fish of the sea.

This book has been long in the making because there has been much to
investigate, much to include. The story of the Sea of Cortez is long
overdue, but the time to tell it is now.

CONTENTS

Useful Information

Maps

NOTE: The maps shown in this book are as accurate as present information permits but are not intended to be used for navigational purposes.

THE STORY OF
The Sea of Cortez

A primitive world of beauty and adventure that begins less than fifty miles below the southwest border of the United States

Less than fifty miles south of the United States-Mexico border, there starts a vast body of water—a rich and enchanting sea bounded on three sides by Mexico, and open at the bottom to the Pacific Ocean. Though this sea has existed since the Pliocene Epoch, though it has been part of recorded history for nearly 500 years, and though it is but an hour by air from Los Angeles, the area is one of the least known places on the globe.

The Sea of Cortez (Gulf of California on most U.S. maps) is the youngest of all the seas as reckoned in geologic years. In many ways this relative youth has made this sea quite different from any other. Her surface is calm most of the time, her depths fish-crowded all of the time. She has a hundred uninhabited islands, some of which are yet to be explored. Her east side, the mainland of Mexico, is sparsely settled. Her west side, the arid, mountainous peninsula of Baja, is also barely populated with humans; but it is alive with burrowing, running, and flying animal life.

If there were other places that could be used as a basis for comparison, describing this extensive slice of Mexico might be easy. But where else can be found the likes of a sea vagabond's beach shack made of palm leaves and driftwood, as well as a resort with Roman baths made of onyx? Where else are there hundreds of miles of roads like El Camino Real that were once traveled by the Indians, conquistadores, and padres, then left to be obliterated by growth for two centuries, then revived? Where else are there grotesque masses of thorned shrubs, dry vines, and bare trees that become transformed by the first seasonal rains into brilliant seas of blossoms, aglow with reds, yellows, blues, and greens?

THE CORTEZ STARTS HERE AT BAJA'S TIP.
The calm of the upper Cortez is not apparent at Cabo San Lucas, where a foam-laced ocean enters the placid, land-protected Gulf of California. This arch is at the very bottom of the Peninsula.

Where else is there a sea as clear as crystal, as warm as a bath, as calm as a mirror? Where else are there waters so full of life that even a beginner can catch a dozen different species of game fish within a period of less than an hour and a distance of less than a mile?

This is a land of contrasts. Its extremes range from sand-swept deserts to tropical jungles, from ragged mountains to valleys of wheat and sugar cane, from thatched huts to grand resorts. Its weather can be soporific or fearsome, its beauty grotesque or lovely. Whatever the extreme, whoever the observer, this is a land capable of charming the most sophisticated and softening the most blasé.

AN EARTHQUAKE-CREATED SEA

The creation of the Sea of Cortez occurred between ten and fifteen million years ago and was a result of violent action along the San Andreas fault zone, which still runs through most of the length of California. When Mother Earth gave birth to this sea, it was with great travail. There was a volcanic swelling, then a catastrophic faulting, in which the earth ripped wide. A large chunk of the west side of Mexico was lifted and wrenched free, forming a new peninsula. Between it and the mainland a gaping chasm opened, and the Pacific Ocean tore into the crevasse, producing a brand new sea.

In the upheaval the mountainous Baja California Peninsula tilted westward along the faulting line. Some of the volcanic peaks along this line split off and slid into the abyss, leaving their tops projecting above the water to form a chain of islands close off the Baja coast.

The gullies between the islands and the Peninsula are called channels. The deep troughs farther out, in the Sea's bottom, are termed basins. One 1800-fathom (10,800 feet) basin was recently found east of La Paz. That's more than two miles deep—and twice the depth of the deepest lake in the world, Lake Baikal in Siberia.

Because of its expansive width and depth, the Cortez was able to absorb some tremendous land intrusions. These included quantities of loose rock and earth that had been transported by the glaciers of the Ice Age before the Sea's formation, as well as sands and silts later washed from the soft slopes of the Mexican mainland or carried down from eroding Baja mountains. As a result of earthquake action connected with the San Andreas fault, whose south end disappears under the delta of the Colorado River, cliffs were shaken loose along both shores of the Sea, sending rock and earth in sizable landslides into the water. (Even today many of Mexico's earthquakes originate in the Gulf.) A small percentage of the water was displaced by volcanoes, which continued to balloon up and to spew over to modern times, forming lofty peaks and new islands. The most recent contribution came from the silts carried into the Sea from the vast watershed of the Colorado River.

Nearly everywhere along the Baja side of the Sea, one or another of these filling activities has created shelves at varying depths. All of the surfaces are now cool and quiet, save for an occasional issue of hot water at several places along the southern shores of the Peninsula.

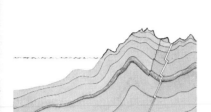

SAN ANDREAS fault caused part of Mexico's west coast to split off Mainland.

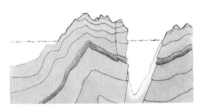

THE PACIFIC flooded into the gap, separating the new peninsula from the Mainland.

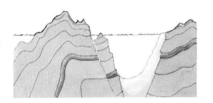

VOLCANIC PEAKS along the gap fell into the chasm, forming chains of coastal islands.

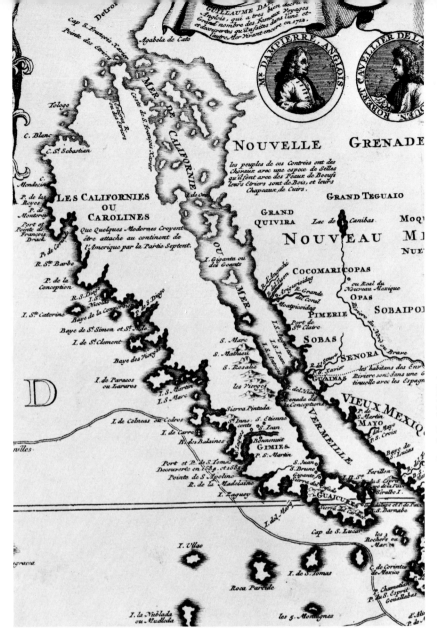

A VERY CURIOUS MAP of Baja
published in 1719, shows this
piece of land ("Les Californies ou
Carolines") to be an island, but
indicates that some explorers of the
time believed it to be connected to the
American continent at its northern end.

For a time the Cortez was thought to have extended up over California's Imperial Valley for a length of more than 1,000 miles, but recent studies of fossils have failed to verify this. The natural dam separating the Sea and Valley is attributed to Ice Age deposits, not to transported Colorado River silts.

INDIANS WERE THE FIRST

The meager history of the Sea and the lands around it is concerned principally with hunters of treasure, with promoters of Christianity, and with seekers of geographical and scientific knowledge. Most of the sporadic endeavors to colonize met with failure, leaving for the record a scattering of primitive artifacts, crumbling missions, and forgotten ranches.

Baja was first inhabited by a people who had moved from Asia across the Bering Strait to Alaska, then down the Pacific Coast of the North American Continent into the Peninsula. In this warm territory they had little need for either housing or clothing, and their ambitions extended little further than satisfying their frequent hunger pangs.

The intrusion by civilized man started when Hernando Cortez, the conqueror of Mexico, dispatched a small vessel commanded by Diego de Becerra in search of the legendary "Seven Cities of Cibola," said to have been the source of the fabulous treasures of Montezuma, the great Aztec ruler defeated by Cortez in 1520. It was a disastrous voyage. Becerra was killed by his crew, who in turn were nearly all slaughtered by Indians when they put in at La Paz. Hearing accounts of the great quantities of pearls at La Paz from the few who escaped, Cortez himself landed there in 1535. He found the pearl stories to be true and outfitted several expeditions.

In 1539 Cortez sent three ships under the command of Francisco de Ulloa to explore further. The expedition sailed north all the way to the mouth of the Colorado River. They discovered that what was called "California" was not an island, as they had believed, but a peninsula, and that the supposed channel was actually a contained body of water. Ulloa named the waters El Mar de Cortez (The Sea of Cortez) in honor of his benefactor. He subsequently sailed around the whole Peninsula to discover the bay which would later be named Bahia Magdalena.

MISSIONS AND BUCCANEERS

The first successful and permanent settlement on the Peninsula was established at Loreto by the Jesuit Order of the Roman Catholic Church under the leadership of Father Juan Maria Salvatierra, who founded a mission there in 1698. Loreto thus became the first capital of both Baja (Lower) and Alta (Upper) California.

One of the most outstanding figures in early California history was the heroic Jesuit missionary, Father Juan Ugarte, who constructed the first ship to be built in the Californias. With only a handful of Indians and a few soldiers, he made a long and perilous journey from Loreto far inland and back over almost inaccessible and mountainous terrain to procure timber. The vessel was completed in 1719 and christened *El Triunfo de la Cruz* (The Triumph of the Cross).

According to church historians, thirty missions (Jesuit, Franciscan, and Dominican) were erected in Baja California. All were built and abandoned by 1854. Very few were ever rebuilt, but in several areas new churches were constructed in the vicinity of the crumbling ruins of the old. There are remnants of all but seven of these early missions. The best preserved and perhaps the finest in Baja is the mission of San Francisco Javier de Vigge, at the village of San Javier, southwest of Loreto.

Some of the missions were believed to have been storage places for vast treasures of gold, silver, and pearls, supposedly hidden there by the Jesuits. It was they who did most of the pioneering of Baja California before being expelled by Spain.

In 1768 the Franciscan Friars, led by Father Junipero Serra, replaced the Jesuits and built one mission on the Peninsula, then moved north to Alta California where they founded the chain of missions that is such a proud heritage of the State of California. The Franciscans, in turn, were

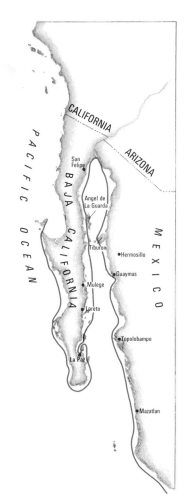

FRANCISCO DE ULLOA sailed north from Acapulco, then around all of Baja.

succeeded in Baja by the Dominicans, who founded nine more missions.

The confusion following the switches of religious orders and the various Indian uprisings left most of the missions deserted. The final blow came in 1829 with the revolution that separated Mexico from Spain, after which Spaniards were deported.

During these early years, Baja California was also a favorite hangout for two other types of visitors—adventurers and pirates. The pearls from the Sea's oysters and Baja's precious metals (augmented by fantastic stories of Indian gold) drew adventurers from all over the world and made piracy in the Sea especially lucrative. Many of the Pacific's notorious pirates sought protection in the Sea's sheltered harbors and left their names on rocks that shielded beaches where they stashed their treasure. Also among Baja's lawless visitors were buccaneers who despoiled Spanish-American treasures, pillaged coastal settlements, and hijacked slave ships.

History tells of the greed of these early adventurers and treasure seekers and of the toll it took in the lives of the natives. In some instances, whole Baja California Indian populations disappeared. The intruders either killed the Indians or forced them to flee.

IN RECENT YEARS there has been another type of adventurer who—unlike earlier exploiters—is understood and sincerely welcomed by the present-day citizens of Baja. These are the sportsmen, boat-owners, and outdoor-loving families from the United States who enjoy what the rugged country and its people offer and take nothing away except happy memories. Between the gentle, humor-loving Baja Californians and these visitors there is a feeling of compatible equality.

Nevertheless, tourism below the border towns is not likely to flourish in the immediate future. There still are vast wilderness stretches so remote that their fishing and hunting have never been tried, their quiet beauty never experienced. And even in some of the frequented places, transportation, accommodations, and services are limited.

NEAR RIO ALTAR, *Tubutama is one of 25 missions founded in Sonora by Father Kino.*

MISSION *San Antonio de Oquitoa is reached by Mainland dirt road from Santa Ana.*

How California Got its Name

The land below the border may have been indirectly instrumental in the naming of the American state of California. The origin of the name "California" is believed by some historians to have been derived from the Latin name Callida fornax (hot furnace) which Hernando Cortez applied to a single port.

So far as is known, "California" first appeared in print in a romantic Spanish novel entitled *Las Sergas de Esplandian* (The Adventures of Esplandian), written by Garcia Ordonez de Montalvo, and published in Toledo, Spain, between 1510 and 1521. In the novel, California was described as a Pacific island — rich in minerals and pearls — and the home of a tribe of beautiful Amazons ruled by a queen named Califia. These fanciful accounts made good reading, but helped to confuse explorers who came looking for gorgeous women, treasures, and an island, probably in that order.

CHOLLA CACTUS

SALLY LIGHTFOOT CRAB

SOLITARY CORAL

UNSEEN LIFE IS EVERYWHERE *in the Cortez.*
*Though you may not see a human face in some parts, there
are always living creatures, both large
and small, above and below the surface of the Sea
and on the land that borders it.*

15

A SEA FILLED WITH LIFE *lies beneath the tranquil surface. On three sides it touches Mexico — a land of fascinating contrasts and extremes. On the fourth side the quiet waters meet the great surges of the Pacific. Everywhere around the Cortez, challenges await the adventurer.*

AN UNEXPECTED JUNGLE *borders placid Rio Mulege, where lush date palms and thick vegetation bring a bit of the tropics to this part of Baja. Even the bird life here differs from that of surrounding regions.*

16 ✸ STORY OF THE CORTEZ

FORESTED HIGH MOUNTAINS *await the hiker, horseman, and backpacker in Baja's Sierra San Pedro Martir, an uplifted fault of granite with peaks that reach elevations of 10,000 feet. Here, along the foot rim of Canon Diablo, you can look east across the San Felipe Desert to the far-off Gulf.*

The Cortez is a Place
of Contrast and Weird Beauty

GETTING TO KNOW
The Land

For a place that in the past has been termed unproductive and arid, there is everywhere a variation and richness of life

From the U.S. border to the top of the Cortez there is a broad, flat plain so arid, barren, and unappealing that a cactus stands out as a landmark and a rattler must strive to make a living. But southward from the start of the Sea, vegetation and wildlife increase down both sides.

Probably the most commonly seen plant anywhere below the border is the cactus, in all its shapes and forms. Cattle, rabbits, and other vegetarians graze on the spineless green fruit of the cholla, abundant the whole length of the Peninsula. Its short limbs pull loose from the parent so easily the plant is often called "jumping cactus."

The most striking cactus is the giant cardon *(Pachycereus pringlei)*. This cactus resembles the Arizona saguaro, but can grow to an amazing height of fifty feet! For centuries the natives have prized the fruit of the sweet pitahaya—both for its fine fruit and because they considered it to be a potent aphrodisiac.

The barrel cactus *(Ferocactus acanthodes)*, which grows to a height of seven feet on some of the islands, is claimed to be a veritable wellspring of fresh water. Though it does not actually give out water, as tall tales claim, its cool white meat will quench thirst when chewed.

An over-enthusiastic visitor could go *loco* trying to understand the strange ways of the numerous cacti. One, the size of a walnut, hides in decomposed granite; then in mid-winter, without rain or reason, it shoots forth a large cluster of beautiful blossoms. The "creeping devil" *(Machaerocereus eruca)* stretches along on the ground, dying and renewing itself, sometimes traveling for miles. There are also several species of the familiar pipe organ cactus which forms such formidably solid barriers that they are often planted for fences.

WANTS ARE FEW AND LIFE IS UNCOMPLICATED.
All around the Cortez, on peaceful little ranches,
people live off the land, raising cattle,
cultivating simple crops, and enjoying a life still
uncomplicated by modern "conveniences."

19

Some of the trees and shrubs have been made use of for centuries as building materials. The palo de arco is the most common of these. The natives cut them into six-foot lengths and weave them upright to form side walls of houses. Palo de arco is also woven tightly into fences that can keep cattle in and prowlers out.

Among the most curious plants is the grotesque elephant tree (*Pachycormus discolor*). Its trunk is bulbous and fat, somewhat resembling an elephant's trunk. Though the wood is almost as soft as cactus and it has no spines, no birds or animals will eat it. Older trees attain a height of around twenty feet, and they spread out horizontally for the same distance. The elephant tree grows from the Midriff islands south throughout the Juanaloa Region.

Only the nature lover or the most curious finds pleasure at the sight of Baja's dead-looking thorn bearers during the dry season. However, within a few days after first rains, there is a remarkable metamorphosis, even among the plants that seem most barren. Buds, some of which swell as large as golf balls, open and a whole countryside becomes blanketed with blossoms that entice bee, bird, and human alike.

During the seasonal dry spell, shrubs and trees that have been introduced from the tropics flourish in Baja's watered oases. There are groves of coconut, date, and other palms, and a variety of fruits such as sapote, guava, mango, banana, papaya, fig, lemon, lime, and tangerine. Wherever the roots of a transplant find moisture, the fruits flourish.

There are also forests of conifers, including yellow ponderosa and sugar

MISSION SITES and locations are noted by: J, Jesuit; F, Franciscan; D, Dominican.

Twelve Regions of Exploration

Early explorers and settlers didn't give definite bounds to areas around the Cortez. Baja was ". . . the land in the extreme west"; the Gulf, ". . . an arm of the Pacific"; Mexico, ". . . the Mexican empire." Today, the political bounds fronting on the Sea are the states of Sonora and Sinaloa on the Mainland, and the State of Baja (lower) California and Territory of Baja California on the Peninsula. Local names for general areas are strictly local. The twelve regions on which the chapters in this book are built will not be found as such on maps or charts; the names are derived from a town, or some special attraction, as noted below.

North End: Centered on old fishing town of San Felipe, in Baja.
Midriff: Centered on islands Angel de la Guarda and Tiburon.
Mulege: Tropical town of Mulege (in Baja), Concepcion Bay.
Loreto: Town of Loreto, site of first California mission.
Juanaloa: Centered on islands Monseratte, Santa Catalina, Santa Cruz.
La Paz: City of La Paz, islands Partida and Espiritu Santo.
Cerralvo: Centered on island Cerralvo, just below La Paz.
Buena Vista: Resort area of Buena Vista, inland town of Santiago.
Cabo San Lucas: Baja's cape region, where Cortez adjoins Pacific.
Magdalena: Magdalena Bay (Baja's west coast), Santo Domingo.
Guaymas: City of Guaymas, inland mountain country on Mainland.
Topolobampo: Bahia Topolobampo, Fuerte River Valley (Mainland).

pine, on some of the mountains above the 4,000 foot elevation. Scrub oaks and cottonwoods are quite common in the northern canyons, and the California fan palm is found in the watered canyons in the south. The wild fig, or higuera, is a showy tree which is characterized by large spreading roots that are ghostly white, as is the trunk. Along canyon walls, exposed fig roots may spread down a sheer rock face for as much as 100 feet.

WILDLIFE AND MILD WEATHER

For a semi-arid country that has just survived a half-century of drought, Baja has a remarkable stock of wildlife wherever there is cover, especially in dense thickets that are impassable to man. Though very few of the mighty herds of antelope of the Pacific lowlands survived the long dry spell, those that did have doubled their numbers in the past few years. There are whole mountain ranges where the bighorn sheep is king of the hill. Although thought to be rare, these skyline dwellers are, according to ranchers, fairly numerous. The mule deer that ranged around the few streams remain plentiful but appear to be smaller in size than their cousins farther north. However, on Isla Tiburon in the Midriff, where deer were hunted continuously, a 300-pound buck is still not uncommon.

Mountain lions, or pumas, range all of the highlands and occasionally make nocturnal feeding forays down over the lowlands. They do very well when deer and wild ass flourish, but filch domestic stock when other animal populations decline. During the drought, varmint-hating dogs stood guard between the farmer's stock and the night-prowling beasts that would otherwise have exterminated the family's meat and gravy crop.

Besides the lions, the worst among the nocturnal thieves are the bobcats, coyotes, and foxes. Then there is a long list of nuisance critters, some of which prefer farm life over the wilderness. Squirrels, ringtail cats, raccoons, and badgers all are quite willing to become pets, if not pests, at least until the mating season. Some crowd right in to integrate or compete with domestic stock and poultry. A family of fat coons may inhabit a cave or burrow just fifty feet from a hen house, and quail and dove often nest in the chicken roosts.

During the drought many of the grass-eating birds virtually disappeared and grass-eating rodents seriously declined in numbers. When the rains started again, there was a sudden burst of succulents, grasses, and many other greens. This brought the grass-eaters back—rabbits, doves, ducks, geese, quail, and a whole checklist of shore fowl.

On the Mainland side of the Cortez, there are several kinds of larger game, such as el tigre, Spanish for ocelot, or jaguar. In the northern state of Sonora, there is a little wild boar called javelina; larger wild boars on Baja (especially in the mountains below La Paz) are nothing more than domestic pigs gone wild. There are also wild asses; but if shot, they are likely to cost $5.00 per head, for all too often they turn out to be a domestic work animal. The wild goats found on three of the Cortez islands are descendants of common milch goats.

Almost everywhere on both the Peninsula and the Mainland there are several varieties of snakes (some venomous), lizards large and small—from

RING-TAILED CAT, *a shy inhabitant of the Mainland and Baja, is seldom seen by people.*

FRESH FROM THE TREE, a papaya is a special treat any time of the day. Large papayas are grown along both sides of the Cortez; they, as well as coconut palms, are both cultivated at the southern end of the Baja Peninsula.

tiny geckos to giant iguanas and gila monsters—horned toads, and turtles. Most of these creatures do their hunting and exploring at night, though they are commonly seen even in the heat of mid-day.

Except for a few cool days in the extreme north end in winter, and some humid and hot periods during mid-summer along the southern Mainland side, the Cortez temperature is generally in the shirt-sleeve range. If the sunshine were not so constant and direct, the loin cloth, as worn by the early Indians, would serve for today's well-appointed male.

For most of the day along the Peninsula, a gentle breeze wafts inshore and is cooled by evaporation of the surface water. To all shore dwellers it is nature's air conditioner, and it overcomes a temperature that would otherwise be uncomfortably hot. Though inland temperatures may soar above 100 degrees, the Sea and its surrounding bench lands seldom exceed 85 to 90 degrees. Except in the Midriff, where waters generally are cooler, water temperatures remain remarkably warm up to mid-November in the upper half of the Sea and to the first of the year in the lower half. In the south, 80-degree water at Christmas, with an air temperature of 82 degrees is not uncommon.

Heavy fogs occur along the Pacific Coast of Baja, but fog is rare around the Cortez. Since the annual rainfall is seldom more than three or four inches, the bench zones of the Gulf are dry as a desert. But unlike the desert, the nights along the coast are pleasantly balmy.

For the greater part of the year the Cortez is dead calm, with tranquil mornings followed by light on-shore breezes in the afternoons. Shortly after sundown, the direction reverses, and the breezes then come down from the cool, mountain altitudes.

Generally the prevailing winds are from the north, but during early July south winds come up intermittently and continue through September. The winds are more complex in the North End, where they are sucked in by an almost constant low pressure, especially from the west, north, and northeast. Most Pacific storms lap over into this Region, creating blows too strong for comfortable cruising. Some winds may last for three days, especially during March and early April. A few heavy blows may occur from early November to early April. Once in about every ten or twelve years the north winds may develop into hurricane proportions and reach as far south as Guaymas. Gales of lesser ferocity subside in and below the Midriff. These Pacific-origin gales bring little or no rain but blast down the lengthy arroyos, especially those in back of Bahia San Luis Gonzaga and Bahia de Los Angeles.

Natives apply the term chubasco to any strong winds or heavy warm rains — although the true chubasco is of nearly hurricane strength. The rains generally occur seasonally in high mountains on the Peninsula, and on the southern Mainland coast between July and December. Rainfall elsewhere is sparse. During this "rainy season" the southern Mainland side becomes quite humid, but the Peninsula remains extremely dry around the shores. Additional rains occur in winter in mountains north of Loreto.

CROSSING INTO ANOTHER COUNTRY

There are several border towns that are used as accessways to the Cortez — from Tijuana in the west to Nogales in the east. As in border towns around the world, which act as a transient stop-over point, most of the inhabitants differ greatly from the people throughout the rest of the country. Although vast numbers of bad elements among the population tend to swell it beyond all possibility of self support, the towns remain a prime tourist attraction, since they are usually the first glimpse of a new country. Weekend visits to the Caliente races and the bullfights at Tijuana and to the real Mexican market at Juarez were once pleasurable trips, but today other attractions have taken their place.

Though Tijuana is doing its best to clean up and dress up, its very name is still synonymous with sin, and despite parking meters, it's far from being a credit to modern Mexico. Anything made anywhere in Mexico, plus many items not made anywhere in Mexico, can be bought in Tijuana.

Mexicali, being the capital of Estado de Baja California Norte, makes every attempt to preserve its dignity. It has reasons for being a large city. It is the center of an extensive agricultural area and has developed considerable industry. Leading citizens of Mexicali are proud that their city is called the "Gateway to the Sea of Cortez."

FANTASTIC inverted-turnip-shaped boojam or cirio is common on Baja peninsula.

The next crossing to the Cortez is at San Luis, a very small town compared with other sprawling border cities. Recently, paved roads have awakened this napping pueblo, and it is trying to adjust to the new influx of people. The crossing at Lukeville, often included in the name of Sonoyta, a town two miles south, is less frequented than the others, and it probably will not develop above the village stage for a long time.

Nogales, a small city straddling the border, is likely to become one of the most important crossings of all, since it is the nearest entry to the Cortez for everyone east of Arizona.

Fortunately, the people of Baja have chosen to forget the invaders that swarmed up the Peninsula in the 1849 gold rush. Except in border towns, very few Norte Americanos were seen around Baja again until recent years, when some daring outdoorsmen began venturing down the Peninsula's hazardous roads and seaways.

TRABAJO MEANS TRAVAIL

Since no two humans are alike, trying to find the unique qualities of a whole population is not easy, but below the border towns of Baja California there are some striking differences in human behavior. With few exceptions, the people are honest, opposed to violence, generous, affectionate, and very happy. They are not as aggressively ambitious, not as industrious, and not as competitive as the people of the U.S., nor do they hold that earning by the sweat of the brow is a virtue. The Spanish word for "work" or "labor"—trabajo—also means "trouble," but it is more meaningful when translated as the English "travail."

When the pueblo or ranch-bred Baja Californian is helping out in an emergency, with no pay or reward expected, he will work twice as hard as when wages are the motive. Omar Khayyam's loaf-of-bread-and-jug-of-wine philosophy appears to be the preferred way of life. "Possessions are good to have," goes a common saying, "but are not worth striving or exchanging happiness for." Around a ranch house you will invariably see many things that need to be done, and the rancher knows it, but, as he says, "There will come a cool day, maybe, when I need to exercise."

Though the gentle people of Mexico are not overly ambitious, according to the competitive standards of the Norte Americano, they are not backward. Too often the first-time visitor below the border jumps to the conclusion that, just because a family lives in a semi-finished house that has been in the same state of incompleteness for many a year, the people are lazy. And often the visitor becomes exasperated at the time it takes to get something done. The point to be understood is that the people aren't lazy—they're just in no hurry. What if the roof leaks? The holes also let the fresh air in. What if it takes Pablo three hours to walk half a mile? He has enjoyed the sights and sounds along the way.

The people of Baja and the Mainland don't worry about *when* something gets done. They enjoy thinking about a job for a long time before starting it, then they enjoy doing the job while they're working at it. This is evidenced by their singing and whistling and constant chatter. They

BLEACHED ROOTS of the native fig (Ficus palmeri) web over rocks, seeking a water supply.

A DESERT LANDSCAPE *during much of the year, the land abounds in color when spring wildflowers bloom. Even when the land is brown and dusty, there is life to be seen — in the small forests of cacti, the occasional green oasis, the rocky tidepools, the brilliantly clear sky, and of course in the shimmering Sea itself.*

GARAMBULLO CACTUS

BARREL CACTUS

SWEET PITAHAYA FLOWER

don't worry about life or its demands—indeed, to them, there are few demands that must be met. In this way they are not far removed from their forebears, the carefree Indians.

The first families of Baja California, or at least those that settled there more than a century ago, were predominantly European; but the majority of the population that followed called themselves Mestizos. They were a mixture of Mainland Indian and European, principally of Spanish blood. The Indians came largely from highly civilized tribes that enjoyed more rigid moral codes than did the conquistadores. The surviving culture that produced the gentle Baja Californian was this, tempered with the ethics expounded by early missionaries.

The very few prisoners in Baja's Territorial Penitentiary at Mulege (nineteen at the time of this writing) are a testimony to the non-violent behavior of these people. Ranchers do not carry guns, but they usually wear large, razor-sharp machetes, which can lop the head off a mountain lion. Except for some antique rifles at ranches, there are very few firearms, and these are largely limited to single-shot .22 rifles owned by youngsters.

Friendship seems to have a more sincere meaning in Baja than in many other places. Old friends—men included—greet each other with a warm embrace. Women never seem forward, but they form close friendships rapidly and express their feelings by a child-like pat or touch that is not at all self conscious.

To find employment, a majority of the young men of Baja have had to leave the Peninsula. This has left an enormous over-balance of women. As might be expected in a country where the females outnumber males (some say 7 to 1), the competition for masculine attention is in a state of restrained fierceness, but is always polite and modest.

EVENING QUIET in Mexico is often broken by the call of the small screech owl.

Bad Men and Good Beer

There is a legend about a small border town 30 miles east of Tijuana, near Tecate. It was once said to be the worst pueblo of the Old West, a refuge for criminals of all kinds until the appearance of a character called "Bad Miguel," a half Yaqui Indian from Chijuajua. Miguel's fame as a super bad-man had preceded his arrival, and when he announced to the town that *he* was taking over outlawry and sin, all the other villains accepted his pronouncement as law. Thus, in a backhanded way, badness became goodness. There was even a song about him that went ". . . When Miguel came, bad men went tame and sneaked up peaceful ways."

The place was not only purged of sin, it was once purged of people, when Indians erased almost every trace of the original pueblo. But after the turn of the century, it revived as a farming center and summer health resort. Today, "Carta Blanca" and "Tecate" beers are brewed there and are of such an excellence to have brought another measure of fame to the peaceful little town. Bad Miguel would not be very happy if he were around there today.

THERE'S A HAPPY LIFE to be led along the sun-drenched shores of the Cortez, and it reflects
in the faces of this Mexican family. Dinner is waiting in the depths for the man who has a knack with a spear
or rod and a knowledge of where the fish are hiding.

LOADING A MILLING HERD *of bawling cattle by muscle power may look — and sound — inefficient; but it does solve a problem when there is no dock, and the job does get done eventually. The animals are lashed alongside a small skiff and made to swim out to a freighter that waits for them offshore.*

Somewhere along the line, after the Revolution down-graded the church, the formal marriage ceremony got sidetracked in Baja. Except among a few wealthy families, living together without benefit of wedlock became the most simple and popular way to mate. Yet, according to many observers, such unions have proved the most durable.

ISLANDS OF ADVENTURE

Down through the ages, adventurers and poets alike have had their fancies tickled by the mystery of uninhabited islands. Man has traveled the lands and seas, searching out and exploring almost every bit of the earth's surface, and now is turning his eyes to other planets. But here in the Cortez are fantastic bits of land that have been ignored for centuries. There are a hundred little-explored islands and as many more pieces of land of various shapes and sizes that could be called islands. Even those that appear as dots on a map may take half an hour to circle in a boat and even longer to scale.

Of immense interest to the adventuresome are the islands above Guaymas, especially in the Midriff, and those down the inner coast of Baja California, terminating with Isla Cerralvo. Some are the remnants of dead volcanoes, but most are the tops of half-submerged mountains that were split off from the Peninsula during the formation of the Cortez. (The numerous delta-type formations along the Mexican Mainland below Guaymas are considered as islands, though in appearance they are monotonously similar. Most are flat and bordered or overgrown with mangrove bushes, except on the outer sea sides.)

Fear and superstition caused early explorers to give a wide berth to many of the "half-drowned mountains" and the "convulsing waters" in the channels around them. Even to this day, natives around the Cortez are afraid to approach some of the way-out places. Tales handed down from the logs, records, and legends of seafarers told of mountainous walls of water gushing through the channels, man-eating sharks and sea serpents, cannibal Indians, wars among the fishes, fowls, and sea monsters, water that turned to blood, magic islands that disappeared and reappeared within an hour's time, and fearsome and bewitched places where wails of anguish were heard as demons charged down island slopes in the night. Astonishing as it may seem, all of these strange phenomena are basically true and have logical explanations.

In the distant past many of the islands were peopled at intervals by Indians. Their dwelling places even now are easily located by following trails of discarded sea shells from near the water's edge up the slopes to the ancient middens or kitchen refuse heaps. It would be interesting to know where these aborigines obtained fresh water, since most of the islands have no signs of springs or wells. Only a few have water, and precious little at that.

While there is considerable vegetation in eroded ravines and on benches, most of the Cortez islands are otherwise rather barren. Those toward the south end of the Sea have thorn bushes and cacti.

ISOLATED ON Islas Partida, Espiritu Santo, the black-tailed rabbit has evolved to all black.

On all except Isla Tiburon in the Midriff, there is a notable lack of the larger land animals, though most of the islands have their share of scorpions, rattlesnakes, mice, bats, pelicans, and boobies. Tiburon has large mule deer, coyotes, jack rabbits, wild (domestic) dogs, rodents, and a few species of snakes. Cerralvo, near the southern end of the Peninsula, has small deer and wild (domestic) goats and cats, and there are deer and some varmints on San Jose, north of La Paz. Coyotes, ringtail cats, and iguanas occur on a few other islands, rattlesnakes are on most of the largest, and various species of lizards are on nearly all. A few small islands are inhabited by large, fish-eating bats.

Vast numbers of sea lions move from island to island, maintaining permanent rookeries on tidal shelves and benches. Prodigious quantities of fish, lobsters, and shellfish inhabit the rock rubble and caves down the submerged slopes.

Myriads of birds swarm over all of the islands; they feed, breed, become over-populated, then migrate to other regions. Several species are known to nest only on the islands of the Cortez.

There is a vital interdependence between the birds and fishes. Diving sea fowls feed on the injured and ill fish, thus helping to keep the schools free of epidemic diseases and the stock healthy in a natural selective-breeding process. The enormous deposits of rich guano fertilize the water, encouraging the growth of phytoplankton.

Except for periodic visits by guano collectors, only three of the main islands are inhabited by man—the islands of San Jose and Carmen by workers in the salt mines, and San Marcos by workers engaged in a large gypsum operation. A few of the islands are overnight campsites for shark and turtle fishermen. The most consistent island visitors are the vagabundos del mar, or sea gypsies, who may spend a week, or a couple of months, depending upon their vague urges to move on.

While there are very few good anchorages for large yachts, almost all of the islands have small boat coves and lees, which are more often on the side nearest the coast.

To those who find beauty in grotesqueness, the islands of the Sea of Cortez are a never-palling wonder. To all who find interest in sea life, their waters provide constant satisfaction.

FISH-EATING BAT impales his prey on long talons — inhabits islands and shorelines.

LEATHER-GARBED vaquero shows off his hand-sewn garments. The heavy clothing protects him against spines of cactus as he rides. His wide-brimmed hat is stitched leather, and wide leather chaps protect both him and his horse from thorns along the trail.

The Face of the People is the Face of the Land

A DESCENDANT OF CANNIBALS, this old Seri Indian woman is one of a small tribe of these people who live principally at El Desemboque on the Mainland side of the North End Region.

THE EVER-PATIENT BURRO *waits for a load of firewood to be secured. Firewood is not abundant, especially on the Baja side of the Cortez, and since it is essential for cooking, every bit counts. Palo de arco trees are a main source, and even dried cactus serves the purpose when necessary.*

EVERYWHERE IN MEXICO *everyone eats tortillas, the paper-thin bread made of corn dough that is the basis of many Mexican dishes. There are few smells as tempting as the aroma of tortillas cooking over a wood fire.*

The People are Friendly and Gentle

DATES ARE SPREAD TO DRY *in the sun at San Ignacio, a welcome oasis in a barren countryside. Many fruits are grown in this fertile valley, but dates are the principal crop. After being sorted and dried, they will be shipped out through ports such as La Paz.*

POTTERY GOES TO MARKET *on a burro. This is a common scene on market day, when people from outlying regions bring their wares to town and spread them out for sale.*

LIFE AND MOVEMENT OF
The Sea

The waters are a living pasture in which life both small and large flourishes as it has for some ten million years

The wonder and magnitude of this Sea, its movements, and its life cannot be expressed in everyday language. New words are needed to describe this strangest of all great bodies of water and the spell-casting phenomena commonly seen here.

There are few similes that can tell of waters that boil up like a cauldron at one end of a 1,000-fathom channel while at the other end, 10 miles away, a giant whirlpool funnels down whatever gets trapped in its swirling surge. Words are weak in describing the richness of life above and below the surface of the water. Terms such as "schools," "shoals," or even "armies" are inadequate to convey the enormity of a 10-mile long horde of game fish feeding on a still larger body of forage fish.

Much of the life and movement of the Cortez is directly related to the tides. As in all of the waters of the world, the gravitational pull of the moon and the sun, especially the moon, creates two high tides within each 24-hour-and-51-minute period of a lunar day. The maximum highs come with each full and new moon. Because of its narrowness, the Cortez has very little tide of its own. But when the high tide of the Pacific rises to 3½ feet —or to 7 feet or more on extreme lunar tides—and must seek its level, a front speeds up the 700 miles of the Cortez in 5½ hours, not as a flow but as a lifting motion. The high-tide front creates a current of 6 knots, or more, and becomes extremely swift (up to 20 miles per hour) when funneled in from the 150-mile-wide mouth of the Sea to the 32-mile width between the islands of the Midriff and again at the north end.

BLESSED WITH NATURE'S ABUNDANCE.
It is not surprising that this vast warm-water
aquarium is said to offer the best deep-sea fishing in
the world. A packed school of barracuda is just
a sample of what moves beneath the quiet surface.

The speed of the surface water in the deep of the Midriff channels also creates vertical counter-currents, which drive down a half-mile in maelstrom-like eddies, then shoot upward for 10 feet above the surface in what is termed an upwelling. This phenomenon is first observed as a wall of water, which later boils outward like a raging mushroom-topped cataract.

When the tidal surge reaches the north end of the Sea, an immense pressure is built up at the narrow mouth of the Rio Colorado, and a wall of water goes racing upstream, causing the river to flow backward. This is called a tidal bore. (There are several other tidal bores in the world; one in the Canadian Bay of Fundy sometimes rises to a height of 50 feet.)

The effects of the bore riding up over the great spring floods of the river have been lessened by the dams that have reduced the river's flow. Nevertheless, these extreme spring highs approach their crests and reach well above the banks of the river, spreading out over the vast flatlands for some 30 miles. When the tide recedes, the resulting mud flats are impassable. Following the rapid drain-off, even the water in the river bed drops to less than a foot deep over some of the long sand bars.

The first of the northbound, extreme high tides starts on the full or new-moon schedule and in the south can be predicted for a few days. However, at the north end, where the high water remains for only 20 to 30 minutes then suddenly drops 8 or 10 feet, the water bounces or flows back, throwing tidal movements all out of regularity. This thwarts attempts to work out tide tables by which highs and lows can be predicted. During half-moon periods, tides and currents are less spectacular and are more kindly toward small-boat launching.

A knowledge of the unique tidal and current conditions in this Sea is vital to the small-boat operator. By riding with currents he can conserve

THE SPEED *of the surface water when funneled into narrow channels creates upwelling currents.*

Spectacular Water Disturbances

Since the Cortez has little or no lunar tide of its own, and since there are no steady winds to push the water around, there is almost no wave action in this Sea. More often than not, it is truly a "painted ocean." However, despite the prevailing calm, there are several kinds of spectacular disturbances which can become dangerous if they build up to major proportions.

Waterspouts are twisting, funnel-shaped columns that extend down from low clouds to the water's surface. Small ones often follow chubascos, and though they can give a drenching, they seldom are of any real danger to a small boat.

Tidal waves, fortunately, are infrequent. They are triggered by earthquakes occurring south of the Sea.

Upheavals are caused by returning currents meeting head-on with inbound currents, causing rough water over an area, but usually not bad enough to cause trouble to a boater.

Upwellings are mushroom-shaped plateaus (sometimes as much as five feet high) that occur over a wide expanse of water. They result from vertical counter-currents welling up from great depths. Though they sound fearsome, they are of little real concern to the boater.

NOT A PRIZED CATCH *for a fisherman, but an interesting display for the Rancho Buena Vista, an ocean sunfish will be added to the resort's collection of mounted specimens. Scientifically named mola mola, the odd creature is caught in all of the warm waters of the world.*

SHRIMP FISHERMEN *sort their catch at Agiabampo Bay. This is one of many areas on the Mainland side of the Cortez where shrimp are plentiful.*

VAGABUNDOS DEL MAR, or sea gypsies, are men who prefer to roam the Cortez alone. You may get close to one sometime, and if you do, you'll find him friendly and helpful, but he will not seek your company. The vagabundos stop their roaming only when they die and are buried on the southernmost tip of Isla Cerralvo.

much fuel and time. On the other hand, he may find his boat actually moving backward when instruments indicate full bore ahead.

The terrestrial convulsions, eruptions, and faulting creating the Cortez, as well as silting, erosion, and water movements, all have had their cause and effect relationships on present-day marine life and fishing conditions in this most fascinating Sea.

As man is said to be related to all matter within his environment, the well-being of the fishes is essentially tied up with all life in the water, as well as its chemistry, plus the sunshine, rain, and gases above it.

A SEA RICH IN FOODSTUFFS

The waters of the Cortez are like a primitive and fertile valley, a meadow where great and small fishes graze upon the food of the sea. It is not by accident that the massive populations of fish and other sea creatures have come into the Cortez. Since its beginning, their ancestors have come to feed and reproduce, and a majority take up permanent residence. For some 10 million years the Rio Colorado carried minerals and organic materials from the far reaches of the Rocky Mountains and dumped them into the north end of the Sea. Deltas were built up. These, in turn, were surmounted by more deposits until the alluvia spilled over to form a bench extending out into the Cortez for many miles. With each series of spring floods, the Colorado deposited more materials in the northern waters.

Other nutriments were and still are brought in by tidal currents and by flash floods washing down from the mountainous terrain on both the Mainland and Baja sides of the Sea.

Man-made dams have now diverted the Rio Colorado to domestic purposes, halting further silt transportation in the north end. However, soluble nitrates, phosphates, and organic foods from the 5,000-square-mile deposit will continue to ooze up into the water for centuries to come, and life will beget life in quantities beyond the imagination of man.

The nourishment provided by the chemicals, along with chlorophyll born from the sun's benevolence, trigger the growth and tremendous reproduction of microscopic marine algae called phytoplankton. (In a single year one diatom is capable of producing 18,000,000,000 descendants.) This thick plant pasture is grazed upon by diminutive animals called zooplankton, which also reproduce in great profusion.

Together the tiny plant and animal beings make up the largest volume included in the "plankton" (from the Greek *planktos*, meaning to wander). Plankton is comprised of all the drifting, more or less passive but living, entities from single-celled life units to large jellyfish and the eggs and larvae of marine creatures of all sizes. Plankton is the basic food supply for all members of the animal kingdom inhabiting water, from unicellular organisms on up to the great baleen whales, which eat as much as 8 tons of it per day. All graze directly on plankton, or indirectly on it, by eating those marine animals that do.

LARGEST OF THE MARLINS, the black marlin weighs up to 1,000 pounds in the Cortez and elsewhere may be even larger. The two stiff-looking fins are a distinguishing feature: On the black they stay open after the fish is caught; on other marlins they close.

A LIVING PASTURE ✳ 39

In the Cortez, the greatest plankton production occurs in February and March at the extreme lunar tides. During these plankton "blooms" the otherwise clear, blue water becomes cloudy, brilliant green, or brownish. Another contribution to the food chain, and an enrichment to marine vegetation everywhere, is guano. In many areas the white icing that covers rocks or entire small islands is harvested for fertilizer. Thus, this gift of the birds benefits nature as well as man.

You don't have to be a bird watcher to be entertained by the almost continuous show staged by the myriads of sea fowls in the Cortez. Except for the cormorants, and a few other species that dive so fast even healthy fish cannot escape them, all are beneficial to both man and the fish populations. Most fish-eating birds take the the maimed or weak swimmers, thus keeping the stock hardy and the population free of epidemic diseases. In the process, natural selective breeding is achieved.

Observing the habits of certain marine birds can add greatly to the pleasure of any trip. A gull may swipe a fish from a pelican, then in turn be struck in the back by a frigate bird, who will nab the dropped fish in mid-air before it hits the water. A flock of pelicans may repeatedly circle up and over a school of forage fish, then peel off in a dive-bombing formation, sometimes hitting the water in perfect unison.

The pelicans (two species, both in the genus *Pelecanus*) are the most abundant of the Sea's near-shore birds throughout the year. They look and act like clowns, with their large beaks and pouches resting on their chests

A Wandering Pasture to Feed the World

By exercising a bit of imagination, we can have some entertaining — though not too far-fetched — thoughts about plankton.

The dictionary defines plankton as the passively floating animal and plant life of a body of water. Many of the members of the plankton colony reproduce by division, which means that one individual becomes two, then four, then eight, and so on, in a very short time. At any one time the total numbers of individuals in a colony is almost beyond belief. Since most fishes and sea-dwelling mammals live either directly on plankton or on others that do, it is a rich and basic food source for all marine life.

Plankton is just as nourishing to man as it is to the creatures of the deep. Several researchers — most notably members of the Kon Tiki expedition — have strained plankton directly from the sea, using a fine-mesh net, and eaten it as it came. Though the gruel-like mass may not make the most tasty meal in the world, it is highly nourishing and could sustain a human.

In the Cortez, perhaps the most numerous and important creatures in the food chain are the minute crustaceans, especially the opossum shrimp, so named because they carry their young in a belly pouch. In food value they are believed to contain more than 75 percent protein and 10 percent fat. At times these shellfish become so thickly concentrated in the top ten feet of the surface, especially around Midriff islands, they appear from the air as a wide, green belt. "It's like swimming in a bowl of oatmeal," said one diver.

A FEROCIOUS-LOOKING FELLOW, *the spiny-tailed iguana (Ctenosaura hemilopha) found on Isla Cerralvo avoids human company. Though of fearsome appearance and imposing size — up to two feet in length — he lives chiefly on insects.*

even in flight. Like cormorants, they form long lines in flight to and from feeding grounds. They dive from heights of 40 to 50 feet. Along some productive feeding stretches, pelicans post lookouts every half-mile or so. When a feeding game fish stirs things up near one of these stations, the lookout flies up, and then dives. This serves as a visual signal, beckoning pelicans from great distances to join the feast.

Of most direct benefit to the angler is "bird work," a tell-tale circling and diving of birds for cripples in a forage fish school when it is being thrashed by a shoal of predators. Experienced anglers keep a keen watch for this aquatic spectacular, for it indicates hot fishing if the area can be reached in time.

The best of all Cortez fishing guides is the magnificent frigate bird, *Fregata magnificens.* When frigate birds are seen circling rapidly or diving, a game fish school is almost always present. The male frigate is a wild looking creature, with his coal-black body, blood-red throat pouch, large, hooked beak, and angular wings that spread to 8 feet. His eyes are black

THE TIDE REALLY GOES OUT in the upper Cortez. The tidal difference here near San Felipe is
more than 20 feet, and the water that laps at the shore when the tide is high may be a quarter of a mile out within
just a few hours, exposing a rippled, unmarked expanse of tide flats.

and fearless. Although strictly sea birds, frigates can't swim and rarely, if ever, light on water.

The most numerous bird 10 miles or more offshore and around distant islands is the blue-footed booby. The booby is not as stupid as it looks, or as its name implies. It will outwit a frigate bird by diving right back into the water with a newly caught fish.

Next in abundance are the terns and gulls. There are close to a dozen species of gulls and half as many species of terns. Terns are recognized by their black cap and forked tails; gulls have squarish or rounded tails. Terns are plungers but rarely swim; gulls swim but seldom dive. Terns are very graceful birds. They follow fast-moving, zigzagging tuna schools and often help the angling boat in the chase. The fluffy feathers on the underside of white gull wings make good feather lures.

There are enormous numbers of other sea birds that live around, or visit, the Cortez. There are also many shore birds, including edible game fowls such as brant, Canada geese, and ducks, as well as large shore birds in the curlew and sandpiper group. Several rare species, and some that were thought to be extinct, may be found in isolated areas of the Cortez. Of special interest to watchers and photographers are the beautiful common egret, the wood ibis, and the blue heron, commonly seen in the jungles around San Blas, as well as in some areas farther north.

"THAR SHE BLOWS!"

Many of the great and small whales, including dolphins and porpoises, visit the Cortez or live there all year. So far, game fishermen have had no interest in any of the order *Cetacea*, except for the great pleasure in watching them perform, as when a hundred or more dolphins leap and gambol around a boat, or when a 50-foot humpback hurls his full length out of the water. Many are the modern fishermen who have echoed the old-time whaler's "Thar she blows!" at sight of a whale-blown geyser. And many are the greenhorns who have felt their hair stand on end when a herd of big finbacks has headed straight toward their boat. It's reassuring to know that large whales seem instinctively to avoid even brushing a boat.

It is the dolphins, in the family *Delphinidae*, that are the nearest things to humans in the water world. No land animal, including man, has better or quicker reflexes, and no other aquatic or terrestrial creature except man exhibits more intelligence or a better memory than the dolphins. Since ancient times, dolphins have been revered as almost sacred creatures, because of their strange friendliness toward man. To this day, sailors will not harm them. There are numerous legends of drowning men being assisted or saved by these highly intelligent animals.

Of the ten or twelve toothed Cetaceans (dolphins, whales, porpoises) visiting or in residence in the Cortez, three are above 18 feet long. They are the killer whale, the false killer whale, and the pilot whale or blackfish.

While stories of life and death battles between divers and giant squid, octopi, eels, and other ferocious sea monsters are generally pure fiction, certain sea creatures, such as sharks, stingrays, and certain whales have earned the great respect of man. But of all marine creatures in the Cortez,

LINKED TO SEA *by his fish diet, the osprey often nests at the top of a giant cactus.*

the killer whale, *Orcinus orca*, is the most fearsome, despite the fact that no attack on a human by a killer whale has yet been recorded. However, there are unconfirmed reports from various sources of human bones being found in a harpooned specimen, of a skiff being bitten in two, and of the powerful, 20-foot long orcas tipping up ice floes to dislodge seals from them.

Like other toothed Cetaceans, killer whales exhibit a high degree of intelligence. Yet, they occasionally run aground, sometimes en masse, and bake to death in the dehydrating sun. The killer whale can be recognized when he slowly rolls along the surface by a large, dorsal triangular fin, up to 6 feet high in the males, and by a large white spot against black on the side of the head. Females attain lengths of 25 feet; males, 30 feet. The name "killer whale" comes from their habit of killing other sea mammals. Their favorite pastime is tearing out the tongues of less vicious whales.

False killer whales, *Pseudorca crassidens*, may give a skin diver a real scare until he learns to distinguish them from orcas, which they resemble. *Crassidens* have a smaller dorsal fin than the true killers and are all black with no white markings. They too are slow-motion travelers that move in groups of three or four hundred. It is estimated that there are more of these than killer whales in the Cortez.

The 20-foot pilot whale (also known as the pot-headed dolphin, or blackfish), *Globicephala scammoni*, is another king-sized but harmless mammal, one that has proved friendly to humans and adapts well to captivity. A member of this species gained fame as the performing "Bubbles" at Marineland, California. The pilot whale also travels in large pods and very slowly. In addition to the bulging forehead, it is distinguished by a long sickle-shaped pectoral fin.

THE BIGGEST SHOWOFF OF ALL

Perhaps the biggest showoff of the whole family is the cavorting (Pacific) bottlenose dolphin. Its Mediterranean cousin was mentioned as a knowledgeable and kindly animal by the early Greeks and Romans. It is most frequently used in public shows and scientific experiments. Scientists even say it has a vocabulary. Bottlenose dolphins are often seen in large pods throughout the Cortez. There are several accounts of the playful 12-footers jumping right over skiffs.

The spinner dolphin is of special interest in that large pods associate with migrating schools of tuna. The pod runs ahead of the school of fish, jumping and twirling like cheer leaders at a big game. The reason for this strange association and behavior is unknown. The mammals do not seem to prey on the tuna, since squid is the favorite food of this dolphin.

There are three other species of the long-beaked dolphins that visit the Cortez, and at least one species of porpoise *(Phocoena sinus)* is found there. It is the smallest of all porpoises. Confusion between dolphins, dolphinfish, and porpoises is common. Dolphins and porpoises are mammals—or air breathers—whereas the dolphinfish is a true fish. Dolphins have long beaks and seem to wear a perpetual smile, whereas the porpoises do not.

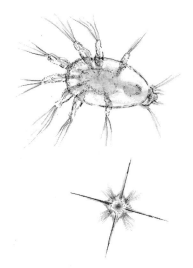

MULTITUDES OF FISH feed on living masses of plankton. Animal forms are shown above.

MINUTE PLANT plankton is enlarged here 300 times. Upper, dinoflagellate; lower, diatom.

LUMINOUS EYES and a flurry of gold-striped bodies indicate this school of grunt — very important to the fisherman as a live bait fish and found throughout the Cortez.

LIKE MONSTERS FROM THE DEEP, *huge manta rays soar into the air and land back in the water with a tremendous splash. It is thought that these gymnastics help them to dislodge parasites, but whatever the reason for the behavior, it's a pretty sight to see a whole school of the huge creatures leaping about.*

The California sea lion is abundant only in the upper Cortez, especially in the Midriff, but most anglers will say that when there are two of these useless fish-hogs around, they are overabundant. This species is the performing "seal" used in shows and circuses. The only purpose the sea lion seems to serve in nature is to keep killer whales fed and happy. The animal could be profitably harvested for fat and other products, though Mexican fishermen hardly give him a second glance. The Chinese utilize four portions of the sea lion's body commercially. They boil the blubber for oil (one animal yields about 20 pounds of oil), render the bladder and bones for glue, work up the whiskers as adornments for bridal costumes, and process the reproductive organs for a rejuvenating medicine.

GIANTS OF THE DEEP

The 80-ton finback whale (*Balaenoptera physalus*) is the second largest animal on earth—being surpassed only by the 100-ton blue whale. Both of these monsters are toothless. They feed on plankton, which is strained through fringed sheets, called baleen, that hang from the roof of their mouths. Finbacks can swim at speeds approaching 20 knots. Watching these bulky creatures threading their way through a maze of jagged rocks without crashing into them is a real pleasure. A small population of some 150 finbacks seems to have taken up permanent residence in the Midriff, where it is not uncommon for half a dozen to join a fleet of small boats.

Whaling proved unprofitable in the Midriff when hunter ships piled up on unchartered rocks or were thrown out of control in upwellings or other currents. The finback's principal hangouts are Canal Ballenas and Canal Sal si Puedes.

Another whale frequently found in the Cortez is the sperm whale, the largest of the toothed whales. Literature's famous Moby Dick was a sperm whale. A waxy substance called ambergris, which is produced in the intestines, was once highly valued as a base for perfume. At one time it sold for $40 per ounce, but today the same amount brings only about a dollar. Ambergris is sometimes found on beaches as a dark, stinking mass, and in that form it is a far cry from perfume. In the Cortez, pods of sperm whales frequently beach themselves for no apparent reason. On April 12, 1953, 9 died on the shore of Cabo Tepoca. On January 16, 1954, 22 sperms drove into the shallows off the town of La Paz, where they died, to the dismay of everyone within smelling distance.

The gray whale was thought to have been wiped out completely by whalers, up to about 20 years ago, when a few were seen heading for Laguna Scammon, on Baja's west coast, one of their favorite breeding and

Modern Expeditions into the Cortez

For many years the Cortez and the lands on either side of it have been explored by scholars and researchers interested in learning more about this fascinating, untouched place of adventure.

The first formal expedition of the California Academy of Sciences (headquarters in San Francisco) to Baja was made in the spring of 1888. Since that time Academy scientists have made many such trips — some by boat, some by plane, and several that traversed the length of the Peninsula overland. Since 1958 there has been at least one Academy expedition each year. These have resulted in a vast accumulation of valuable scientific facts, specimens of Baja's plants and animals, and the publication of a great many papers adding to our knowledge of this remote part of Mexico.

Scripps Institute of Oceanography (La Jolla, California) has made several expeditions into the Sea of Cortez to study the marine life and water movements.

Erle Stanley Gardner, the well-known creator of Perry Mason, has covered Baja thoroughly and has written about his explorations (see Bibliography). He has gone into and around the Peninsula by conventional aircraft, by helicopter, by jeep, by truck, by boat, and on foot. He has explored and, in several books, has recorded his impressions of the breeding grounds of the gray whale at Scammon's Lagoon on Baja's west coast; has discovered and investigated primitive cave paintings far inland; and has even traveled remote canyons and arroyos by motor scooter.

John Steinbeck made an expedition to the Sea in 1941 with biologist Edward F. Ricketts to collect marine invertebrates. The highlights of this journey are described in his book, *Log from the Sea of Cortez.*

The editors of *Sunset Magazine* have long been interested in the Sea of Cortez. They have made many trips to Baja and the West Coast of Mexico and have reported their discoveries and the development of these areas in numerous articles.

FOR UNDERWATER SIGHTSEEING, *La Paz is a favorite starting point and is well equipped to serve the diver. This snorkler is exploring in ten-foot-deep water at Isla Espiritu Santo just north of town in a sea cave that is colorful with seashells, sponges, and coral formations.*

SEA CUCUMBER

SEA ANEMONE

SHELL-LESS SEA SNAIL

calving lagoons. There are other nursery grounds along Baja's Pacific side, and two more on the Mainland near Bahia Yavaros and Bahia Reforma.

There are 30 kinds of sharks in the Cortez, all edible, and 18 varieties of rays. All but six species of rays have a poisonous spine on the top of the tail, whose sting can be crippling. Four species of "electric rays" are capable of delivering a knock-down shock. Around Mazatlan, Cabo San Lucas, and several other places, gigantic mantas and smaller mobulas are often seen making high, flap-jacking leaps or basking on the surface with their pectoral fin tips showing above the water. These fins resemble and serve as under-water wings when swimming. None of the rays is considered as game fish, but very good imitation scallops can be cut from their fins.

Numerous species of snake-like marine eels inhabit the Cortez, but few are caught on bait. The morays (10 species) are the villains of TV and movies, but rarely will they attack without provocation. I am not so sure about the much larger but rare conger eel.

There are several kinds of squid. One species called "giant squid" is actually smaller than the 4-foot specimens brought up by shrimpers. No reports of ship-flipping octopi have been received for the last couple of centuries. In fact, diver-photographers have spent many weeks trying to locate an octopus with tentacles more than 5 feet long.

I have never heard the total figure of species, or at least families, of shellfish in the Cortez. If they were bunched together there no doubt would be hundreds of square miles of them. Among the rock and mud bottom dwellers are fantastic numbers of scallops, clams, cockles, oysters, conches, and water snails from fairly deep water up into the tidal zone. Beds are found almost everywhere except near towns or villages. Three kinds of lobsters, small crabs, and shallow-water shrimp make up the edible crustaceans.

GREEN SEA TURTLE lays its eggs on the beach, and the young head for water when hatched.

WHY THERE ARE SO MANY FISH

For millions of years, great fish schools have migrated up from the tropics to the Cortez to feast on its abundances, then returned to their southerly habitats to spawn young which instinctively retraced the swimways of their parents. Some writers have called the Cortez the world's greatest fish trap, and claimed that the fish schools heading for the Pacific Coast got lost and piled into it. Logic suggests that in a few million years the fish would have learned better. Like the river-running salmon or the fresh-water eels, the visiting fishes are obeying inherited urges to migrate north and south along special swimways, and they appear to be equipped with built-in biological compasses, clocks, computers, and a predestined course already charted. Their ancestors found in these waters a perpetual and endless food supply, favorable water temperatures, protective caves, creviced rock habitats, and brackish backwaters for spawning. So ideal an environment gave them cause for remembering it and set the habit. Many of the species stayed on in the Sea, settled down, and flourished.

In the upper 200-fathom waters of the Cortez, more than 650 species of fish have been officially identified, and there are dozens more in the deep places. Half of those known can be rated as game fish—good fighters or good edible fish that will take the hook.

A casual look under the surface in most areas would reveal a conglomeration of many species of fish, but some sections become occupied by a single, dominant species. Other fish appear to respect these territorial rights even when the entrenched species is weak and defenseless. Some home grounds are occupied on a temporary basis, others seasonally, with many arenas serving as permanent realms.

About a dozen of the most popular species migrate into and out of the Cortez, and a great many more may shift out into the Pacific and back seasonally. But the greater percentage stay put or do their traveling within the Sea. Even on these journeys, schools may go for 500 miles (as in the totuava spawning migrations). Yellowtail and others may travel twice that distance in their seasonal shifts. It is in the enormous migrations that we can see something of the vast quantities of fishes that are supported in this body of water.

SPEEDY LITTLE Sally Lightfoot crab deserves its name — it dashes about as if on tiptoe.

WHERE THE FISH ARE

Most of the twelve regions of the Cortez provide environments which attract sizable to superabundant fish populations of one or more special species. While some of these may be scattered throughout the Cortez and beyond, the water in certain favorable places becomes almost saturated. There are periods when almost every rock area is so crowded it looks as if a fish fiesta were about to break out. There may be twenty such places within a mile, and each may have a hundred or more fish in it. But there are massive aggregations in which the fish must be estimated by the hundreds of tons. These huge schools usually mobilize regularly or remain together most of the time.

Immense populations of mullet occupy most brackish backwaters, but nowhere are they as packed as in the mouth of the Rio Colorado. And no shoaling elsewhere compares with the teeming swarms of Cortez grunion that beach themselves to spawn on the North End beaches. Also seen in this same region, for short periods during the fall months, are concentrations of marlin and sailfish. During spring months, mile-long schools of migrating totuava are commonly seen.

In the Midriff, the nine-month occurrence of California yellowtail exceeds them all in size of assemblies.

At Mulege, hordes of black snook crowd the Rio Rosalia for the winter. California and Mazatlan yellowtail, roosterfish, and other jacks move in large groups, then scatter around the Islas Santa Inez. Just off the mouths of arroyos from this region south, striped pargo house themselves between boulders. Somewhat closer to shore where sand partially fills such boulder areas, ladyfish crowd in.

Sierra come close to getting into a traffic snarl below the town of Loreto throughout late fall to late spring. Roosterfish bunch up in several places in this region throughout the year but may surface only when live bait is presented to them.

While the fish populations of the Juanaloa Region have not yet been fully checked out, massive throngs are certain to be seen in numerous sections. It is a Region of fish-filled reefs. I have found yellowfin tuna abounding on a couple of them during summer and fall. All the shelves of the sector's many islands looked like densely inhabited ant hills. Nowhere have I seen such a profusion of different kinds of basses.

Seasonally in the La Paz Region, schools of various species of jacks—yellowtail and jack crevalle especially—swing in around Isla Espiritu Santo. One of the largest and most permanent hangouts for roosterfish anywhere is in the outer bay at the back end of El Magote. The entrance to the inner bay has long periods of being stirred by swarms of barrilete, with an admixture of sierra and dolphinfish. The deep places in back bays are overrun with bonefish and salt-water catfish. While neither is a good fighter in these waters, the bay's plentiful corvina and black snook are. There are also erratic pileups of sailfish and marlin off the north end of Isla Cerralvo.

The Buena Vista Region is noted for its visiting hordes of warm-water species in the big-game categories. It also hosts other large populations on a permanent basis. Roosterfish, yellowfin tuna, giant needlefish, crevalles, and, in most years, dolphinfish stick around. Then there are throngs of small-game fishes of many hues and kinds.

In the south end during late January and February, there is apt to be more billfish than anywhere else, and great numbers spend most of the year there along with many other big gamesters. In fall and winter the wahoo is more plentiful in the south than elsewhere in the Cortez. But the most compact of all fish masses are the layers around the pier at Cabo San Lucas, where the fish are attracted by the discharges from a fish cannery. Each species has its preferred level, with mullet on the bottom, covered by an almost solid blanket of goatfish. Then there is another layer of salema, topped by several layers of jacks.

Somewhere in warm waters of the earth there may be a region where more kinds of game fish occur, or there may be a greater number of one or two species than in the Cortez, but I have heard of no place where so many fine gamesters are so abundant. All who know something of the world's best fishing regions and who have given this Sea a thorough testing are unanimous in declaring that it adds up to the biggest and most important angling story in the twentieth century. For every kind of angler, from the dry fly purist to the man after monsters, there is a fish to match his art, some so large and powerful that Zane Gray would have been moved to write whole books about them.

PURPLE SEA URCHINS and *starfish dot the shallows and inlets along the Sea of Cortez.*

Where there are so many game fishes to choose from, trying to select the dozen most popular species, for more than a year, would be impossible. Visiting anglers are apt to go all out for a select few one year, then shift their attention the following season. First-timers from California are likely to go wild for their favorite, the large and plentiful California yellowtail. Those from the Atlantic Coast get a bang out of catching an enormous totuava, which resembles and is closely related to the eastern weakfish and sea trout. Inland folks get excited about catching a 150-pound bass, but may feel guilty when they learn that their catch had lived more than half a century.

Before pursuing their favorites, a large percentage of new visitors are determined to catch at least one marlin or sailfish, or both. Until recently some of them caught as many as they could and boastfully brought the big boatload in for photos. Now the resorts and the law frown on decking more than one of each of the billfish per angler.

The history of angling in the Cortez actually begins with this volume, therefore rating the fishes in the various game categories will need time and trial for a decade or so.

The great majority of anglers categorize all edible fish that take the hook as "game fish," giving each kind credit for its extra qualities, such as endurance, power, trickiness, agility, ability to jump, thrash the surface, or make

The Most Dangerous, and a Giant

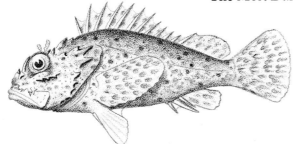

CALIFORNIA SCORPIONFISH, *one of the dangerous boney fishes, has needle-sharp, poisonous spines which can inflict intense pain that lasts from half an hour to four hours.*

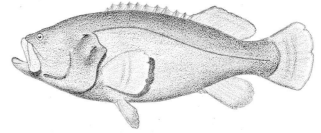

PACIFIC JEWFISH *is a favorite because of size, abundance, wide distribution, good eating. It is the largest native, non-migrating bass in the Cortez, sometimes weighing over 1,000 pounds.*

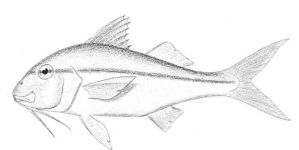

GOATFISH *is not in general use as a live bait, but it is plentiful in a number of areas and is a good bait for big-game fish. The goatfish is neon-yellow when alive but turns red when it dies.*

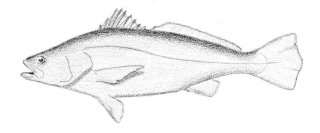

TOTUAVA *weighs up to 300 pounds and is the most sought-after member of the croaker family. Thousands of anglers head for the North End for the totuava's spring spawning migrations to the Rio Colorado.*

long runs. But with all, it is the large size that seems to count most. Though the great marlins and sailfish are not to be depreciated, angling time and effort is and should be divided among a hundred other gamesters. Because of seasonal comings and goings, the various species will generally hold angler interest in the order of their abundance. Marlin may hold the spotlight at Mazatlan and across Baja's tip in late winter and spring, especially in February and March, but yellowtail gets the cheers from the Sea's mouth to Mulege and Topolobampo. This big and powerful first cousin of the amberjack has long been the favored star of Southern California waters, where it rates top billing.

This Sea's own glamor character, the exciting roosterfish, will no doubt develop the most ardent following and a greater number of fans than any other species, when and where live bait has been developed. Nevertheless, no fish in this Sea is likely to outrank the yellowfin tuna. It is a power-loaded torpedo with an unequaled tackle-busting drive. It is known to occur in a few places year-round, but the number of anglers able to get to it is limited, at present.

The image of the magnificent dolphinfish should glow among the brightest, for it is in every way an extraordinary fish and is duly praised throughout the warm water regions of the world. But because it is a villainous thief

Fighters, a King, a Thief

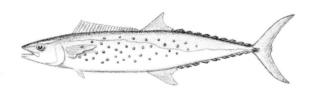

PACIFIC STRIPED MARLIN is the real king of Cortez waters. The aerial rampages of this 150 to 250-pound fighter are an irresistible challenge to anglers. This is the most plentiful member of the marlin family.

SIERRA GRANDE is a great fighter on very light tackle. These are valuable fish to the angler: They provide the best ski and strip bait, and are also good, whole, fresh bait for large fish.

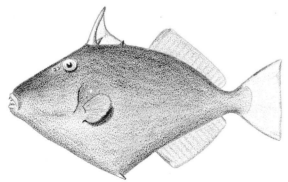

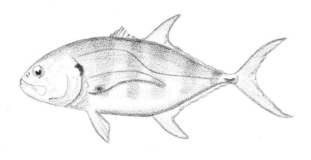

TRIGGERFISH is a bothersome bait thief. "Triggers" sometimes achieve weights of 12 pounds, but even a two-pounder seems heavy when he holds his broad side toward the angler. There are three species.

JACK CREVALLE is widely distributed, can be caught by shore casting. There are several members of the wild, fighting jack family, including the 25 to 45-pound yellowtail, and roosterfish up to 120 pounds.

CLOUDS HANG HEAVY *over distant mountains, and an approaching storm ruffles the usually placid surface of the Sea. Sturdy fingers of cactus stick up from steep, rocky bluffs that drop off sharply here to a ragged shore that is typical of much of Baja's coastline.*

of carefully prepared billfish bait, marlin and sailfish anglers berate and degrade it. The dolphinfish is at once the finest jumper, the most photogenic, and proclaimed by gourmets to be the best food fish.

My choice of the most interesting and most fun fish is the fathom-long, giant needlefish, *Tylosurus fodiator*. It gets the vote because it takes off on the surface and comes bounding in for the bait from a hundred feet away, hits it, and starts a series of Watusi belly-dance movements while jumping two or three times its length. The technique for taking the fish is very tricky. It makes a fine pan fish.

Sierra Monterey and sierra grande are not only fine light-tackle game fish, but they are the most useful of any fish as live bait, fresh-dead bait, ski bait, and other cut baits. In addition, they are food fish par excellence cooked in any way or not cooked at all. They are also good for survival food and water and are exciting to catch.

Although any one of two dozen species may be more plentiful at times and places, the true basses (36 members in the family *Serranidae*) are more

What You Can Do if You Don't Fish

If the Sea of Cortez had no other attractions, its fishing alone would make it one of the most exciting places on earth. But even for the nonfisherman, there is enough adventure and fun at hand to liven a day or a month anywhere along either shore or in between.

Swimming. Most hotels and resorts have their own bathing beaches, though swimming is good anywhere in the Sea. The water temperature is often so close to air temperature that you hardly know which you are in.

Shell collecting. If you know your mollusks (or even if you don't), you can have a field day of collecting shells almost anywhere around the Cortez just by hiking or wading along the water's edge.

Skin diving. Life beneath the surface of the Sea is richer by far than that above. Except in rare seasons of plankton bloom, when the water may become murky, the depths are crystal clear and alive with marine life. Underwater photographers and spear fishermen have a happy hunting ground here, and clams, oysters, crabs, and lobsters are everywhere abundant.

Hunting. Many species of game birds (notably doves, quail, and ducks) are plentiful. Javelina, deer, jaguar, and mountain lion require inland treks. For seasons and regulations, check with any Mexican consulate in the U.S.

Horseback riding. Many of the resorts around the Cortez have riding horses, and any of the country is great riding country.

Shopping. In the main border towns (Tijuana, Mexicali, Nogales), you can buy anything that is made anywhere in Mexico. Farther down on the Mainland there are better shops in Hermosillo, Guaymas, and Mazatlan. In Baja, the only shops are in La Paz and Ensenada.

available on a day-in and day-out basis and in all seasons than any other fishes in the Cortez. This is especially true of the constantly abounding gold spotted bass found in 35 to 55-fathom water, and of the leopard grouper, found in shallow water. The 1,000-pound jewfish, largest of native dwellers, is also in this family.

The true jack family, *Carangidae*, has 32 members, all of them as mean as they look. Included with the yellowtail and roosterfish are the amberjack, crevalles, a host of huge and small pompanos, and species to fit any size of light tackle.

Many anglers who are fond of catching snook will rate the 6-foot black snook as their favorite. Among such species that have developed a following elsewhere are the high-jumping ladyfish, especially numerous in shallow shore waters, the tenacious, tuna-shaped skipjack, or four species of 3-foot croakers in the genus *Cynoscion*—anglers elsewhere know the weakfish, sea trout, and white sea bass as members of this family. Included also in the croaker family, *Sciaenidae*, is the mighty totuava, found only in the top half of the Cortez.

Who knows when the aggravating, bait-stealing, mulish triggerfish, which knows how to slice sideways to get leverage against his tormenting angler enemy, may one day be singled out for its meritorious manners.

There are also several sharks that must be nominated for high rank. The leaping blacktip seems to be the most plentiful, the mako the largest, the hammerhead the most feared (by natives), and the thresher the most showy when hooked. All are good food fish with superb game qualities.

Singling out these few species for discussion should not be taken as discounting or slighting the more than three hundred others, whose qualities may show up in time as superior.

TENANT OF VACANT shells in water, the hermit crab also goes foraging on shore.

MUCH OF THIS BOOK is about fishing, or more properly, angling, an exercise of the mind, body, and spirit, and in the words of its devotees, "unequaled among all of the earthly pursuits." Most of the leaders and prophets of ancient religions glorified the fish. The great monad, most revered symbol of Buddhism, representing moderation and balance in all things, is composed of two fish. The first symbol of Christianity was a fish. In his most holy state, Christ ate fish. The Koran forbids hunting for animals on the holy pilgrimage to Mecca, but advocates fishing.

Fishermen who catch fish to sell commercially are not included in the highly respected term "angler." It is reserved for the ardent or skillful person who catches fish with a hook, rod, and line, and maintains an amateur standing by selling none. The barefoot boy with his willow pole and can of worms is an angler just as much as is a record holder.

The subject of angling should be treated with profound thought, for it is one of the most vital branches of culture. It is a source of humor, but it also evolves a deep and rewarding philosophy. It is a suspenseful drama, a game of skill, a sport, an art, and a most pleasurable avocation. Angling is all of these and more, for it is an escape from a fictitious society to reality, an escape from tensions, grating sounds, and frightening speeds to true, long-lasting serenity.

NO FRIENDS OF THE SPORTS FISHERMEN *are the commercial fishermen who work the Cortez. With huge quantities of game fish being removed daily by the netters, there is little wonder that the big-game fishermen get upset just at the sight of a group like this.*

A LUCKY CATCH *for shark fishermen. There are many of these native crews plying the Cortez. They camp wherever they may be — you'll often see the ramshackle lean-to of shark fishermen on an otherwise deserted island or a stretch of beach. At night their tiny campfires are like small beacons on a darkened coast.*

SHARK CARCASSES ON AN ISLAND BEACH *are a reminder of the time when the hunt was on to get shark livers for vitamins. The hunt is less intensive now, but salted, dried shark meat is a favorite food of the natives, and shark hunters still fish the length of the Cortez.*

Sharks are Handled, but Carefully

MORE UGLY THAN DANGEROUS, the hammerhead shark has not been known to attack man, but there still aren't many natives willing to give him the opportunity!

THE FAT PUFFERFISH *is a novelty item common in Mexican souvenir shops. When he's swimming, he's a normal-looking fish, but out of the water he puffs up like beach ball.*

*A **PENSIVE SEA LION** contemplates the scene from his resting spot on a rocky ledge near Topolobampo. There's no mistaking the sound of a chorus of barks from a herd of these animals. They take a good share of fish from the Sea when they're not relaxing like this or cavorting offshore.*

IN SEARCH OF DINNER, *a flock of pelicans soars smoothly near the water's surface. This is a common sight throughout the Cortez. Also commonly seen are smaller groups, perhaps a dozen or so, winging along in perfect lineup, dipping and diving in unison as they sight their prey.*

Above and Beneath the Surface is an Abundance of Life

NOT A VISITOR *from outer space, this pudgy-faced creature is just a harmless guitarfish viewed from beneath. What appear to be eyes and nostrils are actually olfactory cups which help him to detect the organisms (principally crustaceans) on which he feeds.*

REGION OF THE
North End

Giant totuava in the upper reaches of the Cortez are accessible by trailered boat through California and Arizona

The North End encompasses the top of the Sea of Cortez, from where the Rio Colorado once flowed into the Sea, down to Bahia San Luis Gonzaga on the Baja California or western side, and Cabo Tepoca on the Mainland or eastern side. This region has many attractions but all are overshadowed by the fishing. The star attraction is the giant totuava, largest croaker of this hemisphere, which is caught principally at the extreme north end of the Sea on the Baja side. Other popular species are sailfish, marlin, and dolphin, which occur seasonally on the east side of the Sea, and the great black sea bass, abundant the year around throughout this sector.

I have a special attachment for the North End, since it was there that I experienced a single, adventure-packed day that changed the whole course of my life. It was a day so filled with excitement and enchantment that it caused me to shed my lifetime career and become a vagabundo del mar — a vagabond of the sea — a way of life that has given me many rewarding and fun-crammed years. It was a rags-to-riches story in reverse.

That day was my first on the bountiful and mysterious waters of the Sea of Cortez, and within a few hours I became involved in the most fantastic fishing I had ever experienced.

The time was 1947, a couple of years before the first road had been graded to this sector of the Cortez. Senor Ableardo Rodriquez, former President of Mexico, and his partner, attorney Guillermo Rosas, co-owners of a large section of San Felipe, engaged me to make a survey of the area's angling potential and to help train native shrimp boat crews so they

A BAD PLACE TO RUN OUT OF GAS.
An inland trail near San Felipe in the North End has fewer bumps and ruts than some, but the track across the sand is typical of roads anywhere from below San Felipe to La Paz.

NORTH END *is the region nearest U.S., centered on town of San Felipe.*

could assist State-side anglers who were anticipated as soon as the proposed paved road and accommodations were completed. Eddie Abdo, an opera singer and my fishing amigo, persuaded me to let him in on the venture. We drove down from Hollywood to Mexicali in a pickup and took a shortcut to our campsite, two miles above San Felipe. Senor Rosas had a comfortable and well-organized camp and enthusiastic crews ready for our three months of "work."

The excitement began the next morning, soon after we rounded guano-plastered, 286-foot-high Isla Consag. From a distance the island itself seemed to be quivering, but a closer view revealed only restless activity of immense numbers of birds, sea lions, and other sea creatures.

I had heard sea lions roar, cough, and trumpet many times in the Pacific, but the hallelujahs the sea lions in this assemblage were blasting out sounded like an old-time revival meeting.

There were more than three hundred of the tuba-throated creatures. Great, bewhiskered bulls were busy routing the younger males from their sprawling harems, which filled the tide-washed caves and spread far into the grottoes and benches. In nearby surf a younger, virginal set was performing like a corps of dancers executing a circular ballet routine. Despite the racket, the whole show was one of nature's finest circuses.

It was spring, a period when creatures on the land and in the sea are stirred by a restless agony to get mixed up in some kind of an adventure, romantic or otherwise. It was a time when that latent primitive urge to return to the wilds becomes compelling among kids and codgers, and all ages in between.

The full force of spring was bubbling in both of us as we glided over the velvety blue surface of the Cortez at sunrise. The voyage and the Sea were delightfully strange—it felt like we were cruising on out into the beyond. As the first rays of the rising sun beamed over the water, our reverence for that new day was expressed in Abdo's dramatic and devout Arab invocation. The six-foot-four, 250-pound singer stood atop the wheel house of our shrimper, and facing toward Mecca, gave full thunderous volume to the Mohammedan call to prayer: "Lah illah lah" (There is no God but Allah) . . . "Allah azime" (Allah is great).

Except for the young and neat skipper, our crew of five Mexicans looked like cutthroat pirates, but all assembled on the bow and were so awed by Eddie's ritual they repeatedly made the sign of the cross.

MONSTER FROM THE DEEP

Crew members had hosed the lengthy deck and were working on the opposite corner from our position on the stern, where we had settled for some fishing, when I tied into something that sent vibrations up the rod to my uppers. Whatever I had was as heavy as a log and felt like no other creature I had ever tied into.

Eddie quit fishing and set his rod aside to see what I had hooked. He was amazed when ten feet down in the water there appeared a great and vicious-looking head with beady eyes and gaping jaws set with

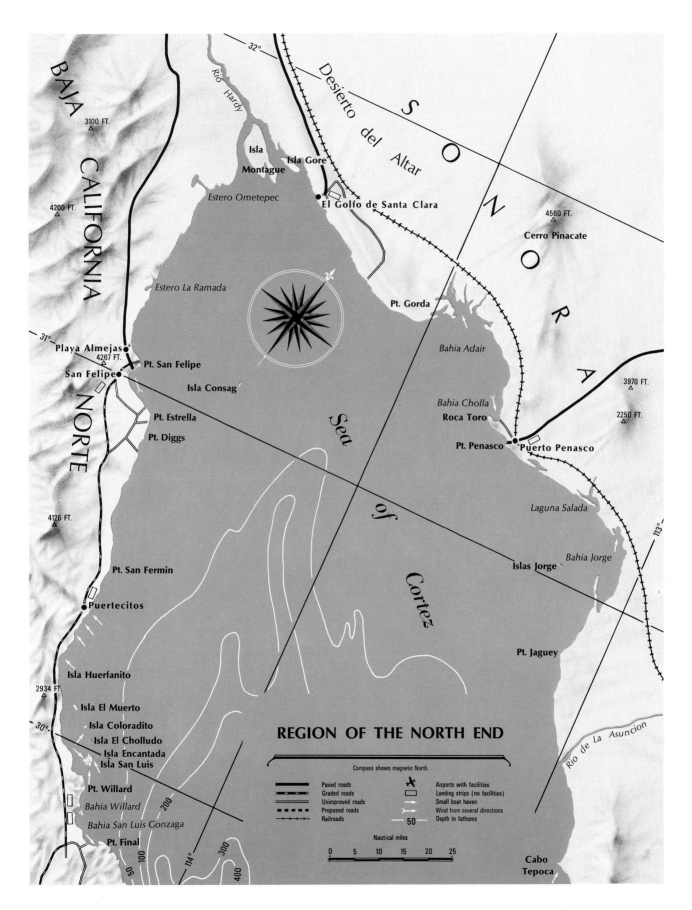

BAJA CALIFORNIA

3100 FT.

4200 FT.

Río Hardy

Isla Montague

Isla Gore

Estero Ometepec

El Golfo de Santa Clara

SONORA

Desierto del Altar

4560 FT.

Cerro Pinacate

Estero La Ramada

31°

Playa Almejas
4267 FT.
Pt. San Felipe
San Felipe

NORTE

Isla Consag

Pt. Gorda

Bahia Adair

Bahia Cholla
Roca Toro

3970 FT.

2250 FT.

Pt. Estrella
Pt. Diggs

Sea

Pt. Penasco   Puerto Penasco

4126 FT.

of

Laguna Salada

113°

Pt. San Fermin

Cortez

Bahia Jorge

Islas Jorge

Puertecitos

Pt. Jaguey

Isla Huerfanito

2934 FT.

Isla El Muerto

30°

Isla Coloradito

Isla El Cholludo

Isla Encantada
Isla San Luis

Rio de La Asuncion

Pt. Willard

Bahia Willard

200

REGION OF THE NORTH END

Bahia San Luis Gonzaga

Pt. Final

100

114°

300

Compass shows magnetic North

Paved roads	Airports with facilities
Graded roads	Landing strips (no facilities)
Unimproved roads	Small boat haven
Proposed roads	Wind from several directions
Railroads	50 Depth in fathoms

50

400

Nautical miles

0   5   10   15   20   25

Cabo Tepoca

glistening teeth. The head was followed by a huge, squirming body that seemed to extend to the depths.

Both of us froze. We were gazing right into the face of a real sea monster. As I cautiously eased it up to the surface, Eddie grabbed the shark gaff, and in one powerful swoop, caught the creature through the throat. The sting caused it to lurch upward, helping Eddie to hoist it aboard. As the slithering monster hit the deck, both hook and gaff came free, and it went skidding straight toward the bare feet of the Mexican crew, teeth snapping like castanets. As one, they gave the fearsome thing one horrified glance, and scurried up the mast pole. And who was the top man on the timber? El Capitan.

The ten-foot denizen proved to be a conger eel (*Muraenesox sp.*), the largest recorded to that date. We soon caught two others measuring over eight feet, which led us to the mistaken belief that they were quite common. Instead of saving the rare specimens for our collection, we committed a scientific error by cutting them into steaks and eating all we could of the white, poultry-like meat. (The only other king-size conger reported to have been caught in the Cortez, to my knowledge, is an eight-footer taken at Mazatlan.)

Moving out to deeper water, we brought up several other kinds of fish, among them a 100-pound baya grouper, a 60-pound spotted pina

When You Cross the Border

All United States citizens who visit Mexico must have a tourist card, obtainable from Mexican consulates in major U.S. cities or at the border. Cards are free for visits of up to 30 days ($3 for single entry visits of 30 days to six months; $5 for multiple entries for six months). No tourist card is required for visits of less than 72 hours to border towns. It is always advisable to carry proof of citizenship, such as a birth certificate, passport, or voter's registration card. Naturalized citizens will be required to present their naturalization papers.

All persons must have a smallpox vaccination certificate obtained within the last three years. Vaccination may be obtained at the border, but in order to avoid inconvenience and possible delay, it is advisable to have it taken care of before you leave home. The information must be recorded on an International Certificate of Inoculation and Vaccination, which must then be certified by an office of the United States Public Health Service.

If you drive a car into Mexico, you will need proof of ownership, or a notarized statement from the registered owner stating that you may take the car out of the country. You will be issued a free permit for the car, valid for 180 days, when you cross the border. Your U.S. driver's license is good in Mexico. Check with your agent before you leave home regarding automobile insurance, since most U.S. policies are not valid in Mexico. You can get a short-term policy when you cross the border.

Check with your nearest Mexican consulate regarding gun permits and hunting regulations. Fishing tackle may be brought into Mexico duty free, and fishing licenses may be obtained at the border or from fish and game wardens in the area in which you are staying.

WEIRD SOUVENIRS *hang to dry on the beach at Puerto Penasco. They are sting rays, or devil fish with the tails and sides slit to form gruesome, skeleton-like shapes. The rays are swept up in the nets of the shrimp fleet. When dried like this, they become tourists' mementos.*

cabrilla, a 125-pound totuava, a large dog snapper, and a 30-pound white sea bass. The sea bass was the only species in the whole day's catch that was familiar from Pacific Coast fishing. It was easily identified and distinguished from its close relatives, the corvina and totuava, by the raised white cord along its belly.

Although several of the fishes that we caught around Isla Consag were closely related to some I had taken in the Gulf of Mexico and the Caribbean, most of our day's catch was completely new to me. We felt that we had been angling in an untouched Eden. Even the behavior of the birds—pelicans, goonies, terns, gulls, and frigates—and the crazy performances of the sea lions seemed different from elsewhere.

Then there were other queer sights, such as the occurrence of thousands of coconut-sized jellyfish, most of them with one to two-inch jacks residing in their tentacles. The jellyfish were so poisonous that a mere touch would have killed other small fishes or given a human a serious sting. On spotting drifting food morsels, the tiny jacks would dash out for them, then scuttle back to resume peeking from under the protective, bowl-shaped blobs. These young jellyfish (floating invertebrate colonies called Portuguese man-o-war) were being moved southward by the current. Scientific reports of six-inch-long jacks seen in residence in large jellyfish at the mouth of the Cortez caused us to speculate on the long and adventuresome voyage the little fish were embarking upon.

On our way back to port, to climax the day in this fish fantasyland, a big marlin grabbed a bone jig I was trolling and made four magnificent jumps before breaking the hook and taking off.

It was the return to San Felipe that added the final touch of sheer delight to this fullest of days. Just a mile out from the village, as we were gliding into the setting sun with a breeze at our back, Eddie climbed to the top of the housing and sang a medley of Mexican songs to express and to share his joy of that day.

Most of the town's populace, awakened from their siestas, came rushing down on the beach, to find out whose highly trained voice was booming out their native melodies. At that moment they would have elected Eddie the jefe (mayor) of the pueblo. In fact, from that time on, every service we asked for was happily granted.

THE GREAT BLADDER ENTERPRISE

Near our camp, two miles above the village of San Felipe, we met an old Chinese, named Quan, who lived in a cave. We were told that he had accumulated an immense fortune by exporting dried totuava bladders to China, where they were ground into a costly powder used to enrichen and thicken soups. In addition, we learned that at the end of World War II, when there was a rush on harvesting of shark livers for vitamins, Quan had salvaged the shark fins, which he also shipped to China.

Many of the villagers had been employed in Quan's fin and bladder enterprises. After removing the bladders, they discarded tons of totuava on the beach and there it waited until a high tide flushed the remains out for sharks to feast on. That's how it worked until a couple of venturesome Californians with initiative arrived, saw the waste, and started a sizable

PUMA'S SWIFT striking force and power constantly peril Mexican deer and livestock.

business. They hauled ice down from the States and trucked the big totuava back to the U.S. where they sold them as "sea bass." We saw the kaput body of a truck that was still being used as an ice storage house for the huge fish between trips.

One of the totuava brought in by a native weighed 303 pounds. It helped convince us that there could be a potentially enormous angler interest in this great and abundant croaker *(Totuava macdanaldi).* We decided to study habits and habitat of the species.

The next day we were back at Isla Consag with a new crew. One of them, Jose Limon, who operated a fishing fleet in San Felipe, had fished totuava commercially near the island so he directed us to their habitat. We found it to be a 20 to 22-fathom narrow, mud-bottom trench, starting about a quarter of a mile northwest of Consag and extending westward. After fishing there with various baits without success, we switched to very small hooks and baits and began catching foot-long corvinas— then suddenly something hit and made off with one of them.

The next corvina caught was quickly switched to my heavy outfit. The lively bait had barely reached bottom when a tug indicated that I had hooked something like a slow-moving submarine. I gave it all the pressure the heavy line would take but couldn't turn it. The contest was resolved not by sensational runs but by matching endurances. Both fish and I were close to exhaustion when he gave up. The catch proved to be a hefty totuava weighing close to 200 pounds. We seemingly could have caught

What to Expect Below the Border

Weather. Along Baja's Cortez coast the days are hot, but dry, and the evenings are balmy. In the cape region, sea breezes often cool the afternoons. On the Pacific side of Baja the weather is cooler year-round, but nights are often foggy. Rains come in late August and September. The Mainland coast is hotter and more sultry, day and night, for most of the year.

Language. Spanish is the language of the land, though many of the Mexican and Indian idioms wouldn't be understood in Madrid. Even a few words of Spanish will let you have more fun, but English is spoken at most of the places you are likely to stay.

Food. Most of the resorts on both sides of the Cortez have their own wells. In the small towns and back villages, don't drink water unless it's bottled; stick to soft drinks or beer (cerveza). Usually the food is not highly spiced, though a fiery chili sauce is served for you to use at your discretion. Fish is served everywhere, in a variety of ways, all of them good. If you ever have a chance to eat turtle, don't miss it. Mexican breads and pastries are very tasty.

Accommodations. In the entire Baja Peninsula there are fewer tourist rooms than an average-size American hotel, though more are being added daily. Rates are generally higher on the Mainland than in Baja. For a detailed listing of places to stay and their general rate structure, see the Appendix.

THE EBB TIDE OF THE UPPER GULF *flows off the land like a great flood rushing into the Sea, but before the land is dry, the flood will sweep back over it again. This aerial view from 9,000 feet shows miles of the tidal inlets of Montague Island, one of two islands at the mouth of the Rio Colorado.*

tons more of these huge and excellent food fish. Instead we tested different techniques for catching them. Lures and dead baits were far less effective than live 8 to 12-inch croakers and corvinas which we caught on the same mud bottoms with totuava.

To allow the baits more freedom to swim around, we used a light, 30-pound test, flexible leader as long as the fish we expected to catch, and a sinker with a hole that would allow the line to run through it freely just heavy enough to hold against the current.

After two weeks in the Consag area refining techniques, we covered the San Felipe sector searching for totuava hangouts. We found one loaded, deep depression, 7 miles southeast of the island, which we suspected was their main swimway, two fairly productive holes nearer the village, another off Punta Diggs, and a shallow, undefined flat, 15 miles north of Punta San Felipe, over which small schools roamed.

One of the most important of all angling techniques developed was "rhythm pumping." This method worked not only for totuava but for all large fish. The art of pumping a fish during retrieving has long been practiced by astute anglers. With this method, the fisherman pulls the rod upward as far as possible without cranking the reel, then cranks rapidly as he lowers the rod.

In the new method, the rhythm is achieved by making three or four half-second halts while pulling the rod up. These should not be yanks, but rather a slight lessening of the pressure on the fish in a regularly timed rhythm. This causes the fish to keep its mouth open and gills closed. Without water passing by its gill filaments, the fish smothers.

The timing of the upward strokes should be regulated according to the size of the hooked fish: the smaller the fish, the more rapid the strokes. While not difficult, this technique must be learned by practice. The strokes should be continued even when the fish stops, or takes off. When most fish begin to smother they usually get panicky and spend their energy in erratic and charging runs. Billfish tend to do more jumping.

Casting from the beaches below and above San Felipe we caught many orangemouth corvina (*Cynoscion xanthulus*) on a variety of light-colored lures by dropping them to the sand bottom and bouncing them on it when retrieving. We tried other baits and found that we did even better with

ELEPHANT SEAL'S improbable nose is a distinguishing feature. They inhabit Isla Guadalupe.

strips of sierra and squid. Fresh shrimp topped both of them, especially after dark. Live bait proved best of all. For corvina, a tidal estuary toward the Colorado River on incoming tides was most productive.

Trolling from a skiff, we accidentally discovered a bait that was subsequently developed to be sensational for trolling. We were fishing about 40 feet from Punta San Felipe rocks, where we saw disk-shaped pompano jumping and flipping on the surface like pancakes being tossed in a griddle. We tried trolling and casting almost every lure and bait without getting a single taker. That is, not until I baited a hook with a small strip of fish and peeled off a couple hundred yards of line. As I retrieved, the two-inch strip-bait began to ski on the surface. A pancake pompano *(Trachinotus paitensis)* grabbed it at once and went into flapping, four-foot-high leaping turnovers.

Monterey sierra *(Scomberomorous concolor)* is the most abundant fish available to anglers in the North End, except from December through March, when it becomes scarce. Each late afternoon, returning from Isla Consag, we watched schools of Monterey sierra jumping in a follow-the-leader pattern as far as we could see in all directions. Even south of this region, where it is superabundant, I have never seen the other species, Sierra grande *(S. sierra)*, display this jumping habit. The sierras are closely related to and resemble the Spanish mackerels of the Atlantic. All are in the true Spanish mackerel family, *Cyblidas,* and are excellent light-tackle gamesters. Sierras are among the best for cut or whole bait. Both Monterey and grande are caught more consistently on white, quarter-ounce Compac feathers, trolled or retrieved at rapid speeds.

BUTTRESSED TRUNKS and cones like wooden puzzles are typical of the native Guadalupe cypress.

A FISH WITH A MESSAGE

Although I had seen and experienced much so far, I was eager to learn even more about the fascinating waters of the Cortez. This desire resulted in my accepting the invitation of Charles Rucker of Los Angeles to join him on an exploration in 1953. Rucker, a pioneer in waters of the Cortez,

The Enchanted Islands

Las Islas Encantadas form a small, six-island archipelago which stretches for 20 miles across the 30th Parallel opposite an unbroken beach, beginning 29 miles south of Puertecitos. Headed by San Luis, biggest and southernmost of the Encantadas, the flotilla-like group includes the islands of Cantada, El Cholludo, Coloradito, El Muerto, and Huerfanito.

Natives explain the reasons for calling the group Encantadas (meaning enchanted or bewitched) this way: First, the current on the west side of the chain runs counter to that off the east side. Second, large rocks (pumice stone, a spongy form of volcanic glass) cracking off Islas Encantadas do not sink, but float. Third, when you sail eastward, you often see a sea mirage: Long after the islands disappear over the horizon, they reappear to their full height.

ALWAYS READY TO LEND A HAND — *for a price* — *San Felipe beach boys haul a lucky fisherman's prize totuava to the beach for cleaning. The usual cleaning charge for these big fish is about a dollar. Totuava spawn and live in the North End, and they are taken all year out of San Felipe.*

previously had scouted fishing between San Felipe and Bahia de Los Angeles. He engaged a sizable shrimp boat for five-day cruises down the coast from San Felipe past Puertecitos to the Islas Encantadas (Enchanted Islands) and on to Bahia Willard and Bahia San Luis Gonzaga. The shrimper carried five outboard-powered skiffs, and accommodated twelve anglers. A crew of seven lowered and operated the skiffs.

At Bahia Willard and Bahia San Luis Gonzaga we fished up to the rugged cliffs until a wind caused us to find shelter on the south side of Gonzaga. Here we discovered a completely hidden cove with an S-shaped entrance. Except for triggerfish and small grouper, we found little else in it; but the outer ledges and benches abounded with species, and I learned to catch several new to me. Included were the roosterfish and two other jacks. The strangest was a 14-inch-long chino mero (*Cirrhitus rivulatus*) which I horsed out from under the edge of a rock.

The name "chino" was given this fish because of the fantastic mask-like design on its face, which is similar to the makeup of a Chinese actor, and because of the odd pattern of large bands resembling Chinese calligraphy that run vertically across its sides. The characters are light brown with a pin-line border in neon-blue.

When I first examined a chino I was reminded of a Zanzibar butter-fly fish that I had read about which had Arabic-like markings on its tail that spelled Lah illah lah (There is no God but Allah) on one side, and Shani-Allah (This warning from Allah) on the other.

When I returned to California I took my carefully preserved chino mero to a Chinese friend, Professor Paul Fung. At first he thought it was a fake and that a scholarly Chinese had done the decorative script.

"This," said the learned professor, "is early Ming style of writing and tells a classical joke: Two farmers, one wife—no peace."

I could hardly wait to take the specimen to Dr. Boyd Walker, the noted ichthyologist. I was naturally disappointed to learn from him that the species had already been described and was thought to be plentiful.

The bass-shaped chino mero lives under rock ledges on shallow bottoms throughout the Cortez and down the Mexican coast. The largest I've seen weighed seven pounds. It is one of the trickiest fish to catch; in addition to the unusual evasive stunts other fish employ when hooked, this one makes use of the lower, greatly enlarged rays of its pectoral fins. When it gets a purchase on a rock with them, it is as difficult to pull as a balking burro. Furthermore, it actually can use the fins to back itself up under rocks.

As a light-tackle game fish, the chino is rated among the top by shore anglers. It is taken on 2-inch strip-bait or small lures hopped along on the bottom near a ledge.

Except for our little cove, we learned that San Luis Gonzaga was a hostile bay, subject to winds from Pacific storms. But Bahia Willard, which is separated from Gonzaga by a sand spit and a small island, had good anchorage on its three sides. Later, when I saw three outboarders get wrecked there, I learned that it, too, could be dangerous for careless small-boat operators.

CENTURY-OLD GIANTS

The slight indentation called Ensenada Grande, at the western junction of the North End and Midriff regions, has a small arroyo separated by sheer cliffs of enormous heights. From the cliffs, water plunges down to a 35-fathom bench, then drops sharply to 300 fathoms. It was on this bench, directly out from the wash, that a commercial vessel was reported to have caught a 500-pound black sea bass. (Some of these great basses weigh up to 600 pounds and live for a century or more.)

After trying chunks, slabs, and whole sierra for bait with no strikes,

BADGER'S characteristic diggings show where he tunnels down for rodents.

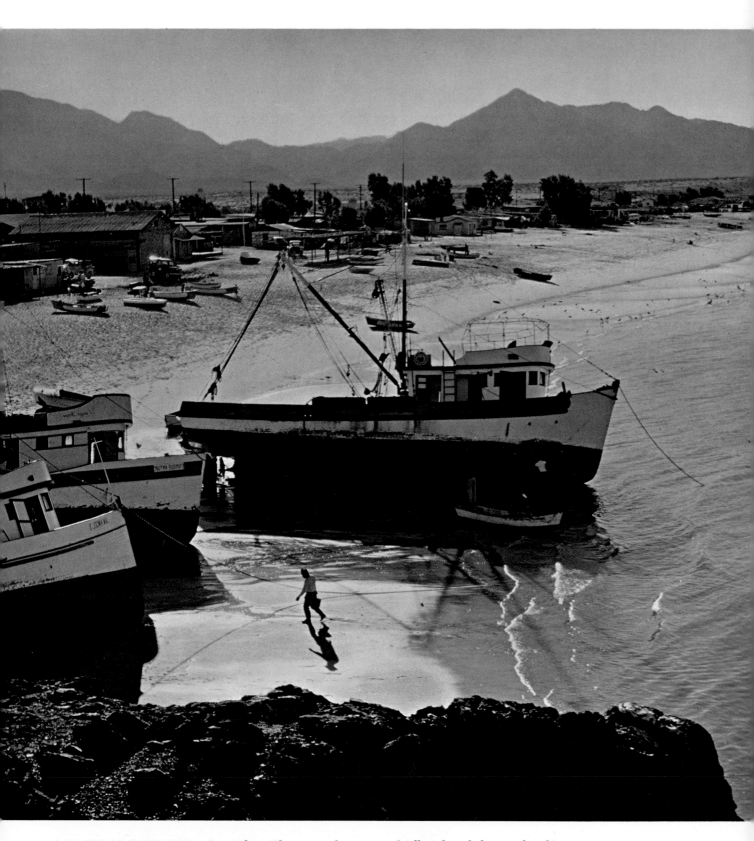

A NATURAL DRYDOCK at San Felipe. The tremendous rise and fall of the tide here makes ship repair easy. Boats are run up on shore as far as they will go; when the tide goes out, they're left high and dry. San Felipe's shore sometimes looks like a graveyard of small boats, but most will be back in service as soon as repairs are made.

THE WAVE-WASHED *shore at San Felipe is easily accessible from north of the border, and the town caters to game fishermen. There are launching facilities, campgrounds, motels, and supplies. A commercial fishing fleet also operates out of San Felipe.*

A VARIED COAST *stretches along the edge of the Sea near San Felipe. It offers sandy beaches, tide flats, a rocky shoreline, and tide pools where many forms of sea life hide.*

 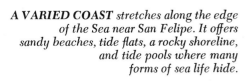

I started prospecting for live bait with strip-bait on No. 2 hooks and discovered that the rock bottom was loaded with foot-long, gold-spotted bass *(Paralabrax auroguttatus).*

As with most fish brought up from great depth, the air bladders of the first two gold spotters extended out of their mouths like bubble gum. We quickly transferred them (hooked under their soft dorsal fin) to heavy rigs and returned them to the bottom. Back under pressure everything was squeezed back into place.

The baits had barely reached their mark before they were gulped by something that pulled like a mule, and the tug-of-war was on. Two of our anglers gave the battle all they had. After an hour of exhausting struggle, one fisherman brought his yearling-size bass to gaff. It took three crewmen and a rope to deck it. The second big black was hauled aboard a few minutes later. Both weighed well over 300 pounds.

I had never heard of such a concentration of big blacks as we ran into here. Almost every one of the live baits that we sent down went into a huge bass, which would try to plunge into its cave, an exercise guaranteed to smash a lot of tackle. But with plenty of extra gear on hand, each of our group hooked, fought, and landed a giant black.

HOME GROUND OF TOTUAVA

While fishing for the blacks, the tidal current changed, and our boat drifted from the rock bottom to a 40-fathom mud flat. My bait was taken by a fish with a power drive as great as that of the big blacks, but it took off for a long run instead of making short dashes.

Although I had caught numerous king-size totuava, I could not conceive of one being at such depth. When the fish was decked and it turned out to be a giant croaker, I suspected that the deep channel was normal home grounds of the species.

The Mysterious Grunion

One of the strangest mysteries in biological science is the timing device that triggers the spawning instinct of the grunion *(Leuresthes sardina).* The spawning run occurs February through May. The fish in great numbers swim close to a sandy beach and remain until the exact crest of the extreme lunar high tide, then swim ashore. The females quickly bore holes with their tails, more than half the length of their five to eight-inch bodies. While they are in the holes, one (or more) of the smaller males bends around each female and discharges milt to fertilize the eggs as she deposits them in the hole. The survival ritual completed, the grunion then flip seaward in time to catch a following, somewhat shorter wave.

Two weeks later, when the next lunar high tide floods over the eggs, they hatch. Swept back into the sea, the tadpole-shaped larvae soon grow into fish.

Grunion can be captured by hand immediately after spawning. In addition to their use as bait, they make an excellent pan fry.

After decking a half-dozen more (and later returning to the same spot at other seasons and finding totuava fairly plentiful), I was willing to conclude that, except during spawning migrations and some short feeding runs, the totuava spend most of their time in the channels of the Midriff and their extensions.

From evidence collected, I surmised that the totuava moved well up into the mouth of the Rio Colorado and spawned shortly before the bore started upstream. The fertilized eggs were carried by the bore into brackish water, where they and the hatched-out larvae were protected from the predators in the salt sea water. The young remained in these less-salty waters for a year or more, feeding extensively on shrimp and perhaps young mullet, also spawned in or near the river mouth.

Since the great tidal bores occurred only on the new and full moon maximum tide periods, forecasting exact spawning dates was easy. After learning that the egg and milt-filled totuava seldom ate previous to spawning, and that afterward they were ravenous, I had only to check the number of days that the schools spent getting to San Felipe to give the calendar dates they would be available there. Years of repeated checking showed that the slow return trip was three days, and that the schools remained in the San Felipe feeding holes from three to five days before moving on. The same calendar held good for El Golfo de Santa Clara, on the Mainland side but occasionally started a day earlier.

Some totuava not quite ready to spawn join the migration and can be hooked going north or coming south. The young (10 to 20-pounders) venturing southward along a line close to shore can also be caught occasionally from spring to fall.

MEXICO'S NORTHERN COAST

The coastal village of El Golfo de Santa Clara is the first settlement below the mouth of the Colorado on the Mainland side of the Cortez. Its potential as a popular angling town will depend upon how effectively laws protecting the diminishing totuava and corvina populations are enacted and enforced. The grunion, usually plentiful, also bear watching.

A paved, 70-mile road from the Arizona border town of San Luis to Santa Clara, and another one branching to it from the San Felipe-Mexicali highway, brought a small boom to the pueblo. A 14-mile extension eastward toward Punta Gorda reaches a stretch of beach, where totuava and corvina come within casting range of shore when thousands of grunion make spring spawning runs during windy high-tide periods.

Close up to Punta Gorda, boaters have two advantages: They can fish the rock reef 7 miles south of the point; and, in case of a blow, they can run into the only deep estuary in Adair, the most westerly of the many esteros breaking inland. Many corvina and some pancake pompano run in and out of here with the tides—tides which reach heights of 22 feet in spring months. Because the tides drain out so rapidly, boats entering other esteros are in danger of being left aground far from water.

The southeastern extremity of Bahia Adair is Roca Toro, which recedes to the north to form Bahia Cholla. The latter has a fairly well-protected cove at its back.

ERRATIC TUMBLING of Mexican jumping beans is caused by small, lively moth larvae inside pods.

FOR BROWSING OR BUYING, *there are plenty of shops in the border towns. There are craft products from all over Mexico — some good, some unbelievably gaudy and poorly made. If you like the graceful shapes and clear colors of Guadalajara glassware, you can bring back a fine collection.*

Border-Town Shopping Can be an Adventure

FRILLY PAPER PINATAS *are fun to shop for. They come in all sizes and shapes (donkeys, birds, bulls, chickens) and a wide assortment of lively colors.*

A BORDER-TOWN FIRE EATER *captivates a young audience. The children are both fascinated and frightened by the antics of this ventriloquist as he climaxes his outdoor show with a spectacular stunt in which he becomes a human flame thrower. This is typical of the carnival atmosphere of the border towns.*

IN THE TIME-HONORED WAY, beans are threshed by throwing crushed pods into the air. As the man whips them around with his stick, the wind blows away the chaff.

Age-Old Trades and Practices are Part of Today

YOU CAN BUY of hand-woven baskets for a few pesos in any Mexican marketplace, and you'll often have an opportunity to watch a basket maker at work.

 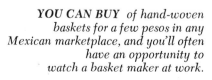

REGION OF THE
Midriff

Camping on a cannibal island — raging currents and upwelling of
the waters — neptunal war between creatures of land and sea

The Midriff is the narrowest section of the Sea of Cortez and contains the
only string of islands crossing it. An isolated belt, about 40 miles above
and below the 29th Parallel, the Midriff reaches from the lower Baja Norte
coast straight across to the Mexican Mainland. Its fifty or so islands are
peaks of large marine mountains projecting from great depths. These submerged mountains, with their underwater gardens of fantastic splendor
and weird dimensions, make this region of the Sea strangely different from
all others. And in the rich waters of the Midriff nature spills over in super-
abundance and evolution proceeds rapidly.

This is a region of violence—deep channels and swift currents create
maelstrom-like eddies and immense upwelling boils—yet there is sublime
beauty. The region abounds in strange fishes, unusual sea plants, and crustaceans that are grotesque and mysterious. Colder than the waters to the
north or south, the Midriff waters provide a vast, natural food factory and
habitat for sea life which prefers cooler water.

The name "Midriff" was chosen for two reasons. First, it is descriptive
of the region's enormous riffles, or great areas of broken water. Then, by
use of a bit of imagination and a map, the entire Sea of Cortez can suggest
a standing woman with a narrow, belted waistline—a chain of islands—
across the midriff.

This island-dotted region is a wilderness encompassing some 5,600
square miles. All of its islands have been virtually uninhabited since the
Seri Indians were officially removed from Isla Tiburon to the Mainland.

NORTHERNMOST OF BAJA'S GREAT OASES.
Cactus on dry hillsides gives way to date palms in a
fertile valley near the town of San Ignacio — after
a good half-day's drive inland from the Cortez. The massive
stone church, completed in 1786, dominates the town.

As of 1965, there were only about 100 people living at Bahia de Los Angeles on the Baja side, a like number at Bahia Kino on the Mainland, and some 200 Seris in two camps above the village of New Kino.

Except for the Hermosillo Valley near Kino, and a few other flat places, the terrain of the Midriff land area is somewhat mountainous. Lofty volcanic peaks, with mountains between them, once sliced off in earth faulting, make a precipitous and awe-inspiring shoreline. Some of the cliffs plunge below the surface 40 fathoms. Others are stepped like pyramids or slope off into crumbling lava piles. Many are pocked with submerged caves of varying sizes. Above the high-tide line there isn't enough soil among the lava and the rubble to provide footing for vegetation. The scant soil and the area's insufficient rainfall sustain nothing but sparse, desert-type cacti and thorn bushes.

LIKE FISHING IN HELL

The first time I saw Bahia Refugio it was as though we had cruised into the outer perimeter of Dante's Inferno. To the dozen anglers aboard our charter boat, the crags, jags, piked pinnacles, and the black, angular shadows they cast, were a shock. Instead of waving palms and tropical jungle, we saw only a half-dozen cacti, a clump of thorn bushes, and an unsightly elephant tree hanging from a bleak cliff. Sinister-looking frigate birds and ungainly pelicans planed overhead.

"Looks like we're going to be fishing in hell," someone muttered.

Despite the grotesque surroundings, there was a soul-satisfying beauty in the tranquil and royal blue water. But even as we beheld it, the surface was shattered, first in a small area, then in another and another until the whole bay boiled as if the dead volcano that created it had come to life and was about to re-erupt. Big fish were causing the ruckus. We did not then know that this was an advance school of the great yellowtail migration, which occurs in April and May, nor that this bunch had just moved in and was competing with the hosts of native fishes and fowls for the massive shoals of sardine and herring that crowd into this bay to spawn.

The crew rushed to lower the outboard skiffs, and within a few minutes all anglers were out in them and getting hookups. It was a sight to witness. Hooked fish were going in all directions, while hundreds of other big mossbacks, milling right around the skiffs, were contesting with pelicans, frigates, boobies, terns, and other sea birds for the forage.

These were avid yellowtail fishermen with experience in Southern California waters, and they had long dreamed of getting into a school that would once and for all provide as much fishing as they could wish for. This time they got it! Before the end of the second day the big forty to sixty-pounders had them yelling uncle and wanting to catch anything but yellows.

The mammoth, 75 to 80-foot, plankton-eating finback whales, second largest of all earth's animals (the blue whale rates first), seem to have found a continuous supply of the food in the Midriff and have become permanent residents. On several trips to the region I have seen pods of from six to

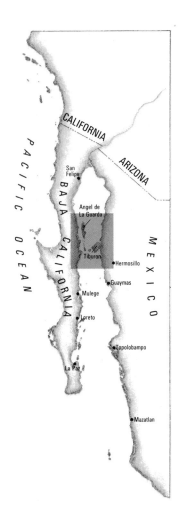

MIDRIFF *region covers both sides of the Cortez and its two largest islands.*

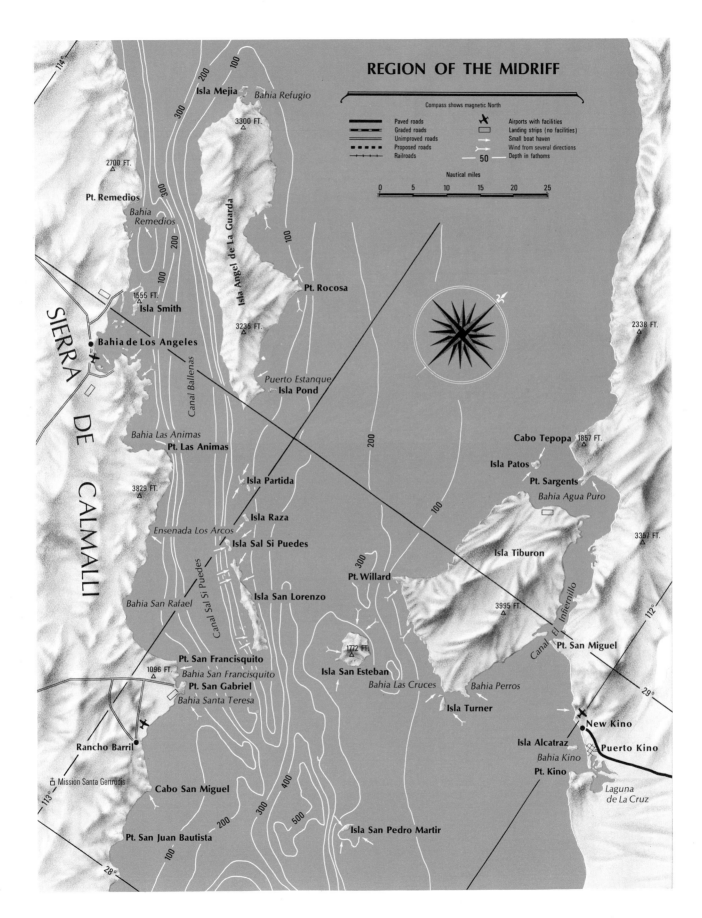

REGION OF THE MIDRIFF

Compass shows magnetic North

▬▬▬▬ Paved roads	✈ Airports with facilities
▬▬▬▬ Graded roads	▭ Landing strips (no facilities)
▭▭▭▭ Unimproved roads	→ Small boat haven
▪▪▪▪ Proposed roads	⇉ Wind from several directions
┼┼┼┼ Railroads	─── 50 ─── Depth in fathoms

Nautical miles

0   5   10   15   20   25

Isla Mejia

Bahia Refugio

3300 FT.

2700 FT.

Pt. Remedios

Bahia Remedios

Isla Angel de La Guarda

1555 FT.

Isla Smith

Bahia de Los Angeles

Pt. Rocosa

3235 FT.

Canal Ballenas

Puerto Estanque

Isla Pond

Cabo Tepopa   1857 FT.

Bahia Las Animas

Pt. Las Animas

Isla Patos

Pt. Sargents

Bahia Agua Puro

3829 FT.

Isla Partida

Isla Raza

Ensenada Los Arcos

Isla Sal Si Puedes

Isla Tiburon

3357 FT.

Canal Sal Si Puedes

Isla San Lorenzo

Pt. Willard

3995 FT.

SIERRA

DE

CALMALLI

Bahia San Rafael

Canal El Infiernillo

Pt. San Miguel

Pt. San Francisquito

1772 FT.

Bahia San Francisquito

Pt. San Gabriel

Isla San Esteban

Bahia Las Cruces

Bahia Perros

Bahia Santa Teresa

2338 FT.

Rancho Barril

Isla Turner

New Kino

Mission Santa Gertrudis

Isla Alcatraz

Puerto Kino

Bahia Kino

Pt. Kino

Cabo San Miguel

Laguna de La Cruz

Pt. San Juan Bautista

Isla San Pedro Martir

112°

29°

113°

28°

114°

100   200   300

300

200

100

300

200

100

50

200

100

300

300

400

500

200

300

200

100

A CHOP FROM A MACHETE *frees date clumps, which are then slid down a rope to a helper on the ground below. Date palms were imported to San Ignacio by the Jesuits.*

DATE PROCESSING *is a thriving business in some regions of Baja. Beyond the drying racks are typical, small San Ignacio houses, made of sun-dried adobe blocks and roofed with palm thatch.*

thirty-five of the huge baleens. They appear to follow well-traveled courses.

On one occasion five skiffs were loaded with anglers fishing a mile or so away from our big boat. Suddenly, the skipper and I saw a dozen finbacks freight-training in from around a point and heading directly toward the skiffs. We had no bell, whistle, or other sound device to warn the anglers. I grabbed a couple of gunnysacks and tried to semaphore them to attract their attention, but to no avail. We decided our only chance was to try to reach the skiffs before the whales did. The skipper gave the old ship full throttle, and the race was on.

In the beginning we had a slight edge. Every nut, bolt, and shaft was strained to the utmost by the full charge of fuel, and the exhaust boiled and belched flames.

We could see the lead bull a hundred yards ahead of the pod, heading directly toward one of the skiffs, where anglers were centering all energy and attention on fighting fish. Their crew boy was busy maneuvering the boat, but when he finally saw the bull bearing in, he began to frantically windmill his arms. The struggling anglers gave him nothing more than a gesture to shut-up.

We expected to see the whale plow into the frail skiff and fling it into space. Instead, the great mammal surfaced so close it seemed he could have inhaled boat, men, and all, then blew up a geyser and sounded. The sudden dive brought his fluke up to the height of a two-story building, and enough water was tossed across the boat to drench the occupants and nearly swamp the craft. So engrossed had the fishermen been that they were quite mystified as to where the water had come from. Later I learned that healthy finbacks rarely nudge boats.

THE BIGMOUTH

On a number of trips, with the help of ichthyologist Dr. Boyd Walker, I collected fish for identification purposes. On one such trip, in an area about 50 by 75 feet in Bahia Refugio, we collected more than 100 species. Included was one new species and another so rare that only three specimens had ever been recorded. Its scientific name is *Opisthognathus rhomalea*, which literally translated means a fish with a large mouth.

This *rhomalea*, with its brilliant yellow and neon-blue dotted stripes, was one of the most beautiful things I had ever seen come out of the sea. When I asked Walker what the common or vernacular name of the fish was, he explained that none had been selected. However, he said, regarding the first *rhomalea* he had seen, one of his students had accidentally misplaced the specimen. On being queried as to the whereabouts of the strange fish, another student asked, "What strange fish?" Walker answered, "Oh you know, that big-mouth bastard."

Walker agreed with my suggestion that, whenever reasonable, a thing should be known by the first name ever applied to it. This seemed a most reasonable situation, so the common name "bigmouth bastard" was adopted.

MULE DEER RANGE *mountain spine of Baja and Mainland, foraging early and late in day.*

TIBURON—THE CANNIBAL ISLAND

Cruising northward through the Midriff one time, we stopped for the night at Isla Patos (Cormorant Island), lying 5 miles off the top of Isla Tiburon and providing shelter from both north and south winds. In the morning we examined the broad north end of Canal Infiernillo. The shallow water had been heated by the small flow through the narrows near the south end. Because of this we did not expect to see anything and so were surprised to find the water rich with many species of small fish.

The tide was low when we got back to the northwest corner of Isla Tiburon, and I noted that the convergence of the warm Infiernillo water with cool water from the depths was a great distance out. During the extreme minus tides, the warm water extended down the full length of Tiburon's west side. While cool water is preferred by many species, it acts as a barrier to some of the more tropical forms. Marlin, sailfish, skipjack, and dolphinfish avoid the cool waters in the other Midriff channels and migrate through the warm waters of this passage.

A few miles down the west side of Tiburon we saw some Seri Indians who at that time were still living on the island in caves near the water's edge. We lowered a skiff for a friendly visit. As we neared shore, a dozen savage-looking men and women charged out of the caves brandishing deadly-looking shark spears. Our gang wasted no time in heading back to the big boat. It was only when we were aboard that our Mexican crew,

"Gulped . . . into Fearful Maws"

Spanish names bestowed upon many of the places in the Midriff seem to have been inspired either through prayers or imprecations: Canal El Infiernillo (Channel of Little Hell), Canyon El Diablo (Canyon of the Devil), Isla Angel de la Guarda (Guardian Angel Island), Canal Sal si Puedes (Channel Get-out-of-here-if-you-can). With its raging water that rises in upwellings and crashes down without warning, this last one was evidently viewed as a channel gone mad.

Water movements in the channels, often more forceful than river floods, are caused by the regular rise and fall of the extreme lunar tides in the Pacific. When the full gush of the tidal currents is funneled into the 32-mile-wide narrows of the Midriff on each full and new moon, a flowing surface is created whose speed has been clocked at 20 knots.

Canal Sal si Puedes, deepest of the channels, and shaped somewhat like the spout of a funnel, gets the full pressure. When the swift, tidal flow heads through it and on up through connecting Canal de Las Ballenas, each land point splits off a slice and ricochets it back opposite the main flow. In addition, a *vertical* counter-current is created that causes the water to revolve from the surface to great depths. When the vertical counter-current gains more momentum than the surface flow, immense whirlpools develop, sometimes 300 feet in diameter. Although early day navigators wrote of small sailing ships being "gulped down into the great and fearful maws," this was, like many of their records, a tall exaggeration.

SUN AND THE SEA await the visitor to the Cortez. Swimming is delightful in warm, gentle waters, and there's welcome shade beneath a ramada if the sun becomes too hot. The Midriff Region is dotted with little islands; the one offshore here is Isla Alcatraz, or Pelican, Island.

who had refused to accompany the shore party, explained that some natives shipwrecked on Tiburon had disappeared, not into the proverbial thin air, but into a pot or barbecue pit.

At that time there were two separate groups of Seris on Tiburon. Those on the south end of the island were slightly less savage. The women wore flounced shirtwaists and ground-dragging skirts. This form of dress was taught them by a woman missionary around the turn of the century. She was said also to have taught them basket weaving. Today they still make and trade excellent baskets.

Since their removal to the Mainland, the Seri men hunt turtles for the market and occasionally work on farms. Otherwise the Seris keep to their tribal habits and live in small huts made of sticks. Scrawny dogs prowl all over the place. Girls and unattached women still paint their cheeks and noses with brightly colored stripes.

Much fiction has been written glorifying the Seris, but I've found them anything but glamorous. Until 1956, the Mexican Government allowed the tribe to remain on Tiburon, with the strict condition that they give up cannibalism. But the mysterious disappearance of a couple of Mexican

WEIRD, DARK BEAUTY *surrounds a tranquil bay on Isla Angel de la Guarda. Black volcanic rock cliffs, with no vegetation except for the stiff spires of an occasional cactus, present a forbidding landscape, but small boats find the quiet, protected harbor (Bahia Refugio) a welcome shelter in a storm.*

fishermen that year prompted the Mexican army to move the whole Tiburon population, then numbering 220, to the Mainland. Today there are a few Seri tribesmen living on a beach above New Kino, and a few others at Desemboque, near Punta Sargents.

SLAUGHTER IN THE SEA

The most exciting of all experiences I have ever been involved in, on land or sea, was a fish pileup. These extravagant mass murders occur during the great spring migrations. They are triggered when long schools of hungry yellowtail, mixed with armies of bonito and skipjack, collide with an even greater concentration of sardines, herring, and other small fishes abounding in the cooler Midriff waters. As the game fish cross the convergent line of warm and cold waters, the smaller fishes take to the air in such numbers they form what seems to be a solid silver blanket two to three feet above the surface.

It is then that every fish-eating creature of the Sea dashes into the fray and runs amok, chomping or disembowling each other in a ferocious frenzy. As a result of this devastating interruption in the well-ordered processes of evolution, the normally calm, limpid face of the Sea is churned in convulsions of mass slaughter. There appears to be a sudden reversal in time, halting all of the rhythmic balances developed by nature over millions of years.

At the start of a pileup the Sea may look as flat and motionless as a pane of glass. Suddenly a small area is disturbed. Within seconds the silver blanket spreads in all directions for a hundred yards or so, lengthening to as much as a mile. Up to this stage the feeding of the hungry migrators seems orderly enough, and such scenes are often witnessed throughout the Cortez. But here in the Midriff it sets off a frantic competition among the fish-eating creatures and all start tearing in as if to get their last meal.

When the pelicans, boobies, gulls, terns, and frigates zero in, peel off, and dive for a share, their excited screams summon clouds of other sea fowl from the distant islands. The bellows of sea lions are relayed from rookery to rookery, until long lines of these creatures come barreling in from all points. Some such signal even seems to be broadcast through the water itself, for pods of porpoise and bottlenose dolphin vault in toward the pileup. Great sharks join the slaughter, tearing and slashing at everything in sight. Huge manta rays, gigantic jewfish, and black sea bass, with mouths large enough to gulp in a beer keg, come up from their 50-fathom caves. All carnivores become as if insane, and they gorge, disgorge, and gorge again. Maddened by the blood and by greed, they slash and rip and kill even their own kind. They gut creatures twice their size and behead the lesser. Even the playful dolphins seem to take special pleasure in the melee, pounding sharks by ramming them in the belly, then leaping high into the air as if to express their joy.

At sight of a fish pileup, the angler accustomed to them becomes the most excited predator of all. No boat can get him into the fracas fast enough, for he knows that any large lure or bait let out in it will get nailed by some monstrous fish. I am unable to think of anything that can build

BROWN PELICAN DIVES *at full speed into the fish-rich waters from cliffs or on the wing.*

up a bigger head of suspense steam than coming around a point and finding yourself facing one of these fish pileups. Every cell and fiber of brain and muscle seem to get a triple shot of adrenalin, giving a "go" signal to some repressed instinct for combat. Some anglers, especially first-timers, blanch white at the sight of a pileup, even at a distance. The most disturbed that I have seen were two greenhorns from Okaboji, Iowa. They had several good reasons.

These two freshwater anglers drove to California to fulfill a longtime ambition—to see the Pacific Ocean. Confused by the Los Angeles freeways they pulled in at Charlie Rucker's tackle store to ask directions to the "sea." To Rucker, the sea means the Sea of Cortez, not the Pacific Ocean, so he gave the newcomers a quick pitch and signed them up for a week's voyage aboard his angling boat. Rucker drove them down to San Felipe, and they were off on the deep.

When they arrived in Bahia Refugio next morning, the visitors were sound asleep. An oldtimer on deck saw the surface begin to boil and recognized the signs of a pileup. He pounded on cabin doors and yelled, "Pileup! Pileup coming! Hit the deck!"

The startled Iowans, barely awake, thought "pileup" meant shipwreck. They pulled on their pants as the skipper bellowed orders in Spanish, of which they knew nothing. Skiffs being lowered thumped against the ship's hull, then backfired on takeoff. Other passengers banged their tackle in the mad rush as they scrambled around the deck.

The Iowans saw loaded skiffs stand on their tails, then race away from the ship. Close-by were awesome, hell-scaped crags and cliffs. Shortly their Spanish-speaking guide hauled them over the rail and into a skiff, handed each a club of a rod with a winch-sized reel, gave the motor some powerful yanks, and off they shot in an ocean-splitting drive. Never did the two suspect that the goings-on were for fishing until the guide attached foot-long plugs to each line and let them out for trolling.

INTERLOPING cormorants are the bane of fishermen when they scatter a school of fish.

A Camper's Island

Isla Angel de la Guarda, or Guardian Angel Island, is the largest Cortez island on the Baja side of the Sea (Tiburon is the largest on the Mainland side). It is 42 miles long, 10 miles across at its widest point, and has a total area of some 350 square miles. The island is uninhabited, except for a permanent population of lizards and snakes.

Francisco de Ulloa discovered Isla Angel de la Guarda in 1539. His exploration route through the upper part of the Gulf took him between the large island and the Peninsula, and evidence seems to point to his having stopped there. Most of the island is mountainous, and the only water is that which settles in hollows during infrequent rains. A few palms grow, but most of the vegetation is cactus. The east shore has gravel shores backed up with steep bluffs, and the west side drops off to a deep channel separating the island from the Peninsula, 8 miles away.

Isla Angel de la Guarda has a good harbor, Puerto Refugio, at its north end. In spite of its arid character, the island's sandy beaches make it a good place for camping or picnicking.

IT TAKES MUSCLE *to drag a heavy fishing boat up on the sandy shore. These are shrimp fishermen at San Carlos Bay north of Guaymas. If you should happen to be on hand when they unload a catch, you can probably talk them into selling you a few. Guaymas is noted for its delicious, very large shrimp.*

Seated in trolling positions facing the rear, they did not see all of the diving birds, sharks, sea lions, porpoises, and dolphins in the furious free-for-all ahead, and thus were ill-prepared to meet events that followed in quick succession.

Action started before the skiff had slowed to trolling speed. A 50-pound yellowtail latched onto a plug and almost yanked the holder overboard. The guide grabbed the leader but could not lift the heavy yellow over the rail. As he was lowering it to reach for a gaff, a sharp, angular fin of a shark sliced in. The monster made one pass and clipped the fish, leaving a bleeding head in the guide's hand.

Hardly a minute later, a barrel-bellied, bewhiskered, bull sea lion popped up beside the boat with a flapping, yard-long fish in his mouth. Gore squirted as he chomped it to bits.

Their outboard plunged into the thick of the carnage. Now the denizens were churning the water like a blow on Lake Okaboji. Through the mess and heading straight across their course, an enormous bottlenose dolphin came hot after a fish. As their paths crossed, the fish dove under the boat and the dolphin took to the air. The panic-stricken anglers ducked as the huge mammal vaulted over, right where their heads had been.

Then came the last straw. A big pelican flying about forty feet up and a hundred yards ahead, got a bead on a crippled sardine and peeled off in a dive-bombing drop. As the skiff sped over the wounded target, the pelican kamikazied full speed onto a tackle box at the feet of the two men.

When the feathers settled, I could see from my position on the big boat that the Iowans had finally broken the language barrier. In wild gesturing sign language to the guide they were unmistakably saying "Get-the-hell-out-of-here-we've-had-it!"

TO THE SEA IN LITTLE SHIPS

For the most stimulating and inspiring adventure to be found anywhere on any kind of a conveyance, I'll vote for a lengthy small-craft cruise of the Cortez. For those with a yen for fishing, swimming, skin diving, camping, or exploring the wilds, or for those who still dream of way-out worlds to see, this is it.

Small-boat cruising in the Cortez is quite different from cruising elsewhere. Here, it is a challenging adventure that approaches early exploration voyages in the South Seas. One of the values of small boats is in the perspective; the smaller the craft, the more the landscapes and seascapes seem to be magnified. The clear, dry atmosphere creates optical illusions, bringing distant objects, though miles away, seemingly close. The feeling of motion is intensified, and even more pleasurable is the sensation of gliding over the water instead of plowing into it.

In small craft, especially those with inboard stern drive or outboards, you dare to fish over hidden reefs and near rocky shores, enter shallow coves and estuaries, anchor close to shore, or even be rolled up on the beach. Perhaps most important is the contentment of knowing that you can squeeze into a small, sheltering indentation or take refuge in a snug lee when a storm threatens.

My first lengthy small boat voyage in the Cortez, with Eugene Perry and a couple of friends who had trailered their 20-foot cabin cruisers to San Felipe, was a charmed one. We cruised in and out of potential calamity as if we had an infallible talisman, meeting with undeserved luck at every turn. Our ignorance of possible dangers was almost total. I had learned very little on my previous big boat trips, since I never asked the native skippers why they sailed only on certain days and tides, why they gave some areas a wide berth, or why they resorted to frequent strange behavior, which I ascribed to local superstition.

Shortly after launching at San Felipe we met adverse currents, and by the time we reached Bahia Willard our gas supply was too low to make Bahia de Los Angeles. But there, fortune started smiling and we were able to pick up enough extra gas from a shrimp boat to get to Bahia de Los Angeles, where we refueled, restocked, and recuperated. From there we sailed to Isla Raza.

At low, flat Raza we saw thousands of white Elegant Terns (*Thalasseus elegans*) fly up, looking like a snowstorm in reverse. We wondered how so many birds could find room to nest on a rock that is less than a square half-mile in area. The *elegans* is believed to nest only on Raza and perhaps a few other islands in the Cortez. He is a showy sea fowl, with a long, orange-yellow bill, and a black-topped head.

We headed south to Isla Sal si Puedes, once cut in two by a narrow

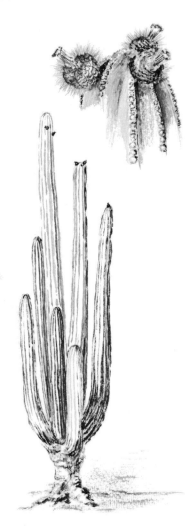

RIBS OF GIANT cardon are used as building beams. Plants can reach 60 feet, weigh tons.

IF YOU ARE INTRIGUED by plants in all their strange and varied shapes, you'll find much to interest you around the Cortez. In this sampling, there's a pitahaya agria (sour pitahaya) in the right foreground; behind it, a yellow-flowered palo de arco and a pitahaya dulce (sweet pitahaya); and in upper left, a cardon.

SHOOT OF SOUR PITAHAYA

FLOWER OF SOUR PITAHAYA

FRUIT OF SOUR PITAHAYA

NOT RECOMMENDED FOR YOUR BEST SHIRT, *but you'll have well-scrubbed laundry if you give it to these girls. This is a typical little oasis where fresh water is available, and there are plenty of smooth rocks. After the scrubbing, the clothes will be draped over nearby shrubs to dry in the sun.*

channel. Over the years, however, storms have cast cobblestones across its middle, separating the channel into beautiful, twin bays. The north side of the island descends rapidly to a great depth. The submerged wall is honeycombed with caves, each elevation accommodating different kinds of fishes. Near the surface we caught yellowtail, skipjack, sierra, and bonito; at the 50-foot depth were snappers, grunts, and small groupers; below that were giant groupers and snappers on down to 200 feet, where huge black sea bass roamed, feeding on foot-long, gold-spotted bass.

This was my introduction to small boating in this Sea, and the trip was a thing of joy from start to finish.

VOYAGE OF TERROR

I have yet to travel with a more cheerful and cooperative group than the one that made my next expedition to the Cortez. Each of the four, 18 to 21-foot, seaworthy outboard cabin cruisers was manned by an experienced man-and-wife team. The men were executives of Hughes Aircraft Company. The teams were: Dale and Eve Frederich, Altadena, California; Harold and Jerry Swenson; Bill and Virginia Harker; and Chuck and Betsy Lundy, all of Fullerton, California. I sailed with the Swensons, and a native deckhand went with the Harkers.

We trailered to Hermosillo, where we fitted out, and then went over to Bahia Kino in mid-November, a month when anything can be expected in this Sea. The arrival of our fleet at the old, half-deserted Kino village created a sensation, and half of the population of 88 persons joined in the fun of getting us launched. It was a gay beginning.

As we rounded the southwest tip of Tiburon, the smooth surface of the Cortez was so inviting we set off on a direct course for Isla Sal si Puedes, where we had arranged to have a larger boat, the *Galeana*, meet us with 500 gallons of gasoline, some ice, and fresh water. We slipped over the dead-calm Sea as in a dream, until we were a few miles north of Isla San Esteban. There the surface was suddenly riled by ravenous schools of big fish. We could not resist halting a while. After more than enough wild hookups all around, we continued north, disregarding some ominous swells. We were only about 11 miles from San Esteban when the first blast of a chubasco struck full in our faces. Had we stayed on course just a few more miles, we would have been dead center of the Sea and beyond the point of no return.

As it was, there was no direction to go except with the wind and waves, which were building by the minute and were well on their way to San Esteban. Before Jerry and I could batten down, half of our loose gear was flying all over the cabin. Nearing the cliffed face of the island, we could see waves driving up the bluffs and breaking back.

All of the skippers knew enough to quarter up and down the waves that were outrunning us. Even then we caught the mighty force and got going in surf-boarding glides. Less efficient and confident helmsmen would not have been able to avoid tangents that would have flipped our boats.

As we bobbed down the east side of San Esteban we had to keep well offshore to avoid the cross-wave backwash. Despite the skippers' alertness,

JAVELINA, *peccary, or wild pig, often travels in groups, kneels warily to drink.*

waves slopped over the transoms and more than once nearly drowned the motors. They coughed and sputtered but always picked up in time to keep our bows pointed south. With a dead motor any of the boats would have been a sure candidate for the cliffs. Making the turn around the southeast corner of Isla San Esteban without getting into the open maw of a trough tested all the stamina and skill the skippers could muster. We were greatly relieved to reach the narrow lee that extended the length of the sheer south end of San Esteban. But there was no sheltered anchorage short of the southwest corner, where nature had built a 40-foot-high jetty that helped to form a cove. To our surprise, we found the *Galeana* already at anchor there. She had been en route to our rendezvous, but at the first ground swells had altered course and fled ahead of the blow. The comfort we felt at the sight of her could be compared to that of lost chicks finding a mother hen.

We made quick visits aboard, took on gas, and hurried to drop anchors, cuddling up as close to the face of the bluff as we could. This allowed as little margin as possible for the boats to swing clear of the rocks. After seeing the huge waves that were breaking over the jetty, we let out a second stern anchor.

At midnight I hit the sack. At 2 A.M., Harold woke me with, "Ray, I think we're in trouble!" It was the understatement of all time.

If I had awakened on Mars I would not have been more astonished. Unearthly sounds blasted into my ears, and my first thought was that the long-dead San Esteban volcano had again blown her top in a major eruption. In the blackness I didn't know that the wind had shifted and was blowing down a canyon with walls that were indented with dozens of great and small caves. In the teeth of the gale these had become shrieking

Get Out of Here if You Can

During the northward run of the surface current through Canal Sal si Puedes, the water is sucked down at the north end and sides, to move southward at the bottom. The current is so swift that everything on the bottom smaller than large boulders is swept away. This action was observed by scientists from the University of California's Scripps Institute of Oceanography, La Jolla, California, when they lowered a TV camera to the bottom of Sal si Puedes. They also found that water temperatures at all depths were the same as a result of churning and mixing during the upwelling periods. (Elsewhere in the Sea, deep water is several degrees colder than at the surface.)

The most frightening demonstration of the power of the counterflow is seen when it shoots up at the channel's south end, exploding during extreme highs to a height of ten feet or more above the surface. At first these upwellings occur in small, circular boils that are about 100 yards across, but they widen at times to half a mile and stretch across all of the channels. As the water spills down from the top of a boil it resembles breakers about to crash into a beach, but instead of one wave being behind the other, they are stacked on up a flat plateau of smooth water.

IF YOU FLY YOUR OWN PLANE to Baja, you'll find many decent landing fields; but plan fuel stops carefully. Between the border airports and Cabo San Lucas there are usable airstrips — but watch out for bumps and holes. This is Bahia de Los Angeles, a good stopover point midway down the Peninsula.

SIPHONING GAS from a fuel drum into a small boat. If you plan a long cruise in the Cortez away from normal refueling stops, you can usually make arrangements to have a larger boat deliver fuel at key points.

pipe organs. The smaller openings screeched and screamed; the larger ones bellowed and roared; the in-between ones howled and wailed.

Suddenly a phosphorescent blanket soared over and dropped onto our boat. It was water. We were soaked, and the whole deck was lit up. Then came another. The liquid sheets were the crests of waves that had been sliced off by the jetty and kept buoyant by the wind. They were rich with tiny lightning-bug-like organisms that give off a bright light.

While all these phenomena were spooky, our real concern was for the boats. The change of wind had pushed our cruiser toward the cliff. One anchor popped off, then the other started slipping. Harold scrambled to the bow and hauled furiously on the good line, kedging the boat out and away from the bluff.

All of our outboard motors, having been repeatedly flooded, were now completely kaput. Another quick switch of the wind hurled the boats toward the powerful current, and both anchor lines snapped on the Harker cruiser. We could see it drifting rapidly, but we were helpless to do anything except blow our disaster horns. Fortunately, the sounds from the caves had let down with the wind shift, and our horns were heard by a passenger aboard the Galeana, who bounded on deck just in time to see Virginia Harker pop up through the bow hatch with a coil of line. The current brought the two boats close enough for her to throw the rope to the man. His two-finger catch saved the Harkers and their guide.

The wind raged for 18 hours, then died as quickly as it had come up. Our damages were the loss of four anchors and a dinghy, a few bruises, and a lot of frayed nerves.

VOYAGE TO MISADVENTURE

Having viewed the chains of islands and broken inner coastline of Baja California several times from the air, I was anxious to explore this little-known side of the Peninsula. The chance came when Charles Cohen, of Santa Ana, California, and Harold Nash, of Los Angeles, organized an expedition of five 18-foot cruisers for a voyage from San Felipe to La Paz. Dr. Phillip Savage, Jr., of San Bernardino, California, was to attempt a crossing from Bahia Topolobampo to La Paz aboard a sixth boat.

Although I suspected that April could be windy, I set sail with Nash. Before we reached Bahia de Los Angeles, four of the boats had run into trouble, and three of the four had to drop out. Two boats ran onto the rocks in Bahia Willard, trying to cruise at night; one cruiser had its anchor pulled and was smashed against a bluff; one motor (Cohen's) burned out in Bahia San Felipe, but the craft managed to limp along.

The boats that got past Bahia Gonzaga hit a ferocious wind from off the coast, half-way between there and Bahia de Los Angeles. We all hugged the high, cliffed shoreline for 40 miles, then going into Bahia de Los Angeles we caught the full force head-on. Fortunately, I had charted the long sand bar stretching across in front of the lodge area. Otherwise we may have gone around, as a freighter had done the previous night.

Cohen's boat was not seaworthy, so he decided to wait for engine parts and a factory mechanic to be flown in. During a noon lull in the wind,

FERMENTED JUICE from century plant produces tequila, a pleasure to native and tourist.

CALM, MAGNIFICENTLY BLUE WATER and a very gentle surf lure shore fishermen to a
lonely stretch of beach in the Region of the Cape. The clean, smooth sands are broken only by a few jagged rock
formations and distant barren hills. Who knows — perhaps they are the first to fish this idyllic spot.

THERE'S ALWAYS MANANA, and no one here is worrying about today! No matter how advanced the people become, it will be hard to convince Mexico's animals that they should give up a refreshing midday siesta.

the two remaining boats took off for the 65-mile run to Bahia San Francisquito. About half-way there, the blow hit us again, and we were forced to lie close to the bluffs for the night.

The next morning we came within 10 miles of San Francisquito when the north-running current caught us. Even with our engines going full bore, we were stopped dead. Our instruments showed us to be making 20 knots, but when we noticed that a point off our starboard appeared to be running ahead of us we realized that we were going backward! By swinging behind the point we got up enough speed to round it and catch a counter-current in the small Bahia Mojarra. Passing two more points in the same manner, we finally arrived in San Francisquito.

After reviewing our log, it became apparent that this course for cruising the Cortez could not be recommended for small craft. Although most of our mishaps had been due to human error, the winds and currents could have been disastrous, especially along the three 50-mile stretches that provided little or no shelter: San Felipe to Puertecito; Bahia Gonzaga to Bahia de Los Angeles; and Bahia de Los Angeles to Bahia Mojarra. Contrasting this course with that from Kino—*across* the Midriff, where there is always a shelter within 7½ miles—made the choice of the best seaway to San Francisquito easy.

Fighting constant winds and currents had about exhausted the full load of gas taken on at Bahia de Los Angeles, so the 500 gallons shipped to us at San Francisquito came in handy. We loaded it and left on a favorable current for Santa Rosalia, where we stopped off before sailing to Mulege. Cohen caught up with us there the next day.

From Mulege we cruised to Loreto, then into the Region of Juanaloa, where we enjoyed our first full day of calm. Below that Region we were again plagued by winds all the way to La Paz, but not enough to cause concern, except for a flash chubasco near Isla Espiritu Santo. From La Paz we went on to Rancho Buena Vista where we were met by Savage. He had miscalculated the force of the current in his crossing from Topolobampo and had run out of gas 15 miles off Isla Cerralvo. Fortunately, he'd been able to obtain enough fuel from a passing yacht to make the resort.

ACRES OF ROOSTERFISH

Time may prove that the live bait research voyage that we made in late June one year was the most valuable trip of all. I learned that whole regions where fish had previously appeared to be scarce at times can, with the use of live bait, be fished with confidence. Some species thought to be rare will probably be proved abundant, while others seldom taken on hooks will no doubt become common in the angler catch. Also, numerous popular fishes can be expected to be caught in seasons when they refuse any but live bait.

This survey was made possible through the assistance of Herb Holland and his son Douglas, of Los Angeles. They had purchased a new 24-foot Ryan crusier and were as eager for the experimental trip as I.

A few of the anglers and resort operators along the way thought our live bait efforts were useless, since some kind of fish can be caught on lures every day in the Cortez. Some were purists who believed that using anything but a lure was cheating. But they decided to join our "sneaky fishing" when we brought in a number of highly prized roosterfish from areas where none had been caught for a month or more and where they

Birds by the Thousands

From late March through June each year, the small interior valleys and usually quiet lagoons of tiny Isla Raza, less than a mile across, are white with birds. Two kinds of terns, the Royal and the Elegant, and huge colonies of Heermann gulls flock by the thousands to nest on this bit of land off Baja's coast southeast of Bahia de Los Angeles. Acres and acres are covered by chattering birds — the gulls evenly spaced about 18 inches apart and the terns in shimmering, tightly packed circles in their midst.

For a time, it seemed that this unbelievable bird population could not survive the efficient raids of commercial egg gatherers who descended on the island each spring. Throughout the season, the nests were kept completely denuded of eggs as the raiders systematically gathered every egg in sight, keeping the fresh ones and carelessly flinging the others aside. It was not surprising that the bird population of Isla Raza decreased alarmingly. In May of 1964, however, President Lopez Mateos heeded the call of conservationists and signed the decree that established Isla Raza as a migratory waterfowl sanctuary, and the annual cycle continues on one of the world's great rookeries.

HE BREAKS OUT OF THE DEPTHS, *and the game is about to begin. It will be an hour or more before this sailfish is brought to gaff — if indeed he is captured at all. One of the most beautiful fish the Cortez has to offer, the sailfish is a much-sought-after trophy for all anglers.*

STRAIGHT UP! A lot of weight is airborne here. Just a quick glimpse of glistening blue-black beauty, and he's into the water and off again.

AT LAST, the prize is aboard and the battle is won. More numerous than marlin and rated next in esteem, the sailfish is favorite for mounting because of the large, royal blue dorsal fin.

were thought to be entirely absent. We repeated the roosterfish performance at Mulege, Loreto, and Rancho Buena Vista. It was so impressive that most of the resort owners at each place started preparations to install live bait equipment.

Native boat crews at Loreto were not surprised when we trolled favorite lures through an area and saw no signs of roosters. But when we let out a couple of live mullet in the same place and about a hundred yards of surface was suddenly ripped by the cock-tail fins, they were amazed. The big fish became frantic when they made passes and missed the illusive mullet. After each near-miss, half a dozen roosters tore after the prized morsel. This competition stirred a whole school into thrashing the surface. We had never seen roosters in such a frenzy, and this was the prevailing condition throughout our trip.

At Buena Vista we ran into acres of roosterfish. We stopped, cut the motors, and tried casting our lures, with negative results. Then as a couple of boats loaded with lure-casting anglers came alongside, we cast out a couple of eight-inch, live salemas and retrieved them rapidly. Gangs of roosters, plunging after our baits, provided our audience a show of exciting fishing and gave us an hour of triumph not for our skill but for our live bait inspiration.

There were dozens of other fish species equally eager to attack live bait. Amberjack up to 100 pounds proved far more abundant and ranged farther north than I had suspected. White seabass, seldom taken in the Midriff, appeared to be plentiful when shown live bait. Mazatlan yellowtail were caught at the Santa Inez islands. Giant needlefish showed up everywhere from Mulege to Cabo San Lucas. The high-jumping, black-tip shark, surgeonfish, and tripletail, rarely taken on anything, all responded, even during the month of July when these species are especially choosy and spooky.

In the cove alongside Punta San Telmo, one of the highly productive arenas for big-game fish, we netted young herrings, or anchovies. The mature members of these families had moved out to sea, although around some islands we found them close to shore. Small 12 to 14-inch needlefish were plentiful. At night they cruised around our light beam, where they were suckers for our long-handled dip net. They made excellent bait for big game.

In outfitting our cruiser for this expedition, Ryan and others had designed and installed special equipment, not only for capturing and holding live bait, but for other conveniences as well. Among them was a two-foot by four-foot fish landing and cleaning shelf. This was balanced and braced on the rail and flushed with running water supplied by the bait well pump. When not in use, it could be collapsed snugly to the inside of the railing. All caught fish were brought directly onto the shelf for clobbering and bleeding, then were dropped into a wet gunnysack hung just above the water line, where they awaited the time for cleaning. This avoided messing up the deck. The process of evaporation from a continuously wet gunnysack hung *out* of the water, kept the fish almost as fresh as in an icebox.

Installations for the bait apparatus included a 4-cubic-foot bait well (a small, portable, plastic tank would serve), a black circular net (which we suspended from one of our trolling outriggers and submerged under a bright

NERVOUS-LOOKING eared grebe skims the water, abruptly diving deep for fish.

spotlight for night bait netting), a long-handled dip net, two small dip nets for baiting up, and a 4 by 4-foot collapsible receiver to hold the bait outside overnight.

As an added safety measure in case both engines conked out, we could have rigged our outrigger trolling poles and our overhead canopy to serve as a square sail.

With our powered inboard stern drive, and by taking outside courses in favorable currents, it took us only three days to run from Buena Vista to Kino. But on the shortcut from Punta Virgenes (just above Santa Rosalia) to Isla San Pedro Martir, there was a period when we made ready to hoist our sail. The big motor died, and a wind came up too strong for our 15-horsepower outboard. Having made port on a previous occasion by rigging this kind of a sail, I sort of welcomed the chance to repeat it. With good reason, the Hollands were shook up, but not enough to keep them from tearing into the motor and quickly getting it back in temporary working order.

ISLA SAN PEDRO MARTIR

Isla San Pedro Martir—which lies 20 miles south of Isla Tiburon—can fittingly be described as the Grand Central Station for migrating fishes.

The migratory movements seem to follow the edges of two 400-fathom trenches that bend in and join near the island. One trench slants over from the Baja California side, the other extends up from the center of the gulf. At low tide the cool water, laden with forage fishes, swings down to encompass the area and spreads out a welcoming buffet for the hungry traveling schools. Fish pileups are common during the low-tide periods of late spring and early summer. Often the feeding orgies are stretched out two or three miles, especially on the westerly side.

Yellowtail and barrilete skipjack are the first arrivals, to be followed a month or so later by striped marlin and dolphinfish, then by black marlin, sailfish, yellowfin tuna, and other tropical forms. Some remain to overlap the newcomers. Most are chummed northward when the receding tide transports the food supply. Diving birds can be seen following the schools as they fan out toward other islands of the Midriff.

Martir is also surrounded by native bottom dwellers, but the precipitous shelving and caves off its western point seem to be especially loaded with black sea bass at 40 fathoms, baya grouper at 20, and other groupers, cabrilla, snappers, and a host of different species at lesser depths.

Although the clownish, brown booby bird, *Sula brewster*, may be seen in small numbers on several islands of the Cortez, Martir belongs to them. A few other sea birds visit the island, but boobies hold possession.

A reception committee of a few dozen boobies often flies out several miles to greet an approaching boat. Although almost silent during the day, at night they stir up a racket that sounds like a full tribe of Comanches on the warpath.

The small indentations on each of the three, mile-long sides of this triangular island provide shelter from all directions. These, plus many other advantages, should stimulate enthusiasm among operators of very small craft and make Isla San Pedro Martir a rewarding fishing arena.

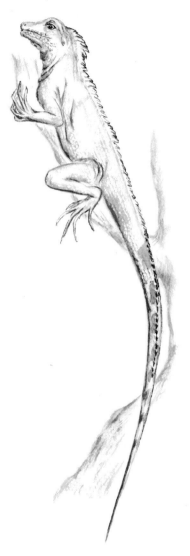

DRAGON-LIKE in appearance, the large, spiny-tailed iguana is a native of Isla Cerralvo.

AN IMPRESSIVE JOB OF MAKEUP decorates the face of a young Seri Indian woman. The design is painted in bright colors and, in typical Seri Indian fashion, it begins just below the eyes and covers only the lower portion of the face — like a Moslem woman's veil.

IT TAKES EFFORT to get acquainted with the Seris, but once their confidence is gained, you'll find them quite friendly. The tribe has almost died out, but there are a few Indians left at Puerto Libertad.

The Cannibals are Peaceful Now

LOOKING LIKE A GROUP OF BEDOUINS, several Seris rest on the sand. Unlike Bedouins, however, the Seris are not nomadic. They live in very primitive shelters at the edge of the beach. Although the buildings that show here are deserted, the Seris do not live in them, preferring a more simple outdoor existence.

CARVED DOORS *front the old San Ignacio mission church. Other mission buildings around the town's plaza house government offices. One is a school for Indian children.*

San Ignacio is an Oasis in the Desert

A COOL RETREAT *from the heat of a Baja day, the San Ignacio mission was long a base for exploration of the Baja frontier. Four-foot-thick rock walls keep the inside refreshing all day long.*

MOST PHOTOGRAPHED OF THE BAJA MISSIONS, *San Ignacio is a fine example of mission architecture.*
Unlike the adobe mission buildings, the rock walls of San Ignacio have not crumbled away with the years, and the
mission today is in a remarkable state of preservation.

*A **BLUE-FOOTED BOOBY** guards her fuzzy youngsters. The mother booby lays two eggs but usually raises only one chick. The birds don't often see people, but when they do, they pay no attention. You have to watch your step as you pick your way among them, for they will not move until you're right on top of them.*

Boobies are Always Around

SIX WEEKS OLD, *these boobies trust stranger. Some of the older chicks object a bit to being picked up, but their beaks are dull and their efforts feeble. Most are passive, and just sit wherever they are put.*

SPECTACULAR IN THE AIR, *boobies dive from heights of 60 feet. Spanish sailors tagged these birds with the name "bobo," or dunce, and the name has stuck in its English version.*

FATHER, MOTHER, AND BABY *are an unconcerned family group. Father booby, in front, is light-headed and smaller than mother — or the baby. The young booby will keep his white fuzz for eight weeks. When he loses it, he'll be down to his parents' size. Parents stay close by except when fishing.*

REGION OF
Mulege

Along a sleepy river, a dozing town hidden away in a lush tropical setting of flowering vines and swaying palm trees

The town of Mulege (pronounced moo-la-*hay*) is a storybook pueblo hidden in a valley of charm and beauty, in complete contrast with the arid and thorned wilderness that surrounds it. It is an unspoiled slice of old California where only the fish, and the fishermen after them, move with any degree of alertness.

A hundred pages could be written to describe the many intensely interesting things that can be done today in Mulege, and a thousand pages to review the strange and giddy goings-on in its past history. Whole books could tell how, in 1705, the Jesuit Padre Juan Maria Salvatierra founded a mission there. How, after the Indian population disappeared, the place would have been given back to them if any could have been found. How it revived and became a prosperous copper mining town with creditable business buildings and dwellings surrounding a plaza. How, in 1847, the Battle of Mulege was fought, in which U.S. troops captured and annexed Baja California but lost it back to Mexico by a most fortunate diplomatic blunder. How, in 1870, Mulege came close to being deserted again when richer copper ore was found at Santa Rosalia and almost every man, woman, child, and burro moved there. And, finally, how a snook shook the village awake from a century-long siesta.

Mulege is halfway up a lush valley of date, mango, and other tropical fruit trees. Clearings for vegetable gardens are spotted here and there, and are watered by artesian wells and springs that fill an artificial lake, the headwater of the Rio Rosalia. The palm-fringed river has fresh water for the first mile, then is brackish with mangrove borders for 2 miles.

DATES SLIDE FROM A TREETOP AT MULEGE.
As the date picker in the tree sends a bunch of dates down the rope, his "anchor man" below pulls taut to break the fall. This helps to keep the dates on their stems and saves gathering them off the ground.

MULEGE region is centered around the tropical town of Mulege on the Baja coast.

Many years ago there were some cases of malaria in Mulege, but, according to natives, the U.S. Health Department came in and eliminated the disease-carrying mosquitoes. Since then a large crew of Mexican Government sprayers passes through each year and gives every house and fresh water section a thorough treatment, thus keeping most insects cleared out. This practice is conducted throughout the Territory. The Region is now so free of ills that retaining an M.D. there who isn't an avid angler is a problem. The one nurse who operates the small hospital told me that in order to get something for her monthly reports she keeps herself busy circulating around town patching up the stubbed toes of barefoot kids.

The Mulege Region offers delightful river cruises, clamming, shell collecting, picnic excursions, rousing fiestas with gay music and dancing. You can also go horseback riding or skin diving in search of sunken ships or to hunt for lobsters, turtles, and shellfish. There's water skiing and swimming off white sandy beaches in calm water that's usually about 80°.

While this region provides these and other attractions for all kinds of people, to me it is an area of ever-new explorations, unexpected adventures, and piscatorial abundances. An angler can stand on one rock and catch 21 different kinds of game fish. He can battle 6-foot-long snook in the river and sail to nearby islands for a go at dolphinfish, sailfish, marlin, mako, black sea bass, and jewfish, or troll near shore or in the estuary for roostertail, bonefish, tenpounder, sierra, skipjack, bonito, jack crevalle, giant pompano, snappers, yellowtail, corbina, and 80 other fine fishes. Here too, a Nimrod finds convenient fowling along a river for ducks, and around the little fields for doves and quail, which frequently so clutter yards the Mulege housewives have to carry long switches to shoo them away while feeding their chickens.

All this is in a locale that is only 350 air miles below the California border but more foreign to U.S. visitors than most places in Europe. It is an area with a character unchanged over two centuries, an area inhabited by some of the most hospitable and friendly people I've ever known.

THE SNOOK SHOOK THE TOWN

My first introduction to Mulege was in 1955 when I got mixed up in an incident that the natives will long remember and which I shall never forget.

It started when the late Octavio (Sal) Salazar, owner of a small inn, wrote me that the river there was loaded with tarpon. Since I knew of no scientific record of tarpon occurring in the Pacific except near the mouth of the Panama Canal, his story was both baffling and irresistible. As soon as possible I caught a plane at Tijuana for Santa Rosalia, where Sal met me in his pickup truck for the 41-mile drive down to Mulege.

Three hours later we rounded a parched and barren hill, and I got my first view of the totally unexpected tropical oasis that is Mulege. The profusion of lush green was almost unbelievable. Continuing on through a narrow pass we were suddenly right in town.

Before us spread a dozen blocks of crumbling stores and houses, some engulfed in trees and vines. A half-dozen burros nibbled at the grass grow-

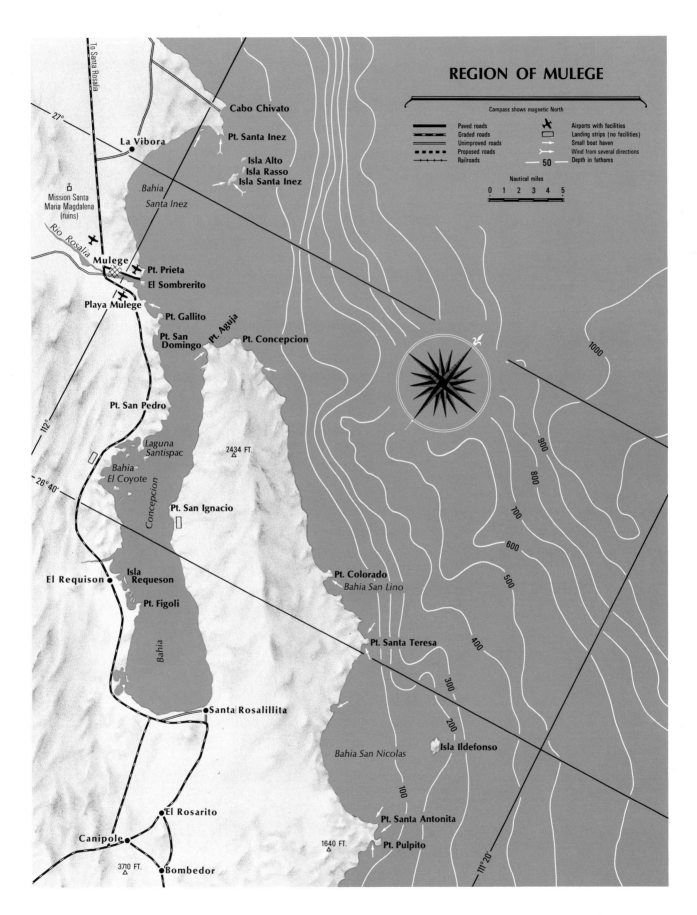

REGION OF MULEGE

Compass shows magnetic North

Paved roads	✈	Airports with facilities
Graded roads	▭	Landing strips (no facilities)
Unimproved roads	➤	Small boat haven
Proposed roads	≻	Wind from several directions
Railroads	—50—	Depth in fathoms

Nautical miles
0 1 2 3 4 5

To Santa Rosalia

27°

La Vibora

Cabo Chivato

Pt. Santa Inez

Isla Alto
Isla Rasso
Isla Santa Inez

Bahia
Santa Inez

Mission Santa
Maria Magdalena
(ruins)

Rio Rosalia

Mulege

Pt. Prieta
El Sombrerito

Playa Mulege

Pt. Gallito

Pt. San
Domingo

Pt. Aguja

Pt. Concepcion

Pt. San Pedro

112°

Laguna
Santispac

2434 FT.

Bahia
El Coyote

26° 40'

Concepcion

Pt. San Ignacio

Pt. Colorado
Bahia San Lino

El Requison

Isla
Requeson

Pt. Figoli

Bahia

Pt. Santa Teresa

1000

900

800

700

600

500

400

300

200

Santa Rosalillita

Bahia San Nicolas

Isla Ildefonso

100

El Rosarito

Canipole

1640 FT.

Pt. Santa Antonita

3710 FT.

Bombedor

Pt. Pulpito

111° 20'

ing in the streets. One of the animals was saddled. This was the only indication that the place was tenanted. Later, a few citizens emerged from their afternoon siestas, living proof that the town was occupied.

Sal informed me that the Mulegians had been almost completely without crime or sin for half a century, and were constantly being reminded that these things did not pay, by the old and impressive mission on one side and the territorial penitentiary on the other, both on hills overlooking the pueblo. We drove over for a closer inspection of the prison. I learned that it had five guards, 150 cells, and housed 19 prisoners, all lifers (the highest number since the Revolution, which speaks well for human behavior in the large Territory of Baja California Sur). Some prisoners are allowed out every day at 7 A.M. to go to work or to fish. At exactly 4:30 in the afternoon, a guard blows on a conch shell and all prisoners promptly return for the night. None, I was told, had ever tried to escape, because they never had it so good.

On our tour of the village Sal pointed out many historical ruins. Along the river bank was a group of shacks housing shark fishermen and their families. At that time the population of Mulege was about seven hundred. There was about an equal number of burros and dogs, turkeys and chickens, cattle, pigs, and mules. Coyotes and bobcats also were crowded in on a coexistent plan.

Preparations and arrangements had been made for me to go after a tarpon, that huge, mysterious fish Sal had chummed me with. That very night I found myself out on the river aboard a dugout canoe with a couple of native spear fishermen. Although I had brought plenty of tackle, the natives

Excursions Around Tropical Mulege

Everyone who visits Mulege should spend at least one day on an excursion (preferably by water, although you can get there by road) to Bahia Concepcion, the deservedly famous inlet just to the south of town. There you can dive for scallops and lobsters, scoop up clams and oysters by the bucketful, and, if you wish, sleep out overnight on a beach of your own discovery.

The town of Mulege itself is noted for many things, among them the mission church, built in 1766, on a high point upstream from the rest of town, and the federal prison, on a hillside north of the plaza. At the latter, the prisoners — who may have jobs or families in town — come and go almost at will.

If you stay at the most modern of the five lodges, you have the use of a putting green and a swimming pool. From its elevated position on a mesa near the river's mouth, the resort commands a view of inland mountains, orchard greenery across the river, the seemingly limitless Cortez, and the entrance to Bahia Concepcion. Oldest of Mulege's places to stay is a typical Mexican patio hotel in town. If you want to go all-out native, you can stay in the palm-thatched cabanas of the Playa de Mulege, right on the beach south of the river — you sleep on wide, firm cots with pad mattresses; your floor is the beach.

AN EXTRAORDINARY GAME FISH from the palm-fringed Rio Mulege. This is the giant black snook, and the waters of this peaceful little river teem with them. Not uncommon are fish six feet long, for this is the largest of the snooks found in America's tropical waters.

claimed that the fish could not be caught on hook and line. Our foray, scheduled on the dark of the moon, was timed so we could meet the incoming tide around midnight and ride it back through the village. The frugal townspeople, having learned not to waste kerosene, had long since retired, and not a glimmer of light could be seen along the shore.

NIGHT OF THE BIG PANIC

I sat in the middle of the dugout between my crew of two. The oarsman paddled quietly in the stern, without a ripple of water to break the silence. Only the far off chirps of a katydid could be heard. It was like moving in a vacuum as we slowly glided past overhanging palms and mangrove branches. The spearman stood on a small board across the bow with a lightweight, iron harpoon in one hand and a miner's carbide lamp in the other. We had reached a stretch in front of the sleeping fishing camp when the spearman's scanning light beam came to rest on what first appeared to be a submerged log. As it shifted forward, a great forked tail fin disclosed it to be an enormous fish.

Cautiously and quietly, in rapid, whispered commands to the paddler, the spearman got the boat into flanking position. He took careful aim, drew the harpoon back the full reach of his arm, and with a mighty heave drilled the denizen just under the dorsal fin without hitting any vital organ.

In a split second the little river was ripped asunder. Mangrove bushes thrashed as violently as in a chubasco. A sheet of water geysered over the dugout as the fish exploded up and over the canoe just past the spearman's head, the impaled harpoon whipping past within inches. The man emitted a screaming stream of Mexican profanity.

The oarsman on the stern began bellowing commands to the spearman, who had all he could do to keep vertical while holding the straining harpoon line. The line suddenly zipped under the boat and nearly tipped us all into the river, and I found myself yelling louder than either of them.

The still night was shattered by the splashing, our yelling, and the echoes bounding from hill to hill. Fishermen and their families came pouring out of the nearby camp to the river bank to join in the uproar. They boomed their advice, out-cussing the spearman in razzing, hog-calling tones. This hullabaloo in the middle of night triggered a chain reaction among the town's dogs, which were quick to join in. Their yelps and howls caused other creatures to sound off. Pigs squealed, turkeys gobbled, chickens cackled, all in frantic alarm. Jackasses and burros brayed, horses whinnied, and a multitude of coyotes and wild birds added their bit.

On penitentiary hill, the single night guard was awakened by the terrifying clamor. He switched on all the prison floodlights and grabbed his conch horn to bugle out the full guard.

That did it! The citizenry panicked and took to the hills, the caves, and the mission. If the hard-of-hearing padre had awakened and started pealing the bells, I might have hightailed it for high ground myself.

Throughout the fracas I had seen no more than flashes of the huge, jumping fish and could think of no aquatic creature except a tarpon that would trigger such a ruckus. After considerably more thrashing and churning the waters of the river in a desperate effort to free itself of the spear, the great fish was finally subdued and dragged to shore. The native kibitzers crowded around.

By the light of the carbide lamp I could now see a turned-up snout and black stripe along the body. No tarpon this, but the largest black snook I had ever laid eyes on! It measured 5 feet 7 inches from snout to tail fork, a whole foot longer than the world record snook. Of course, it could not qualify for a record because of the way it was caught.

The important thing was that this little river had in it one of the most extraordinary of all game fishes. And it was no ordinary snook. This was the giant black snook *(Centropomus nigrescens)*, called robalo prieta in Spanish, largest of all the snooks inhabiting the tropical waters of America, attaining a length of 6 feet and a weight of at least 80 pounds!

Sample seining showed the waters to be loaded with an unequalled abundance of the giant blacks. All I had to do was to catch one on rod and reel and I'd be the world champion snook catcher. I trolled the river and cast from shore, using every kind of plug and feathered lure in my tackle box. No snook was interested. I tried using strip-bait. Nothing!

Frank Dufresne, Pacific Coast editor of *Field and Stream,* heard about my failures and flew all the way down from Olympia, Washington, with

DANGLING PODS and bell-like blossoms identify common trumpet flower (Tecoma stans).

an assortment of plugs, lures, and flies that had appealed to Florida snook. With these, we fished at sunup, at sundown, and at midnight. We fished at low tide and at high tide, up and down the river. All we got was a royal snooking.

Over the next two years, we returned to Mulege again and again to try new techniques. Still nothing happened. Nothing that is, until I goofed and got a 12-pound-test line snarled in a birdnest. As I retrieved my line, the river suddenly burped with a great, boiling belch at my mullet bait, as if a hippopotamus were doing pushups under the surface. I knew I had me a snook, and I was sure there was a world record on the end of the line. But once more I goofed. In the excitement I screamed "arpon" (harpoon) instead of "gancho" (gaff). Before I could retract, my Mexican guide nailed the potential champion with an iron spear and my snook was disqualified for any record claim.

I did gain some satisfaction when I learned that the snook measured 3 feet 5 inches and weighed 48 pounds, well over the world record snook taken on a 12-pound-test line. But even more important to me was proof that giant robalo could be taken by rod and reel on live bait. The trick was simply to drop the bait down, not by casting, then pull the skiff away for a hundred yards and slowly retrieve.

ISLAS SANTA INEZ

The group of three islands 8½ miles out of Mulege and the point 2 miles from the north island, all bearing the name Santa Inez, form an arena for big-game fishing.

Except for one good cove and beach inside Punta Santa Inez, there is little landside attraction. However, there are gigantic, submerged, shelving bluffs that descend to 100 fathoms, 2 miles off the islands, then sharply down to 400 fathoms. Here and in the labyrinth of reefs around the islands there are enormous fish populations.

The theory that marlin, sailfish, tuna, mako, and dolphinfish migrate along such ledges was strengthened when I contacted these fishes in early June along this trench wall. I had made a few runs in the area and around the islands on some of the first, risky boats out of Mulege and found splendid fishing, but on the Nash-Cohen and Ryan expeditions (see the chapter on the Midriff) some new discoveries were made. Those were years when the pelagic red crabs had blanketed the sector, providing such a great amount of food for the large fishes as to allow forage and young fish to escape. The vast schools of fingerlings, linked like chains, radiated in all directions throughout the upper half of the whole Mulege Region.

We cruised the length and breadth of the clear, shallow Santa Inez area and saw the greatest numbers of big fishes any of us had ever seen spread over such a large area. Someone remarked that the many species of game fishes moving over the 4 by 7-mile bottom resembled the traffic in Times Square. This was the first time I had any kind of an opportunity to envision the enormous quantities of fish that really inhabit the Cortez, and I saw that they multiplied beyond the limits of my imagination.

DEFENSIVE ODOR *of the little spotted skunk wards off even a big enemy like a coyote.*

LOOKING UPSTREAM *on the Rio Mulege: A jungle of date palms stretches back toward distant flat-topped lava mountains. The only sounds are the rustle of palm fronds, the trickling of water, and the calls of tropical birds. Downstream, the river is a brackish tidal estuary where you can try for the big snook.*

WHERE OYSTERS GROW ON TREES

Bahia de la Concepcion itself is a huge body of water. It is separated from the Sea proper by a mountainous peninsula that peaks up to more than two thousand feet. On the east side of the bay, between Punta Concepcion and Punta Aguja, there is a short, rugged, and broken shoreline with extensive submarine gardens that provide good habitats for fish, scallops, and rare shellfish. Halfway down is a fishing camp with a tiny, rough airstrip. Except for a half-dozen families with small goat herds, and a few men at the fishing camp, there is no habitation around the whole bay.

About 10 miles down the west side of Bahia Concepcion is Laguna Santispac. Here, cockle-size clams can be gathered by the bushel. They are found in the foot-deep estuary that flows in and out of a circular, mangrove-rimmed lagoon abounding with small Colorado snapper and mullet. This is also the spot where it is said "oysters grow on trees." True, the tide-washed trunks of the mangrove bushes are covered with oysters, but they are so small a hungry hombre would starve trying to get enough meat for a mouthful.

Adjoining Santispac southward are a couple of similar coves, then the enchanting Bahia del Coyote, with its shaded beaches and shoreline looking out to half a dozen sizable islands. A small islet at the south end of the group has been eroded and carved into weird tidal grottoes and caves. It is a meeting place for hundreds of man-o-war birds.

The protection given Coyote by the islands makes it the best yacht harbor between Santa Rosalia and Bahia Escondido, and a delightful spot for way-out camping. Weary land travelers also usually stop here for a refreshing rest. There are a great number of golden grouper around these

RELATIVE of raccoons, *the coati's name means nose-to-belt, its sleeping position.*

The Open-Door Prison

No sentries stand in the corner towers of Mulege's prison — a weathered old building atop a hill north of town. This is the territorial penitentiary, but it is a prison that is unique. Inside the walls, it is about what you would expect: dark, unlighted, airless cells opening onto a bleak central court. But the cells are without gates or doors, and the inmates wander freely in and out — usually gathering around the one water source, a tap in the center of the court, to talk about their day's activities. And the daily activities of Mulege's prisoners differ markedly from those of prisoners elsewhere. Each day of the year, at sunrise, a soldier stands atop the hill and blows on a giant conch shell. The great wrought iron gates of the prison entry swing open, and the prisoners head for town — to visit families or friends, work at a daytime job, or just loaf around Mulege's plaza. They are entirely free until the evening, when the conch shell is blown again and they must return to their walled world to while away the hours until the gates open for them again the following morning.

islands and along the rocky shoreline south of them. Black snook are also plentiful in the estuaries of the half-dozen lagoons between Coyote and Concepcion's south end.

One of my most productive trips into Bahia Concepcion was made aboard a modern shrimp boat. When a cooperative Mexican skipper dragged Bahia del Coyote for me, I counted 19 species of game fish in addition to a quantity of rare shellfish which came aboard with each shrimp haul. The grab-bag disclosed many surprises, among them large numbers of snappers, especially shallow-water striped pargo up to 40 pounds, deep-water ruby snappers, and giant Colorado and dog snappers, known to tip the scales at over 60 pounds. There were also numerous oddballs, such as large halibut, creole fish, and goatfish, which we had been unable to hook. But what really shook me was a haul containing a 100-pound totuava. This suggested the possibility that somewhere along the 200-fathom drop-off east of Punta Concepcion there was an environment well suited for this king of the croakers. There was also the chance that they spawn in the back-bay lagoons.

On a later voyage, we gave the 25-mile-long Concepcion a good going over and found some highly productive fishing holes in certain parts of it. We went ashore to examine the lagoons and found them ideal for snook and brackish enough for totuava and snook spawning.

The mud banks at the head of the lagoons housed massive colonies of small, bait-size fiddler crabs. Each of these odd little fellows has one claw almost as big as his body, which he holds up and jerks like a hitchhiker's thumb. We collected a hatfull of them and chummed small snappers to the bank. Within a few minutes, the ravenous fish were taking the crabs right out of our hands. The tide was too low at the time for fishing those backwaters, and I shall never be satisfied until I get back at high tide and work the lagoons with the "mitt" crabs as chum and bait.

We found groupers around and over all rock areas, with striped pargo even more plentiful from the surface down to 40 feet of boulder-covered bottom. Casting gray-blue or whitish plugs from a slow-moving boat was almost as successful as using large, round chunks of sierra or other fishes. Strip-bait was too often stripped by triggerfish. Chunks were taken quickly when dropped to the bottom and left motionless. Later I tried this method among boulders off the mouth of arroyos and washes throughout the Cortez and seldom missed finding them loaded with pargo.

A LIVING TIDAL WAVE

On one trip to Bahia Concepcion, Frank Dufresne and I, with the assistance of Bill Lloyd of Playa de Mulege, were trying to make contact with one of the gigantic basses off the point. We were hooking small grouper by the dozen, but nary a big one. Our patience was about exhausted when we saw what appeared to be a shipwrecking tidal wave speeding toward us around the point.

OPEN-CROWNED cottonwood tree (Populus fremontii) has reddish catkins, bright leaves.

IT TOOK A SPECIAL BOOM to get this one on deck. You'd never get a big fellow like this on board a small cruiser without some mechanical assistance. The fish is a baya grouper, and they run 200 pounds or more.

Having seen the havoc one of these waves (rare in the Cortez) can create, I frantically yelled, "Tidal wave!" Even while Frank and I were retrieving our lines, Bill had revved the motors and was turning to head for a cove.

Keeping our eyes on the racing wall, we saw a strange sight. In the white, breaking top of the roller we spotted a huge fish, then another, and another. Finally we realized that the whole wave was caused by thousands of yard-long roosterfish leaping over one another in a shoal about a quarter of a mile long. We stopped the boat and switched to casting tackle. Despite the heat of the day, our teeth were chattering with excitement as we waited for the wave to pass our boat so we could tie into the monsters.

The roosterfish got up their dorsal fins, their rage, and a lot of spray as soon as they were hooked. In fact, one of them looked like a crowd as he thrashed the waters all around the boat. We got three on at the same time. If anyone had seen us jumping around trying to keep the fish apart, they would have thought that we were a troupe of circus clowns.

The migrating wave rolled right on back into the bay for half a mile or so, where the fish seemed to end their journey. Since then I have repeatedly seen schools of migrating roosterfish traveling in this manner.

SAVED BY SEA GYPSIES

A frightening experience occurred when I was returning from one of my early cruises into Bahia de la Concepcion with Dr. Earl Hershman, of Long Beach, California. We were aboard an old tub of an outboard, totally unseaworthy, when we met a stiff blow near the mouth of the bay, which is usually flat. In those days, our native skipper knew very little about outboards, Hershman less, and I nothing.

We were making almost no headway against the wind and the 12-foot waves that threatened to flip over our 16-footer. Suddenly we were shoved down the face of a roller, the stern plunging under until the outboard and transom were completely swamped. There wasn't a cough, not even a death rattle from the old coffee grinder. We may as well have been cruising in an iron bathtub with the plug open. What's more, we were being pushed straight toward the flat face of a perpendicular bluff.

We urged the skipper to drop the anchor. He did, but it didn't help. There wasn't enough line to reach half-way to the bottom.

Each wave added more water; there was no use bailing. All we could do was peel off and swim for a niche of a nearby gravel beach. Even then, there was but a small chance of avoiding getting our brains bashed out on the bluff.

We were just about to hit the water when a couple of vagabundos appeared out of nowhere on shore and shoved a little dugout down the beach into the face of the fury. How they got to us, took us aboard, and landed us ashore in that raging blow, I still don't know. The anchor of our abandoned boat somehow connected 50 yards from the bluff, and a change of wind direction left it floating in the lee.

SCARLET BLOOM of poinciana or flame tree is followed by fern-like leaves and huge pods.

FAMILY LIFE is not too bad for prisoners at Mulege. Many have jobs and families on the
outside and can leave the prison during the day. When the conch shell blows at sundown, they head up the
hill. Here a prisoner's wife and child visit him inside the prison walls.

This Penitentiary Welcomes Wives

A PRISON IN PARADISE, penitentiary
building sits on a hillside
north of the plaza, where it overlooks
a tropical scene.

JUST REACH IN AND PULL HIM OUT! *In clear pools like this, there is little difficulty spotting enough fish for a meal. Tide pools hold many surprises: there are seashells to collect, if you wish; or you can simply enjoy the sight of magnificently colored fish gliding through the depths of a huge, natural aquarium.*

DIG WITH YOUR FINGERS *to get clams from the lagoons of Bahia Concepcion. Your feet may tell you where they are thickest.*

Shellfish are in the Shallows for the Taking

THE "CATCH" *is mostly butter clams, with a few darker Pismos. This pile is just the beginning; the final haul fed all the hotel guests.*

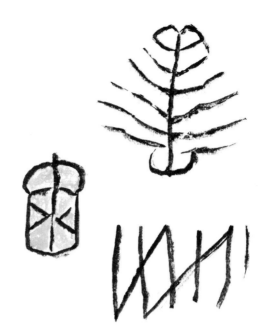

REGION OF
Loreto

First mission and capital of all the Californias in a peaceful village where yesterday and tomorrow have little meaning

If I had never seen Mulege, I would now be applying most of the glowing words I wrote of it to the Region of Loreto. Included would be superlatives about the lofty mountains, the spreading palms and tropical fruit orchards, the quaint town, the simpatico people and their customs, the great hunting potential, and the fabulous sport fishing up and down protected Canal Carmen and around Islas Coronados and Carmen.

Loreto was the first settlement made by white man on the Peninsula, and for more than 130 years it served as the capital of both Alta and Baja California. When the Californias were divided in 1772, Loreto was retained as the capital of Baja California, and Monterey was established as the capital of Alta California.

The story of the establishment of Loreto in 1697 by the Jesuit Padre Juan Maria Salvatierra is told by the historian of the Jesuit Order, Don Francisco Javier Clavigero in his *History of (Lower) California*. Clavigero recounts that Father Salvatierra and his party of nine men (including three Indians) sailed in a fleet composed of a "loaned galiot and a small vessel" to the port of San Dionisio, a small bay whose capes "form a mouth 15 miles long," and which had an abundance of fresh water. Here the exploring party made camp, then erected a "great bell tent" which had been given to Father Salvatierra. In front of the bell tent they placed a cross decorated with wildflowers. The image of the Virgin of Loreto was carried in procession from the galiot to the tent. Then the historian adds, "From that time forward, that miserable camp as well as that port was known by the name of Loreto."

THE QUIET OF MORNING AT LORETO.
Fishermen prepare to leave for a day on the Cortez
as the sun brings a tinge of pink to the
early-morning clouds. In the distance, Isla
Carmen is a dark shadow on the horizon.

Loreto also was the starting point for the mission builder, Padre Junipero Serra, who is credited with the establishment of a culture in Alta California that survived Indian uprisings, white man's wars, gold rushes, western outlaws, pestilences, and politics, and left an enduring civilization.

THE NINTH LIFE OF LORETO

Eight times in her nearly three centuries Loreto has been devastated and deserted as a result of earthquakes, pirate raids, and chubascos, and eight times she has prevailed. I was witness to the agonizing travail during the ninth and most recent rebirth of the pueblo surrounding Nuestra Senora de Loreto—the flooding chubasco of 1959.

I had visited Loreto several times prior to 1959 and found its dwellings dilapidated and crumbling. The mines were depleted. The area had experienced a 50-year drought. The place and its population were withering. Then came the 1959 chubasco — hurricane winds flattened or blew away most of the decaying, thatched cabanas. Thirty inches of rain swelled the dry wash of the upper Arroyo de Las Parras, and the raging torrent jumped its natural bed and tore down the main street of Loreto, giving it a thorough purging.

The inundation could be termed a heavenly blessing. The destruction and misery, quickly and for the first time, brought in the Mexican government, not only with temporary relief but with large-scale public works. Among these projects were the construction of a rock dike to protect the town from another disastrous flood, and a dock, which, the populace hoped, would encourage shipping.

Loreto was rebuilt around its original central plaza and acquired a new office for the mayor, a new post office, and a hospital. The imposing dignity of the Mission of Nuestra Senora de Loreto was restored; and its old bells, an early gift from the Spanish throne to the loyal city, were put into place. Residential plots were cleared of rubble; new cabanas were built; flowering shrubs and fruit trees began to flourish; and the whole place put forth a fresh, clean, and attractive face.

Part and parcel of the rebirth of the old town have been the influx of sport fishermen and other tourists. To serve these visitors and the increasing numbers of townspeople (now 1500), small new enterprises are being developed. Especially important is The Flying Sportsmen's Lodge, with its 3,000-foot runway for small planes, located 1 mile south of Loreto. It offers filtered mountain water, a dining room with food flown in from the U.S., a tackle shop, swimming pool, and other tourist services.

Thus the chubasco of 1959 was Loreto's rebirth into her ninth life, which now seems destined to be a prosperous and enduring one.

The silts brought down by the flood and dumped into the Sea could be assessed as the chubasco's most valuable contribution to Loreto's future welfare. They have stimulated the development of a flourishing food supply for the forage fish and for the young game fish that were spawned in nearby bays. Thanks to continuing rains, fresh-water seepages are still appearing along the shore. These are causing an enormous growth in the mullet population, which attracts and supports an ever increasing number of game species,

LORETO *region marks the site of the first of the California missions.*

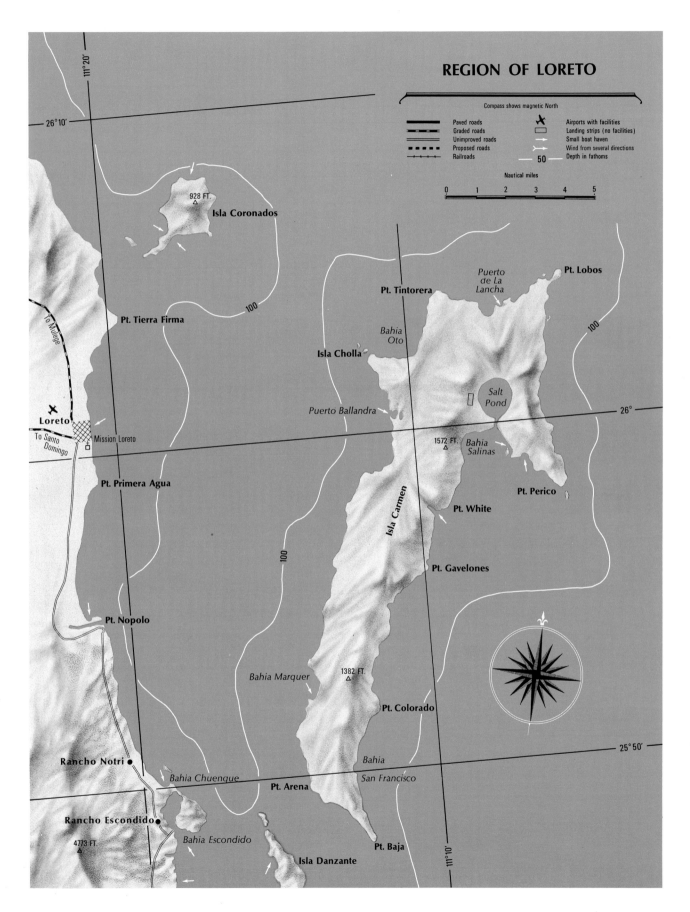

REGION OF LORETO

Compass shows magnetic North

Paved roads
Graded roads
Unimproved roads
Proposed roads
Railroads

Airports with facilities
Landing strips (no facilities)
Small boat haven
Wind from several directions
50 — Depth in fathoms

Nautical miles

0   1   2   3   4   5

26°10'

111°20'

To Mulege

Loreto

To Santo Domingo

Mission Loreto

928 FT.

Isla Coronados

100

Pt. Tierra Firma

100

Pt. Primera Agua

Puerto Ballandra

Pt. Tintorera

Bahia Oto

Puerto de La Lancha

Pt. Lobos

Isla Cholla

Salt Pond

26°

1572 FT.

Bahia Salinas

Pt. Perico

Pt. White

Isla Carmen

Pt. Gavelones

100

Pt. Nopolo

Bahia Marquer

1382 FT.

Pt. Colorado

Rancho Notri ●

Bahia Chuenque

Pt. Arena

Bahia San Francisco

25°50'

Rancho Escondido ●

4773 FT.

Bahia Escondido

Isla Danzante

Pt. Baja

111°10'

YOU MUST GO OVERLAND *to reach San Javier, and it's a memorable experience. The road climbs through Arroyo de las Parras, past waterfalls, native fan palms, and idyllic, amply watered ranches. Allow 3½ hours for the 22 miles each way, and hire a truck that is able to negotiate the very primitive road.*

especially roosterfish. Not only have more of the gamesters been caught since the big flood, but the seasons have lengthened by three to four months.

Much of Loreto's future progress will depend upon the strength it can draw from neighboring developments. There is the great farming area of the Santo Domingo Valley, only 32 miles away. Towering 10 miles to the south of Loreto is the massive 5,800-foot mountain, La Giganta, abounding in deer, bighorn sheep, puma, and varmints—truly a happy hunting ground. Promising also is Loreto's proximity to the wild and romantic Region of Juanaloa, beginning just 12 miles below the town at Bahia Escondido. Loreto is connected by a ferry boat to Guaymas on the Mainland and angling boats ply the big-game fish waters. All this helps build the region, but the backbone of the economy is maintained by the angler patronage attracted by the many and diverse kinds of fishing.

FISH-EATING DOG

On one of my earlier trips to Loreto (before the 1959 chubasco), sudden, strong breezes forced me to cancel my plans of taking a boat for the big game fish and unexpectedly gave me a most pleasurable fishing day. The unexpected turn of events also impressed me with the value of having diversified fishing interests. The angler who is limited to only a few days should always be prepared to switch his pursuit from heavyweights to welters, in case a two or three-day wind keeps boats grounded. A good policy against being bollixed by a blow is always to take along a complete spinning outfit and a flexible mental attitude. With only three days to fish, had I been set on catching billfish or nothing, I would have caught nothing, since the wind lasted just that long.

Al Green, lodge host, suggested that we pack spinning gear and lunch and drive down to Ensenada Nopolo, 7½ miles south of Loreto. Nopolo is a spot where mountains spring up from the Sea and where the tides have carved out a delightful baylet and chiseled a grotto the full length of the 75-foot cliff that forms the point. On the way we passed a long mangrove-banked lagoon loaded with mullet, snapper, and other small fishes. (Since 1959 this inlet has become a stream which empties into the back of Nopolo.)

At the cove we spread our equipment on a table-high rock shaded by a great overhanging ledge. A flooring of almost flat rock, which stood about a foot above the high-tide line, extended back for 10 or 12 feet. Despite the rough sea outside, the water of the cove was dead calm and we were completely protected from both sun and wind. No more ideal shore fishing spot could be imagined. We looked down 20 feet into the clear water that came up to the sheer wall of the ledge. What we saw sent us scrambling madly for our spinning tackle.

My first cast was with a white Compac feather. It landed between the tonsils of a huge sierra, which promptly peeled off 100 yards of mono and began performing some astonishing leaps. Twenty minutes later I landed him—a thirteen-pounder. It was the largest sierra I had seen.

Meanwhile, Al had connected with a jumping ladyfish (ten-pounder), the aquatic Nijinsky of near-shore waters. Along with the snook and bonefish, the ladyfish rates as one of the favored game fishes in the Gulf of Mexico, Florida, and the southern half of the Atlantic Coast, where it attains a length of 3 feet and a weight of 8 pounds.

In keeping with our uninhibited fishing enjoyment, each jump executed by a fighting fish was accompanied with loud and enthusiastic yells from us. The racket, bounding from the cliffs, sent a herd of passing goats into a stampede for the bushes. Not only the goats, but the native herder and his dog seemed shaken by the wild sounds coming from such a lonely place.

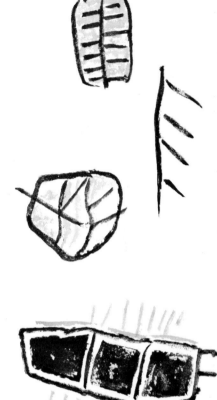

CENTIPEDE and beetle shapes appear in very old cave drawings 5 miles from Loreto.

The Wind that Strikes Fear

While the Cortez may be called a slice of the best of all possible worlds, it is not without its share of earthly hazards. About once every five or six years, devastating chubascos (rain and wind storms reaching almost hurricane force), sweep up from the south. They usually smack the tip of the Peninsula and slam into the southern Mainland, more often during the rainy season of July, August, and September, and occasionally in October. They rarely extend as far northward as the Midriff. Radio warnings (citizen band) of their approach are broadcast in Spanish several hours in advance.

Some of the resorts around the Cortez literally tie their roofs down when a chubasco is on the way. They put cables or ropes over the thatched roofs in all directions and either anchor the ends to stakes driven into the ground, or secure them to huge stones or weights.

The big brindle mongrel raced into our niche and halted right in front of me. He gave me an evil-eye stare and curled his lips, showing a set of teeth that would have been a credit to a Bengal tiger. Thinking that the animal was ready to dismember me, I froze.

Al yelled, "I know that mooching perro. He's not going to bite; he's just smiling for a hand-out."

I was on the verge of tossing our whole lunch to the beast when Al said, "Throw him a fish."

I complied, and the dog gave it a couple of chomps, swallowed it, and once more displayed his dentures. The glutton held his smile until I threw him another, and still another.

The old goat herder hung around for a while to watch. He no doubt considered us trabajo loco for making so much ado over what he considered to be trash fish.

ROOSTERFISH AND DOLPHINFISH

The most dramatic proof that roosterfish (*Nematistius pectoralis*, also called pez gallo or papagallo) are plentiful during the summer months—which have always been considered an off-season—was given during my live bait expedition when we stopped over at Loreto. Just prior to our arrival in mid-July, roosters had been profuse and were taking almost any lure offered. Extravagant reports from anglers returning stateside had caused a rush of roosterfish enthusiasts, and the resorts were crowded. But suddenly it seemed that the roosters had flown the coop, and the anglers' disappointment at not being able to catch a single pez gallo had reached the stage of anguish.

We arrived from Mulege with about two dozen live mullet in our tank and hurried on down past Ensenada Nopolo to Rancho Notri. Knowing this to be roosterfish country we tried to locate the schools by trolling some sure-fire lures, but nary a tail fin showed.

We then selected a mixed rock and sand area near the mouth of an arroyo, stopped the boat, and let out our lines with a couple of 8-inch mullet. They had pulled off no more than 50 feet of line when a dorsal fin sliced the surface. A second one appeared, and we had two hookups.

The ruckus stirred up by those two 30-pound roosters aroused the competitive instincts of the whole school. We hooked roosterfish as fast as we could pay out live bait, until it was all used. Releasing all but half a dozen of the largest, we rushed back to the resorts with our papagallos and boasted like a bunch of showoffs. Our real motive was to impress the resort managers with the importance of installing live bait, but we overdid it and succeeded only in making everyone unhappy with his own bad luck. Nevertheless, a live bait business was in operation by the next season.

Loreto's present fame was started by the discovery that immense numbers of marlin migrate into the region in late May or early June and that sailfish come in 4 to 6 weeks later. Both remain through July, but then return from the north for a fall run that lasts from September through November, sometimes even through December. Sails often remain throughout the summer. Mako, yellowfin tuna, and dolphinfish accompany them.

AGILE GRAY FOX climbs trees to escape bobcats. Foxes live on rodents, berries, insects.

STOP TO GOSSIP *is an important part of the trip to get water. It takes practice to master this balancing feat, but these women are experts.*

IT'S A LONG WAY TO GO FOR A DRINK, *but the task of getting water from the arroyo is an accepted part of life on this ranch near Cabo San Lucas. All water for use in the ranch house is brought from the stream by this age-old method. Laundry is done at the arroyo — accompanied, of course, by a bit of pleasant socializing.*

A PALM-THATCHED HAVEN, *the Hotel Oasis sits in a grove of palms at Loreto. The rooms are modern, even though the buildings are made of the same kind of thatching used for the little native houses. Even the pillars are palm trunks, and the whole blends quietly into its tropical surroundings.*

Amberjack and a number of other jacks follow a similar calendar but remain all summer. Yellowtail are plentiful in all months except July, August, and September. There is a year-round population of yellows that have gone native just outside Rancho Notri in Bahia Chuenque.

The most compact concentration of sierra I have yet seen (some up to 14 pounds) occurs repeatedly a half-mile out from Ensenada Nopolo. Sierra and barrilete skipjack seem to spend the year in one part or another of Canal Carmen, as do a great number of other small-game species.

Swarms of small-game fish occur around Islas Coronados, 6½ miles above Loreto. Sailfish, marlin, and dolphinfish swing in close to this island for late spring and fall runs and occasionally they will even venture up and down Canal Carmen.

Each nook, point, and reef in this section seems to have a different environment, and each is especially suited to one or more species of fish. Even the different kinds of groupers, cabrillas, and snappers are somewhat divided. The porous, honeycombed lava and limestone rocks found around this most recent of the active volcanoes in the Cortez make interesting novelties. Skindivers can find clear water on one side or the other of Coronados most of the time.

The area becomes congested seasonally near the south end of Canal Carmen with roosterfish, yellowtail, sierra, and barrilete. But the strangest, most consistent fishery is on the great grouper reef that extends out from the northeast corner of Isla Carmen.

Isla Carmen, a 17½-mile-long mountain projecting up to a 1,570-foot peak, has both an interesting history and present day attractions. Small boaters can find numerous protected baylets suitable for shore camping. Shellfish and lobsters can be gathered near promontories and landheads, but divers will be disappointed if they expect to locate black pearl oysters. Though the oysters once produced great riches, they all have disappeared.

Inhabited for many centuries by Indians, then completely deserted by them, Carmen was for a while host to cattle herds, brought by the Spaniards. The one continuous enterprise from ancient times is the salt works in back of Bahia Salinas. Forty thousand tons of almost pure salt are produced annually by the rise and fall of the tide in a volcanic crater. At one time, as many as 400 people were engaged in harvesting and shipping it.

WHERE GROUPER GATHER

To the angler, the 1½-mile reef that stretches eastward from Punta Lobos is the island's most exciting area. Billfish and other big-game fishes come in close to this reef, but even more important is the seemingly inexhaustible supply of huge Cortez grouper (*Mycteroperca jordani*) that inhabit this rock shelf.

For a score of years I have fished the reef and have repeatedly seen commercial handline fishermen haul in tons of these 40 to 80-pound Cortez basses. Hordes of anglers out of The Flying Sportsmen's Lodge have converged on this spot year after year. Yet, with all this intense fishing, there are no signs that the monstrous bass population is being depleted. This sustained yield is difficult to understand, since 30 years, or more, are required for fish to gain such sizes. One possible reason for the continuing plentifulness could be that the precipitous walls surrounding this 12-fathom rock pile (which drops sharply to 100 fathoms, then on down to 300 fathoms) are pockmarked with caves for miles around — providing living areas for countless numbers of grouper.

Despite their abundance, the old mossbacks are not easy to deck. After learning the unique method of hooking them, your biggest problem is getting them clear of the rocks. They seem to hit the bait at a downward angle and keep on going until they're under a ledge. Once the leader becomes fouled, getting the fish to move out is very difficult.

In general, I use light tackle and fish easy. But here, heavy equipment and a lot of muscle are required for even a small measure of success. My favorite bait is a 1½-foot sierra hooked in booby-trap fashion (two hooks). To keep the line from twisting when the bait turns over and over, attach a heavy sinker ahead of the long swiveled leader. Drop it to the bottom, then quickly lift it 6 feet above the entangling rocks.

Generally, in bait fishing the fish is given plenty of time to swallow the hook, but with the double-hook rig the angler can strike the moment he feels the big tug or sudden hit. To keep the heavyweight's head up and out of the rocks, apply rhythm pumping and maintain it until he comes to gaff.

APPEALING BANDIT of streams and shores, the raccoon exists by plundering fish and birds.

THE LORETO MISSION *has a modern touch: A clock has been added to its bell tower. The bells from the mission are usually the loudest noise heard in this peaceful little community. The oldest of the bells dates from 1743, but the tower itself is newer.*

OLDEST OF MISSIONS, *Loreto was the start of the chain. Little remains of the original building, which was severely damaged by several earthquakes and has been almost completely rebuilt.*

This is the First Mission of the Californias

INSIDE THE CHURCH, *worn wooden bars, handsomely but simply carved, cover deep-set, shuttered windows. Thick walls keep out the heat of the day.*

A BARROWFUL OF FISHES *at the Flying Sportsman's Lodge. Some will appear on the lodge dinner table, but many will go home with the happy helpers. The big fish is a baya grouper.*

The Bounty of the Sea is a Rich One

SOMEONE WAS LUCKY! *Assortment includes a skipjack, a yellowtail, and a leopard grouper. They're all good eating, though not as good as some other fish taken in the Cortez.*

HE'S HEADED FOR THE STEW POT! *By whatever name you call him — caguama, or tortuga, or turtle — he'll make a delicious meal. Turtle stew and turtle steaks are favorite dishes in Baja, and sometimes a stew is prepared and served right in the turtle shell. The tender steaks resemble veal.*

REGION OF

Juanaloa

Home of the fictional Amazon women — the Cortez' most tranquil and beautiful region — the smallest human population

Gold taken back to Spain from the treasures of Montezuma and accounts of the riches of the Seven Cities of Cibola effectively recruited volunteers for New World expeditions of conquest, but it took a propaganda story sent to Spain from La Paz by a Cortez scribe to start the biggest scramble. The clerk wrote of having fraternized with an Indian woman of such great stature and dimensions that the conquistadores called her Juan (John). But the scribe, impressed by her "elegance of face and form," preferred the feminine, Juana.

According to his romantic report, the Indians of the La Paz area had kidnapped Juana from the "domain of the Amazons" north of La Paz. The domain was described as a kingdom without men, except for a few males occasionally captured for breeding purposes.

In this reino de felicidad ultimo (realm of ultimate happiness), the beautiful maidens wore nothing but small aprons made of black pearls. They dined on exotic tropical fruits, wild honey, game, and sea food, and fished from rafts as they sailed out to nearby islands. This reino, termed as "second only to the Celestial Paradise," was said to have precipitous and impassable mountains, a forested, flowering shoreline, three excellent bays, numerous baylets, and several islands in a sea of constant tranquillity.

To me, the clerk's account of the giant women and their early paradise had seemed as fictional as Montalvo's imaginative novel, *Las Sergas de Esplandian,* in which he told of the goddess-like Amazons. That is, it had *before* an expedition during which I got a panoramic view of the region.

SERENITY AND BEAUTY PREVAIL.
No sign of civilization shows here on Bahia
Tambobiche — except for the mysterious hacienda across
the bay (in center of photograph), home to someone
70 years or more ago, but quiet and empty now.

145

From a hilltop on Isla Catalan I could see almost everything described by the clerk, and, except for the "Amazons" themselves, nearly every detail was the same.

There were the sheer walls of the Sierra Giganta, crowned with domes, spires, and minarets like the profile of a Moslem city, defying all landside invaders. There was the wooded bench aglow with yellows and bright greens, gradually sloping down from mountain base to beaches of white sand, and protected and divided by multicolored landheads. There were three fine bays, Tambobiche, Agua Verde, and Escondido.

Propaganda or not, some of the tales were well documented so far as geography was concerned, so I concluded that this magnificent place should be given bounds and named. The clerk's comely Juana was given credit with the phrase loa de Juana (praises to Juana). Taking poetic license, I transformed this to Juanaloa for the name of this most romantic region of the Cortez.

Except for Indian legends and scant records left by Francisco de Ortega this region has been given nothing more than a few scratches on the pages of history. Ortega named the islands in 1633 during a pearling and treasure hunting venture, and in his report to Spain he told briefly of an encounter at Bahia Escondido with giant Indians whose dancing and flute-playing impressed him. Much later, the region had two shore ranches named Juan and Juanita, but there is little evidence left of them.

INDIAN GOLD, SPANISH TREASURE

On my early small boat voyages into this area, I learned that the population had dwindled to about fifty, including the itinerant vagabundos del mar, who are especially fond of isolated places. These unfettered souls have minds so free of concern that they can give over their days to thinking up preposterous stories to tell. Although their tales often start with fact, they usually end far out in soaring fantasy.

I must admit, however, that an old vagabundo I met at Bahia Escondido left me talking to myself. His wild story concerned the many mineral-filled hot springs along the coast of the Peninsula, and, in particular, the sulphur spring that had led to the large sulphur and copper industry at Santa Rosalia. Knowing the truth of the copper story, I was hooked, and he knew it.

He told me that much of the gold brought into the Loreto mission by Indians had been taken from a secret spring of boiling-hot salt water. Its overflow had left boulders along its stream plated with gold, which could be scraped off in quantity.

He also said that Spaniards had secretly followed the Indians and were about to locate the spring somewhere close to Punta San Telmo. When the spies were discovered, the Indians quickly filled the spring and its stream with rocks, hiding all traces of the gold-bearing water. A short time later, all of the tribe died. The spring has never been found, "till this day . . . maybe," he concluded.

As the old man was about to shove off in his dugout, he seemed to suspect that despite my show of interest I was skeptical. He dug deep in

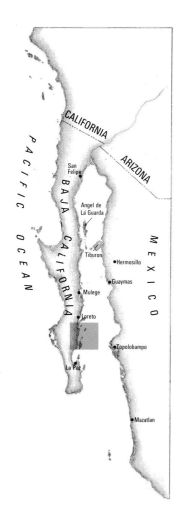

JUANALOA is the serene region, with Isla Monseratte and Isla Catalana.

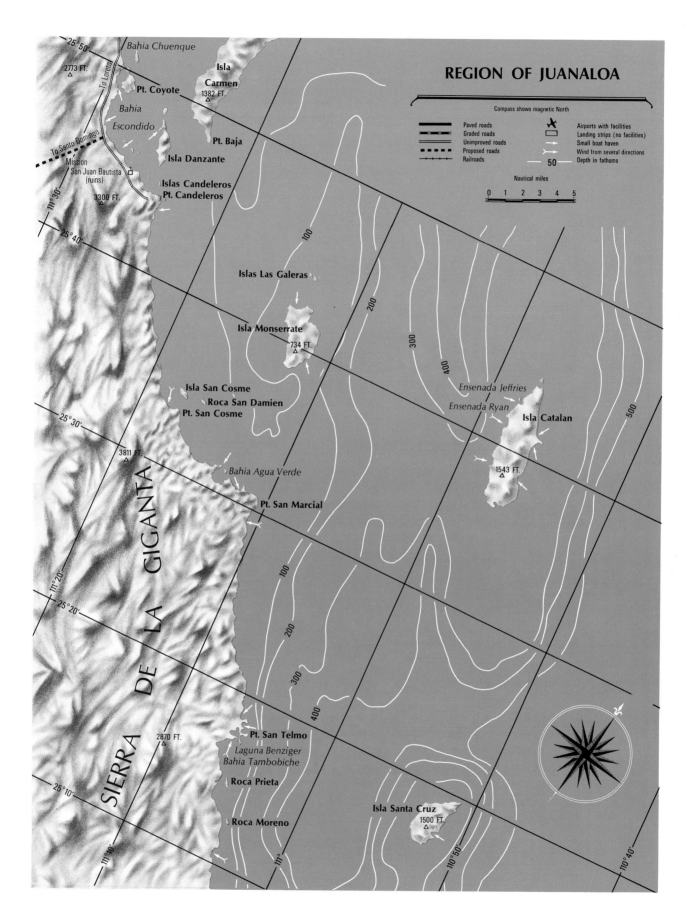

REGION OF JUANALOA

Compass shows magnetic North

Paved roads	Airports with facilities
Graded roads	Landing strips (no facilities)
Unimproved roads	Small boat haven
Proposed roads	Wind from several directions
Railroads	Depth in fathoms
50	

Nautical miles

0 1 2 3 4 5

Bahia Chuenque

2773 FT.
△

To Loreto

Isla
Carmen
1382 FT.
△

Pt. Coyote

Bahia
Escondido

To Santo Domingo

Pt. Baja

Mission
San Juan Bautista
(ruins)

Isla Danzante

3300 FT.
△

Islas Candeleros
Pt. Candeleros

100

Islas Las Galeras

200

Isla Monserrate

734 FT.
△

300

400

Isla San Cosme
Roca San Damien
Pt. San Cosme

Ensenada Jeffries
Ensenada Ryan

Isla Catalan

500

3811 FT.
△

Bahia Agua Verde

1543 FT.
△

Pt. San Marcial

100

200

SIERRA DE LA GIGANTA

300

2870 FT.
△

400

Pt. San Telmo
Laguna Benziger
Bahia Tambobiche

Roca Prieta

Roca Moreno

Isla Santa Cruz
1500 FT.
△

his pant's pocket, then thrust a tightly closed fist in front of me. Slowly opening it, he disclosed a small, oblong pebble that was plated with gold.

But it was his parting farewell that left me muttering. It was, "Vaya con Dios . . . acaso" (Go with God . . . maybe).

JUANALOA IS A GENTLE REGION; its waters are kept tranquil by rows of protective islands and reefs, and its wooded shores are sheltered from chubasco winds by a crescent-shaped mountain barrier. The land is watered by subterranean seepage from high mountain lakes. The atmosphere is dry, with no fog or dew. Tides seldom reach the maximum of four feet, and the flow of near-shore currents is barely noticeable.

Juanaloa is one of the safest areas of its size in the Cortez for small craft and for large yachts that have instruments for keeping clear of rocks and reefs. Around the islands and along the shores there are many lees and coves with fair to good anchorages. The total area encompasses some nineteen hundred square miles. The western boundary includes the steep walls (rising to 2,500 feet) of the Sierra Giganta. Roca Moverno marks the southwest corner, and Rancho Notri the northwest corner. The easterly boundary includes Isla Catalan and the small group of Las Animas islands. Within these boundaries there are four major islands, a dozen smaller ones, and numerous large rocks that almost anywhere else in this or any other sea would be termed islands.

Also within the bounds of this Region there is a great choice of fish and fishing. Some southern forms extend their range north to overlap that of species that venture no farther south than these waters. This mixture of species takes place because of a blending of temperatures — the cold water of the deep basins around the outer islands is upwelled by swift currents, thus maintaining a cool temperature favored by fish from the north, while the quiet, shallow water near shore remains a warm and suitable habitat for fish from the tropics.

PURPLE *blossoms precede the delicious yellow fruit of the papaya carica.*

ENCHANTED BAHIA ESCONDIDO

I had never become aware of the mystic magnetism of the Bahia Escondido seascape until one day when I got an early morning view of it.

As the sun lifted, the islands and landheads appeared to rise above the surface of the sea and hover there. If there had been a mist or fog concealing the tide line of the islands, I could have understood the illusion; but the atmosphere was perfectly clear and dry. There wasn't a drop of dew on the shrubbery.

Some of the landheads along the broken shore line below the site of the present dock looked as if they were islands. Two chains of near shore islands seemed to converge a few miles southward. The glow of the early morning sun tinged the light gray cliffs with pink but intensified the yellows and greens of vegetation growing from the foot of the mountain to the edge of the bay. Shadows criss-crossed the faces of the bluffs, showing them to be corrugated and gouged. Mountain peaks stood out against the sky like a carefully carved cameo.

SCARCELY A RIPPLE stirs the Sea as these commercial net fishermen head out into
Bahia Bocochibampo on the Mainland. Sunlight sparkles on the water, and clear sky forecasts a hot day
ahead. It's hard to resist an early-morning dip in such peaceful surroundings.

ENTER PARADISE, *just beyond the large, upthrust rock that marks the entrance to beautiful Bahia Agua Verde. Turtle fishermen camp here on sheltered beaches, and bighorn sheep roam the mountain tops. Long ago, the mission builders had a foot trail from Loreto to Agua Verde, but the Sea is the best approach today.*

The enchantment was shattered when a long file of pelicans glided in, banked into a descending spiral, then peeled off and blasted the surface. This started other birds from nearby islands and bluffs. At the same time big fish rose in pursuit of forage fish.

The sub-surface waters from the arroyos provide enough water for good forage grasses for the abounding bird and animal life. When this fresh water seeps into Bahia Escondido, it also helps create an ideal spawning and brooding ground for black snook, roosterfish, and several other game fishes, as well as for mullet and small species of bigmouth bastard. In a bait haul made by an old vagabundo and his younger partner, we saw fingerling snook and a half-dozen big blacks. Within the bay there seemed to be several types of environment suitable for the growth and protection of small fish. There were rock and cobblestone areas, mud and sand bottoms, and mangrove thickets.

There now is one deep mouth to the bay (65 feet wide by 9 feet deep) at the south end, but sometime in the past there were two other entrances at the north end. It is believed by some that these openings were filled with cobblestones by mission Indians, but it is more likely that raging chubascos filled the gaps — similar to what occurred at Islas Sal si Puedes and Espiritu Santo. No matter how the dams were constructed, they make Escondido one of the finest yacht and small boat harbors in the Cortez, and the Escondido area probably will attract hunters, divers, and anglers for years to come.

On various trips into the Juanaloa Region I have been able to visit and study all of the islands and the fishing around them. Each has its own special character, but the one similarity among all of them is the enormous quantities of rock-dwelling basses, snappers, and highly colored exotic fishes. Most of the islands also have their quota of sea bird roosts and nesting spots.

The almost barren, 3½-mile-long Isla Danzante, with a maximum elevation of 450 feet, is like a hen's wing, forming and protecting the outer Bahia Escondido. In the narrows of the 1½-mile-wide channel between this island and Carmen, the current becomes too swift and rough for a boat to head into during extreme high tides. Some interesting Indian middens and flowering shrubs can be seen in the gullies in back of Danzante's west side cove and behind a beach south of it.

The most delightful seascape in the region is formed by the convergence of two chains of islands — Los Candeleros, which consists of three large and many small isles extending from Danzante's southern tip to Candeleros Point, and a string of isles and rocks running nearer the mainland to this point.

On a trip to Bahia Escondido with Dr. Boyd Walker, I not only learned that several species of fish spawn in the bay, but also discovered that sleeping in certain places could be an unnerving, as well as a hazardous, experience.

To escape the racket of squawking waterfowl and thrashing mullet, Walker and I selected a spot some distance back of the bay for a campsite. We had been asleep for only a short time when we were startled awake by the barking of three big dogs kept by a ranch a mile up the

RATTLELESS RATTLESNAKES on Isla Santa Catalina give no warning before striking.

A Rattlesnake that Doesn't Rattle

You'll encounter plenty of interesting creatures in and around the Cortez, but one you are not likely to come across anywhere except on the island of Catalana is the rattleless rattlesnake, scientifically known as *Crotalus catalinensis*. Elsewhere you may find the Baja California rattlesnake, the speckled rattlesnake, or the red rattlesnake, all of which have a series of rattles (actually remnants of previously-shed skin), which vibrate when the snake is alarmed. But on Isla Catalana is the only known rattlesnake that is not endowed with the usual warning system. *Crotalus catalinensis* has only a rudimentary rattle at the end of his tail — not enough to announce his presence. In other respects, however, he is a true rattlesnake. So step with care if you decide to explore Isla Catalana!

FULL OF CONTRASTS *you expect in Baja: a lush garden spot in a cliff-walled arroyo. This is Comondu, an oasis on the long drive from the border to La Paz.*

TWO COMONDUS—*San Jose Comondu, pictured here, and San Miguel Comondu—are connected by this road. Several large springs in the canyon above the town provide water for an oasis of sugar cane, date palms, papayas, mangoes, oranges, grapes, and figs.*

arroyo to guard their chickens from the teeming varmint population. The yelping kept up, then grew louder and more determined as the hell-bent hounds got closer. I grabbed a flashlight and snapped it on just in time to see a bobcat leap right over me. When I sat up to get a look, a hound came sailing overhead, then another and another. It was only after I had served as a hurdle for the fourth time that I realized my sleeping bag was lying across a varmint freeway.

The next morning the rancher told us that two smart wildcats were working the area, and that their strategy was for one of them to draw the dogs off into a chase while the other snatched a chicken.

While we were having breakfast with the rancher, one of the same dogs flushed a javelina from under a nearby bed and chased it across a clearing. As soon as they reached the bushes, the pursuit was reversed. The little porker, her bristles sticking out like a porcupine's quills and her tusks glistening, chased the hound right back into the house, under our table, and on under the bed. Only a kick on the snout halted the enraged pig.

The owner of the ranch had imported this and two other of the game animals, which had become pets instead of going wild as they were supposed to do. (The javelina is native to Mexico's Mainland but is not common to Baja California.)

TWO FACES OF ISLA CATALAN

The two masks used to symbolize the drama — one forever smiling, the other expressing agony — could very well represent the two faces of Isla Catalan. The face that looks into Juanaloa is as serene as the rest of that happy region, whereas the one looking eastward displays a forbidding countenance that clearly and most certainly defines the outer perimeters of the reino de felicidad ultimo.

My first expedition to this little known island, which is 26½ miles from Isla Carmen, was organized by boat builder Dale Jeffries, and was made aboard one of his marlin cruisers out of the Hotel Cabo San Lucas resort. Harold Nash, with whom I had made the voyage from San Felipe to La Paz, joined us for the trip. After fitting out at La Paz we cruised northward past large Isla San Jose, triangular pyramid-shaped Isla San Diego, and barren Isla Santa Cruz. From there we could see mysterious Isla Catalan looming up like a giant's haystack.

Except for one gap, the whole 7½-mile-long east side of Catalan is a vertical wall of solid rock, rising to nearly a thousand feet in some places. Various kinds of sea birds have made nests in the wall wherever they can find a niche or footing.

Two small springs are the only sources of fresh water on Catalan; some small palm trees grow near one of them. The break is deep and narrow, and rubble from it has formed a rocky peninsula that extends out for more than half a mile. On the sides of the cobblestone promontory, small craft can find good lees protected from all but easterly winds.

Near the low extension we saw hundreds of pelicans lined up in close formation along the edge, waiting expectantly for a school of jacks to flush anchovies up onto the gravel beach. Rounding the rock-strewn reef and

THE REDDISH, *short-tailed bobcat (Lynx rufus peninsularis) lives in Baja scrub thickets.*

shore at the north end of Catalan, we got our first glimpse of the splendid coast line extending down the full length of the west side. Calm baylets reach back from several points, and as we cruised southward each new cove seemed to extend deeper into the island.

RIDICULOUS FISHING

We eased into a tight inlet about a mile and a half below the north tip, dropped anchor in a patch of sand, and paid out enough line to get ashore. We were especially impressed by the vast numbers and kinds of land birds. Having no animal predators, Catalan provided the most perfect bird sanctuary imaginable. In addition to finches and other tropical singers, there were dwarf white-wing doves, blood-red cardinals, and woodpeckers. We also saw a pair of ravens and a couple of hawks. Most of the nests of the

TIGHTLY SPIRALLED pods give screw bean mesquite its name. It grows near water holes.

Twenty-Two Sailing Tips

The U. S. Coast Guard as well as several motor companies put out numerous publications on boating in general, but the Cortez has its own set of rules. The following tips apply to any region in this Sea, and their observance will make any voyage safer and more enjoyable.

1. Make up a list of equipment and supplies and check it carefully on loading the boat.
2. Post a complete list of everything that should be repeatedly checked (all moving parts, wiring, hull, intakes, bilge and other pumps, instruments, containers), and refer to it daily.
3. Provide for battening or lashing down every item aboard.
4. Get advance weather reports.
5. Chart an alternate course, in case of a shift in the wind.
6. Learn the principle of quartering in rough water.
7. Employ visual navigation.
8. Travel with a companion boat in sight.
9. Do not cruise at night.
10. Start cruising south on a high tide, north on a low tide.
11. Remember that Cortez has: less forceful currents and upwellings on half moons; less wind before noon; fewer strong winds from May 15 to August 1 on the Baja side.
12. In inshore winds, cruise well out from the shore; but in offshore winds, stay close in.
13. Be aware of coves ahead to run to in case of a sneak blow.
14. To beach a boat in a choppy sea, keep the stern toward land.
15. Don't overestimate gas range in adverse currents.
16. Keep in mind that charted as well as uncharted rocks are not disclosed by wave action. (This Sea has no waves except those that are caused by winds.)
17. Sail into bays where counter-currents run, to avoid delaying, head-on currents.
18. Enter coves and round points slowly and cautiously.
19. Choose anchorages with care.
20. Avoid anchoring in massive sea vegetation, which may foul intakes or props.
21. Allow for a great drop, or rise, of tide and let out line accordingly.
22. Keep in mind that "this trip is for having fun."

smaller birds were built on the ground instead of in trees. Their food and moisture apparently was obtained from seeds and fruits, among which were flowering barrel cactus with its lemon-like fruit, and the cardon which produces clusters of chestnut-like burrs which split open to expose a bright red and very sweet meat resembling that of pomegranate.

Lacking time to examine the whole island, we switched to exploring the fishing and found a submerged ledge sloping out from the western shore crowded with fish. Whatever bait or lure we let out while trolling was hit immediately. Even the bright McMahon snaps connecting the two lengths of leader were grabbed at almost continuously by small fish. Among the large fishes, basses of all sizes up to a hundred pounds were the most numerous, with groupers dominating.

To enable us to release our hooked fish easily and harmlessly, we hammered the hook barbs down. To avoid catching small fish, we increased the size of the hooks up to 12/0 and let out tidbits weighing 8 or 9 pounds. To our astonishment, these huge baits were gobbled by gigantic grouper and jewfish before 50 feet of line had been paid out.

For both Jeffries and Nash, this was the first time their desire to haul in monsters had been satisfied. After a couple of hours and a dozen rounds of furious battles, Dale released an 80-pounder, then threw his rod on the deck. Loudly and fittingly he expressed his saturation of it by declaring, "This is ridiculous."

We quit fishing, slowed the boat, and just looked down into the clear water at the hordes of brightly colored moorish idols, angel fish, surgeon fish, wrasses, parrot fish, and other small exotics. Out near the edge of the bench where the deep water magnified size, the mighty jewfish appeared to be as big as buffaloes, as they glided in and out of caves and recesses.

A short distance out from the reef we saw dolphinfish, yellowfin tuna, and needlefish, all leaping above the surface in pursuit of small flyingfish. In one chase a large tuna and a frigate bird seemed determined to beat the other to an airborne snack. It was a photo finish — a collision in a cloud of spray. We expected the frigate to come up minus a head, but it was he who won the prize.

Most thrilling of the races was one in which a bloodthirsty dolphinfish, hot on the tail of a surface-skiing halfbeak, came vaulting up in loops 40 feet long. Half a dozen times we saw the halfbeak take off in a head wind, with its pectoral fins extended to catch the up-draft, and clear the surface for a 100-yard glide, then, with a couple of flips of the enlarged lobe of its tail fin, take off again. Just as the race came up to our port side and it appeared that the little flier was about to lose, he made an abrupt right face, headed straight for our boat, and dived under. In the sweeping turn, the dolphinfish skidded and lost ground. By the time he zoomed in, a feather we were trolling zipped across his path, and mistaking it for his prey, he nailed it hard and good.

Off our starboard we could see the halfbeak rise and resume skiing on toward a distant shore, to live and be chased another day.

The activities of the birds were even more energetic. Among the strange goings-on was their odd behavior in following a course running due west from the north end of Catalan. On this crowded fly-way, a constant flow of

SHOWY ANGEL'S TRUMPET *is adorned with musky smelling, erect, foot-long flowers.*

pelicans, gulls, terns, cormorants, and boobies, was maintained. Rather than take off on a shortcut from the south end, they all flew up the full length of the island to get onto the very narrow fly-way.

It was with regret that we left this fascinating island. Returning to it to finish the exploration became my number one aim.

RETURN TO EDEN

My wish was fulfilled the following year, when I returned to Isla Catalan in mid-summer with Mike Ryan. While the trip was primarily set up as a serious charting survey, I gave Mike all kinds of reasons why we would have to spend several days on the island.

As soon as we dropped anchor in Ensenada Jeffries, Ryan hurried ashore to examine every object above the tide line. He noticed some old and weak seagulls, wading in the shallows, and they seemed totally unconcerned by his presence. Nearby were seven or eight dead gulls, and a heap of bleached skeletons, all of the same species. Remembering stories of elephants going to a certain hidden valley to die, Mike reckoned that this might be a last resting place, a seagull Valhalla.

While Professor John Rowan and his two students, who were on our second boat, spent most of their time with what they called the "crazy fishing," Ryan and I roamed over the rocks, up mountain slopes, and down hills covered with low, flat-top trees. One of the valleys had a white cobblestone wash so lengthy and straight it looked like a paved highway. The July temperature was made delightful by a constant and quiet breeze from the sea during the day and a stiffer cooling draft down the valley from the mountain top at night.

From the brow of a high hill I could see the whole Region of Juanaloa and pondered the thought of building a cabana on this far-away island where I could enjoy, and be forever inspired by, the grandeur of that vista.

If the Region of Juanaloa were ever really the realm of Amazons, then Agua Verde, being the central bay and the most attractive, would probably have been its capital. The palm trees and tropical shrubs are larger and more profuse here than in any other area.

Locating Bahia Agua Verde is simple enough when cruising along close to the coast, but hitting it directly from Isla Catalan requires keen navigation. Bold landheads above this coast line and deep recesses between can confuse a first-time visitor. Cruising north, the navigator should note that the coast from Punta San Marcial runs northward for ¾ mile, then westerly for 1½ miles to an outer division of the overall Agua Verde. After crossing this division, there still is another 1½ miles to the entrance of the larger, more protected part of the bay, which in turn is divided by a knoll, a reef, and an offshore rock. The cove formed on the east side of them is protected from all except north winds. The best small-boat haven is a snug inlet on the west side of the bay, half a mile in from Punta San Pasquel.

On my shore visit to Agua Verde I saw an old ranch house in a grove of tall palms on the west, and in back of the bay there were four smaller houses. They were occupied by friendly ranchers who said that they were the descendants of a general who had fought with President Bonito Juarez

FIFTEEN-MILE-an-hour short sprinter, the roadrunner is a good hunter of rattlesnakes.

TRANQUIL AND COOL, *this sea cave south of Loreto is large enough to enter by boat for an afternoon of shaded, still-fishing. There's very little tide movement, so you don't have to worry about being marooned.*

in 1858. According to them, the great liberation President had rewarded their ancestor with a land grant here.

The foothills, which build up to steep mountains 13,000 feet high, begin less than a half mile back of the water line. Bighorn sheep are occasionally seen on the bench, and according to the ranchers they are more abundant on the mountain top here than elsewhere on the Baja Peninsula. Herds of mule deer, mountain lion, and other game are plentiful.

YELLOWFIN TUNA

There may be other places where you can catch several big-game species within the bounds of a single cove, but I have not heard of one that has more varieties than the cove adjoining Punta San Telmo, called Puerto Gatos. It also is the only place I know, except for the Rancho Buena Vista Region, where a permanent population of yellowfin tuna remains close to shore. The importance of this cannot be overstressed, because this race of tuna, in the 200 to 300-pound class, poses the greatest challenge to anglers of any fish in the Cortez.

All of the other big-game fishes, such as blue and black marlins of a thousand pounds or more, are frequently caught, but as of this writing, out of the hundreds that have been hooked, no rod and reel fisherman has been able to deck a 200-pound Cortez yellowfin.

Yellowfin tuna occur some distance offshore throughout the Cortez up to the Midriff. When hooked in deep water they sound and take all the line with them, but in moderately shallow places they take off for surface runs exceeding 1/8 mile. If the Sal Telmo area had no other attractions, the

GOAL OF A ROUGH BUT BEAUTIFUL DRIVE to San Javier is the church — finest example of mission architecture in Baja and the only original California mission church that remains intact. It was finished in 1758, ten years before the arrival of the Franciscans. The church is built of stone in simple Moorish style.

yellowfin tuna would make it famous; but there are other reasons why it should become renowned, not the least of which is its excellence as a port for small craft.

On previous voyages, lack of time and fuel shortages had prevented me from seeing Punta San Telmo at close range, but on the Holland live-bait trip, getting intimately acquainted with it became a must.

As we approached the point's deep red bluffs and saw the array of colors, we slowed down just to gaze. Sailing around the south side of the point, we discovered the entrance to an enormous hidden lagoon tucked behind the bluffs. The lagoon appeared to spread over a vast area extending close to the red landhead. Mangrove bushes and other bright green and yellow vegetation along the edge suggested that the water was brackish. We were completely enchanted with the place even before examining the good anchorages in the cove.

We saw nothing that reminded us of civilization until we cruised partway back into Bahia Tambobiche. There, beyond the beach a mile away, stood an old and mysterious looking two-story house — the only bit of evidence that modern man had been here. A roughening sea, however, prevented us from further investigation and halted our plans to go ashore.

We saw a school of large needlefish burst out of the water and scatter in all directions. Hooking one of them and trolling it through the middle of the commotion, we learned the reason for the disturbance. It was amberjack, and we decked a 68-pounder.

Our second pass with another needle brought an enormous jewfish to the surface. Doug Holland went after him with a diving lure on extra-heavy tackle, and to our complete amazement, tied into a 70-pound yellowfin tuna. Fortunately, there was enough line on the large, 6/0 reel to allow us to get the boat up to full speed for the long chase.

Although I had caught several yellowfin close to shore at Buena Vista, I had never before seen one back in a cove. This odd occurrence of tuna became clear when we took fathometer sounding and discovered a 50-fathom trench extending from the 100-fathom line to near-shore, similar to the submerged canyon near Buena Vista.

Having no live bait left, we found that most of the big-game species along this front preferred light-colored lures.

After exhausting ourselves fighting these monsters, we sailed in to examine the two mooring spots and dropped anchor in the south niche. It was so well protected that a growth of seaweed flourished, and we felt sure it would be a most productive spot to "make" live bait.

When we let out our net and light, hordes of little fish too small for bait swarmed in, but the large, mature herrings and anchovies we had seen during the day seemingly had moved out. Eventually we did get a supply of other bait species. A lot of foot-long needlefish and halfbeaks would cruise around outside the net, then make a dash through the middle to grab a pinhead anchovy. Doug became an expert at catching them with the long-handled dip net. As live bait they proved to be the hottest of all for many kinds of large fish, including roosterfish, marlin, and dolphinfish.

The fishing was so exciting we used up more time than our schedule allotted, and we had to leave the area without examining the landside. I was sorry since this was the only lengthy stretch around the Cortez that I had never explored.

CHUBASCO!

Although generally calm, the southern and outer extremities of Juanaloa do get blasted by a chubasco on rare occasions. In late September of 1964 I got caught at the southwest corner, in the open Bahia Tambobiche aboard a 24-footer, in a surprise blow that could have ended my allotted days right then. In my eagerness to explore the large lagoon paralleling the north side of this bay and to get a close look at the house of mystery, I violated almost all of my own rules on what not to do on lengthy cruises.

Bill Benziger, owner of Loreto's Hotel Oasis, was almost as anxious as I to learn more about the little-known place. When Bill volunteered to take Harry Merrick, Los Angeles photographer, and me on one of his fast, inboard, stern-drive boats, we threw a minimum of supplies aboard and took off. We had planned, or misplanned, to sleep on board, to live off the sea, and to chance picking up a few gallons of gas at a couple of ranches. Although this was the season for probable storms, no one mentioned checking radio weather reports.

Juanaloa was at her tranquil best, and our spirits soared as we planed down past her fairyland islands and shore line. The water was so still we

CRISP, CRIMSON pulp of organ pipe cactus fruit is edible, borne in heavy summer crops.

had to keep a lookout on the bow to watch for hidden rocks. We pretended to ignore a thunderhead that was boiling up to the south.

Then it struck! A sheet of lightning, a blast of thunder, and a raging crash of wind hit us like a runaway missile. We were caught and committed in the middle of that open bay, with no chance to run against the wind and towering waves or to retreat to the protected Puerto Gatos.

At first we thought we could ride out the storm by anchoring far enough offshore to avoid the breakers that boomed up as they rolled into the shallows. But that idea took flight when a cloudburst deluge came paralleling in and a cross-wind hurled us into the trough, threatening to swamp us. To add to the fury, one of our two anchor lines snapped and the other became as taut as a guitar string. Quick decisions were necessary. All hands agreed to stay with the boat.

We cut the remaining anchor line, then, to fight the cross-wind, revved the motor full bore astern until we hit shallow water and were in the midst of the towering breakers. Just as we were about to catch the force of the largest wave, we cut the engine and lifted the stern drive. The boat, riding the face of the wave like a surfboard, picked up speed. As it shot into shallow water, all hands jumped overboard and shoved stern-in toward land. It was a successful beaching but not one I'd care to try again.

THE HIDDEN HACIENDA

Since the boat was safe enough, we headed on down the shore to examine the mystery house.

Nearing the premises we forded a raging stream that had flooded down a mountain gap. Our goal turned out to be a ghostly brick shell that looked as if it had weathered chubascos for a century. In back of it were ranch houses and an emergency airstrip, none of which was visible from the bay.

About a dozen young men appeared who claimed to be descendants of the original occupants, the De la Toba family. They explained that the brick house, once a fine hacienda, had not been occupied for the past 70 years. They offered to butcher a fat kid for us. We eagerly accepted and took the meat back to camp and slowly barbecued it over coals.

At daybreak the next day the wind let up. The morning high tide was at least two feet lower than the extra wind tide that had given our boat a lift high up on the beach. For a while, we were stumped over how to get ourselves waterborne, then I remembered a method of beach launching that is probably as old as Noah's ark. First we dug a boat-wide trench, three feet deep, alongside the hull and down to the water. Then the next high tide, we tipped the boat into the ditch and shoved it out for an easy launching.

Back on the water we discovered snook, corvina, mullet, and several other species to be abundant; and we guessed that they spawned in this great lagoon. The De la Toba boys had told us that ducks and other waterfowl came in vast numbers to winter in the backwaters. Since neither they nor anyone else had a name for this fine body of water, we christened it in honor of our host, Laguna Benziger.

WEIGHING LESS than an ounce, the spiny pocket mouse feeds on seeds of the desert holly.

A SCRAWNY-NECKED ROOSTER heralds the sunrise in the stillness of a Loreto morning. The town has not yet awakened — except for the braying of burros, the barking of dogs, and an occasional "oink" from a wandering pig.

READY FOR TAKEOFF, *a group of pelicans stands poised on the rocks until their hearty appetites send them flying off in tidy formation after a school of forage fish. They won't have to search very far in the rich waters of the Cortez.*

HE SIGHTS A TASTY MORSEL

MAKES HIS UNGAINLY DIVE

DOWN, WITH A BIG SPLASH

A RATHER UNSIGHTLY NEST, and two top-heavy baby pelicans. The fuzzy white youngsters will soon grow into balance with their large bills.

Pelican Watching is an Endless Pastime

A SCOUTING EXPEDITION that will undoubtedly pay off with dinner. Crystal clear waters are a help, but it's remarkable how the pelican can spot his fish. He seldom misses on his dive.

WHILE THE FISHERMEN ARE FISHING, *the rest of the family can enjoy a day of shelling in crystal clear waters or walking on clean, sandy beaches. This cove at Nopolo, south of Loreto, has plenty of shells, especially fine sand dollars, and a lovely beach. You can reach it by taxi.*

Near-Shore Waters are a Wealth of Marine Life

SO MANY TO CHOOSE FROM! *As each day passes, you'll become more and more selective. The ones you found the first day are sure to be surpassed before you leave for home.*

UNBELIEVABLY CLEAR *and deliciously warm, the Sea is almost irresistible. Swimmers will be tempted to stay for hours on the mirror-like surfaces of quiet coves like this one near Guaymas.*

HERE COMES TROUBLE! *A wild-looking sky like this one often warns of a chubasco, with raging winds and crashing waves that send small boats heading for shelter. But a surprise blow can catch even the most able skipper — and such was the case when the author and his party had a harrowing escape from the Sea at Juanaloa.*

A Shipwreck Can be a Lesson Learned

HIGH BUT NOT DRY, *the storm-beached boat was pushed up on shore. In the driving rain, the photographer relied on an underwater camera to photograph the launching operation, which starts here with the digging of a channel.*

A HUNGRY TRIO feasts on barbecued kid contributed by sympathetic ranch owners who took pity on the stranded group with their boatload of soggy rations.

ALL HANDS HEAVE, and in she goes! The rain still pours down — and the underwater camera still clicks away — but the worst of the storm is over and it's time to be underway. The little boat is tipped into the channel, and from then on, it's an easy matter to float her smoothly out to deeper water.

REGION OF

La Paz

Baja California's principal settlement — the quiet, old city of peace with a fascinating history of pearls and pirates

La Paz, the City of Peace, lies just above the 24th Parallel, and is southwest across the Cortez from the Mainland region of Topolobampo.

Although the area was visited as early as 1533, La Paz did not become a permanent settlement until 1811. Twenty years later it was made the capital of all of Baja California. It now serves as the seat of government for the territory of Baja California Sur. And for anglers and hunters in search of high adventure, La Paz is the hub, the meeting place, the center from which to spread out to remote waters and hunting wildernesses.

On my first visit it did not take me long to decide that if I ever settled down, La Paz could easily be the final port. One swing around the old city, a sail out past the shoreline and islands, a glimpse at the great fields of basking marlin and sailfish, and my mental note for the future was made. Immediately I felt a close affinity with the people of La Paz, the surroundings they had created, and their way of living. This feeling extended to their type of homes and offices, built around large patios abloom with flowers and fruit trees, and to the old-style Mexican markets with their bright craft displays and mounds of tropical fruits. I was constantly amazed to find that art shops, which always appeared to be closed, were filled with genuine native artifacts, imported perfumes, and novelties—all of them at bargain prices.

The list of La Paz's other attractions that appealed to me is almost endless. I liked the mixture of French, American, and Mexican foods at the hotels; the grand old mission cathedral and its fine altar; the President's winter palace, and nearby public beach; the shading Indian laurel trees

THERE'S ALWAYS ACTIVITY AT THE PIER IN LA PAZ.
Busy all day long, the waterfront serves commercial
shipping, privately owned craft, and sportfishing
boats. The cargo being loaded here is grain which has
been trucked from the Santo Domingo Valley.

169

that form canopies over downtown streets. I liked the gay fiestas given on the various saint's days, which take the place of birthday parties. Since almost everyone is named for a saint and since there are so many saints, these shindigs keep the population dressed up and jumping almost every night of the week.

But what got to me most of all was the soft and caressing climate. While it caused complete relaxation of mind and body, it also stimulated sensations I had seldom noticed since I was very young. My responses to every thing became beautifully sharpened, and I found myself being charmed by little things that hadn't affected me since I was a kid.

On my first trip to La Paz I stayed at the old but gay Los Arcos Hotel. Cocktails were served on an open roof garden overlooking the bay, from where I watched dozens of dugout canoes in full sail riding down the winds called coromuels. Beyond the inner bay I could see El Mogote, a sand peninsula sawtoothed with many inlets that were fringed or hidden by brilliant green mangrove bushes. Beyond that was the royal blue outer bay, and out on the horizon, Isla Espiritu Santo.

Below, half hidden in a lush grove, was the romantic Malecon, a broad street along the sea wall, bordered by towering coco palms on the bay side and Indian laurel on the other. Strolling couples slowed their pace to linger within the sound of the love songs played by the Los Arcos roof garden orchestra.

I dined luxuriously in a flower-banked patio. Anglers occupying the tables were diverted from their food by the waitresses, who were trained to swirl their skirts at each turn and perhaps accidentally touch a diner's shoulder with a plump bosom while bending over to pour his coffee. They were always chumming but never hooking their grouper-eyed customers.

PEARLS AND PROGRESS

The early history of this region is best told in periods of pearl searches and colonizing attempts, starting with the vain undertaking by Hernando Cortez, in 1535. None of the several colonizers got a foothold until the first mission was erected in 1720. It lasted less than 30 years, then melted into the earth.

There were occasional visits to La Paz by pirates, privateers, and merchantmen; but the real continuity of the town did not get started until after most of the Indians had been killed or had died of introduced diseases. In 1811, Juan Espinosa moved in with a small group and settled down in permanent residence. He was followed by an influx of English, French, and Norte Americanos.

Sustained by pearling and mining operations, the pueblo of La Paz developed to accommodate 814 persons by 1830, when the capital was moved there from Loreto. When Lt. Gould Buffum arrived with the United States Army of Occupation in 1847, he noted that the eternal summer climate and natural beauty of the place would make it ideal for retirement, "even though the natives had independent minds regarding morals."

Both the pearling and mining industries flourished for many years, then everything crashed. The mines played out, and the pearl oysters died off

LA PAZ includes the city of La Paz and the two islands Partida and Espiritu Santo.

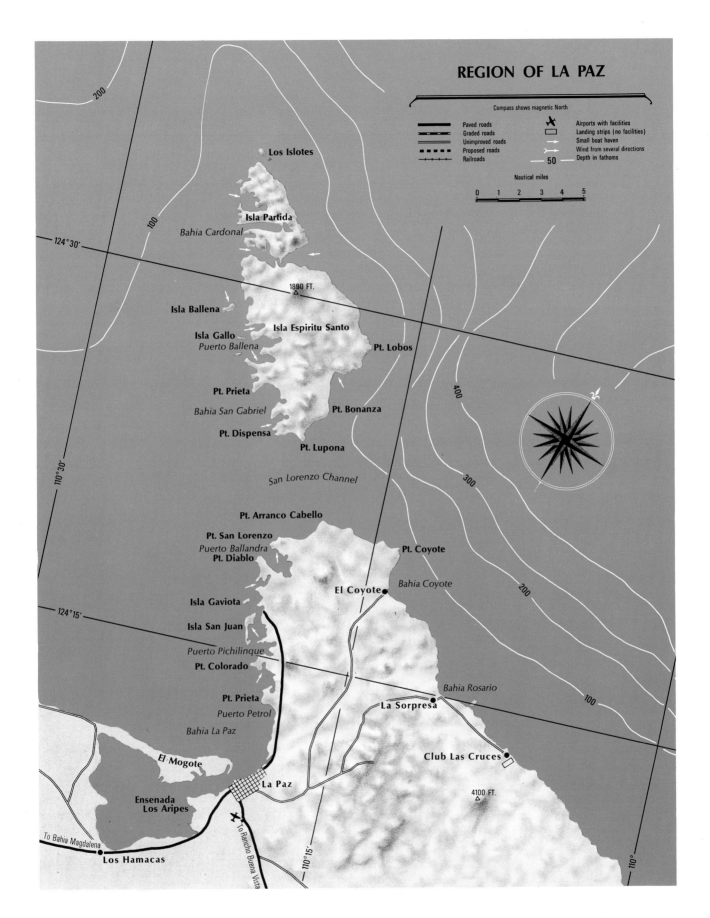

REGION OF LA PAZ

Compass shows magnetic North

Paved roads
Graded roads
Unimproved roads
Proposed roads
Railroads

Airports with facilities
Landing strips (no facilities)
Small boat haven
Wind from several directions
50 Depth in fathoms

Nautical miles

0 1 2 3 4 5

200

100

Los Islotes

Isla Partida

Bahia Cardonal

124°30'

1880 FT.

Isla Ballena

Isla Espiritu Santo

Isla Gallo
Puerto Ballena

Pt. Lobos

110°30'

Pt. Prieta

Bahia San Gabriel

Pt. Bonanza

Pt. Dispensa

Pt. Lupona

San Lorenzo Channel

400

300

Pt. Arranco Cabello

Pt. San Lorenzo
Puerto Ballandra
Pt. Diablo

Pt. Coyote

Bahia Coyote

El Coyote

200

Isla Gaviota

124°15'

Isla San Juan

Puerto Pichilinque

Pt. Colorado

Bahia Rosario

100

Pt. Prieta

Puerto Petrol

La Sorpresa

Bahia La Paz

Club Las Cruces

El Mogote

La Paz

4100 FT.

Ensenada
Los Aripes

To Bahia Magdalena

To Rancho Buena Vista

110°15'

110°

Los Hamacas

in an epidemic that began around 1940. Occasionally, cattle from back-country ranches were shipped out of La Paz, and a small amount of cotton and a few other farm products provided subsistence for dockhands. However, the economy was not lifted out of its long depression until anglers began to discover the big-game fish potential. About that time the town's principal businessmen, the Ruffo brothers, brought a fleet of marlin cruisers and Mayo Obregon started the Trans Mar de Cortez Airlines. By 1953 a boom period was on the way.

Rapid growth of the early sport fishing industry at La Paz can be attributed to Trans Mar's vice president, Ernesto Coppola, and their public relations director, Guillermo Escudero, both of whom knew the value of publicity. Having long been an enthusiastic outdoorsman, Coppola had fished, hunted, and gone skin diving around the shores and islands of most of the Cortez.

When I first arrived in La Paz to study the fish and fishing, Coppola became my sponsor and provided help or persuaded others to furnish me with every possible facility. Escudero assisted as my traveling companion, and his knowledge of out-of-the-way places and acquaintance with local people saved me much time.

These two farsighted men must be given credit for awakening the La Paz citizenry to the great potential of the region. La Paz and the whole southern territory had misgivings about unbridled "progress" that would change their happy and easy way of life. Thanks to the foresight of the pioneering Trans Mar officials and the modern and progressive managers of Aeronaves de Mexico, who took over the operation of the airline in 1962, orderly development became the aim of all civic leaders.

An era of modern elegance was ushered in with the construction of the Hotel Los Cocos. It sits in a spacious grove of coconut palms on the bay shore. It has a swimming pool, a miniature golf course, a large, outdoor dining veranda, excellent food and service, and its own pier and fleet.

THE PRICE OF PEACE

La Paz has suffered some king-size growing pains. At one time its narrow streets became almost chocked with taxicabs. About the same period a sudden switch from cotton to wheat farming in the Santo Domingo Valley brought hundreds of grain trucks through the town, down to the dock area. The traffic snarl was frightening. In any other Latin country it might have started a revolution.

The condition became even worse when a large herd of cattle was driven in for immediate shipment. The Malecon and streets leading to it were virtually lost to view; and for a city that had never before needed traffic laws, much less a traffic cop, the pileup was catastrophic. The town was full of cattle, and the harbor was full of ships; but no more than two boats at a time could get to the dock to load the animals.

The wild range cattle raised havoc until they were all driven to the beach. Following an old custom still practiced all around the Peninsula, the animals were forced to swim to the anchored ships, where they were lifted out of the water and aboard by a line tied around their horns.

A GNARLED monstrosity, the Baja elephant tree has yellow, papery, peeling bark.

DOLPHINFISH OR MAHIMAHI — *by either name, this is considered by many to be the best of all the game fish. It takes a longer fight to boat a dolphinfish than it does to land a marlin. A big one is tenacious, and he'll put up a terrific battle. This is the delicious food fish the Hawaiians call mahimahi.*

173

Prior to these mixups but not too far in the past, La Paz also was shaken by some other visitors. Twenty-two berserk sperm whales floundered into the bay like a fleet of submarines heading for drydock and ran aground on the shore. Tugboats tried hauling some of them back out to sea, but they obstinately swam right back onto the beach to die. A Pharaoh's plague couldn't have been worse. The awful odor from one dead whale is enough to gas a square mile, but the fallout from 22 of them — wow!

To avoid such a revolting development, the citizens gathered together every pan, pot, and kettle and turned out en masse to cut up the huge mammals and render out the blubber. Two days and nights they worked, and by the third day the smog that had built up was reckoned to be the biggest stench in all history. It was a fry to remember, and a smell to forget.

THE LADIES OF LA PAZ

From reading its lurid history, I had somehow expected La Paz to be somewhat of a roaring, lawless frontier town. I found it quite the opposite. Never have I encountered people more gentle or more sincerely friendly, especially the women.

There is a personal reason for the affable conduct of the women. There are five women to every man, and open competition for male attention has become quite fashionable. The women's manners, however, are refined. This niceness is maintained even in the highly charged atmosphere of the traditional promenades each Sunday and Thursday evening at the old plaza and at the new, less attractive Promenade Square, a concrete promontory that projects out into the bay from the Malecon.

According to the custom, eligible young men, including perhaps some visiting anglers, stroll leisurely around the plaza clockwise, in pairs, or groups. The senoritas parade counterclockwise, and at the moment of confrontation they smile and allow their shifting eyes to halt for an extra, understanding second on favored candidates. In this exchange of glances, the restraint is admirable.

Only after the promenade is finished and the dance music begins does a young man cross over to the girls' side, seek out the senorita who gave

THE DESERT pack rat's prickly burrow of cactus spines or burrs discourages most predators.

A Refuge for Pirates

The most believable pirate treasure stories around the Peninsula are those told of Bahia Pichilinque (Bay of Pirates), 12 miles out of La Paz. It was the most popular hideout for buccaneers of all of the Baja ports. Many of the notorious pirates who roamed the Pacific made repeated visits to this concealed and comfortable place. Captain Cromwell, the sea marauder for whom the offshore winds, coromuels, were named, was said to have lurked in Pichilinque where he could always get a good wind outward at night and inward during the day. This tale has been doubted, but no one doubts the legend of the French freebooter who buried a ton of silver somewhere in the area.

him the inviting gaze, and ask her to dance. If the chemistries mix, they will sit out a couple of dances. After the ball is over, quien sabe?

My first visit to La Paz was in late September, when billfish start their lingering migration southward. The area between Isla Espiritu Santo and Punta Coyote and on out to Isla Cerralvo was crowded with sailfish and marlin. Elsewhere I had hunted for many hours or days to locate a billfish, but here fins could be seen in all directions. With so many fish to work with, I soon learned that Zane Grey-size gear, still in popular use, was not necessary here and that I could handle the largest billfish on very light tackle. I promptly spread word that the region was the greatest billfish area of all time.

On a return visit in late December I learned that I had previously blundered in writing about the great numbers of billfish. I hadn't taken into consideration that the runs could be seasonal, or that they could be just the opposite to those at the better known Mazatlan, across the Cortez. As a result of my broadcasting the misleading dope, La Paz hotels were loaded with anglers expecting big game, when none was to be found. What I didn't know at the time was that marlin were plentiful 75 miles south of the city.

Feeling guilty, I engaged an outboard skiff and operator, packed some light tackle, and set out in desperation to catch whatever fish were around. If I couldn't make amends, I still could prove that the area had plenty of good all-around fishing.

At that time native skippers had not learned to troll for small game. Mine was puzzled when I let out a quarter-ounce feather lure and insisted that he keep the skiff moving at 6 to 8 knots. We hit a school of large, arm-long sierra and almost filled the boat. By slowing our speed and running close to the beach and stretches of mangroves, we caught several corvina and a couple of sizable snook.

We cut the day short, tied all of the fish along an oar, and paraded from the beach right through the Los Arcos lobby to the kitchen. The fishermen along the route were duly impressed and proceeded to scour the town for light tackle for the next day's fishing.

THE ONLY REASON I don't claim that La Paz waters provide the best fishing anywhere is that the numbers and kinds of fishes are equalled in other

DOG-LIKE ONLY in appearance and size, the coyote is seldom seen by day, often heard at night.

PALM-LINED AND INVITING, the waterfront drive (Malecon) in La Paz is a favorite place for strolling. The wide thoroughfare borders the beach for a mile or more, and in the balmy, breeze-kissed evenings, both visitors and residents turn out to promenade along its length.

Cortez areas and even surpassed in some seasons. However, I believe that with further fishing exploration, especially with live bait, these minor gaps will be narrowed. The use of live bait in the region has proved that there are populations of powerful game fish that have barely been noticed.

Morning fishing around Islas Espiritu Santo, La Partida, and Cerralvo has hardly been tried. In my limited survey I found numerous large schools and also pockets of several members of the jack family—including amberjack, yellowtail, crevalle, green jack, threadfin, and horse-eye pompano —on one side or the other of all three islands. During the summer, most of these fish showed little or no interest in trolled lures and baits, but responded quickly to live bait during early morning and late afternoon hours. Although the basses and snappers have long been fished here, their habitats are little known.

During the height of the seasonal runs, both marlin and sails spread halfway in to the outer La Paz Bay and become so thick, fleet owners used to guarantee a billfish hookup, or no charge. But early and late in the season the fish were too far out to get to with time left to fish them. Anglers who did try gave up when no fins were seen. Now, with knowledge of the position of the swimway and newly developed techniques for deep fishing, billfish can be contacted with assurance.

I have contacted several roosterfish along the shore on both sides of Punta Coyote. It seems that the large population off the Mogote narrows are year-round residents and that they become infiltrated with dolphinfish and other species most of the year.

Immature black snook have been caught all around Ensenada Los Aripes (inner La Paz Bay) on small lures. Collected specimens suggest that they spawn in the back reaches. This plus divers' reports of 5-footers indicates that La Paz could become a favored black snook area.

NOT A TRUE parasite, *Tillandsia* attaches to trees but absorbs airborne food and water.

Crossing the Cortez by Ferry

Plying the Cortez between La Paz and Mazatlan, the modern car ferry *La Paz*, with space for 370 passengers and 115 motor vehicles, provides an easy and interesting connecting link between the Mainland and the towns, resorts, and fishing areas in lower Baja. It makes two round trips a week, leaving Mazatlan on Tuesdays and Saturdays and La Paz on Sundays and Thursdays.

The trip takes overnight, and you have a choice of four classes of accommodation: *Salon* provides reclining seats at $4 per person; *Turista,* cabins for two, without bath, at $16 per person; *Cabina,* cabins for two or four, with bath, at $28 per person; and *Especial,* luxury suites at $50 per person. Rates quoted are one way and do not include meals. Salon and turista passengers have a cafeteria, the other two classes a dining room. Rates for vehicles are based on length: about $30 one way for a compact car, $44 for a long car, proportionately more for trailers and larger vehicles.

A MIDDAY QUIET *settles over La Paz when shops and markets roll down their shutters and everyone heads home for a leisurely lunch and siesta. Occasionally, through a partially opened door, you can glimpse a lovely, restful patio, filled with colorful potted plants in the true Mexican style.*

The Peace of La Paz is More than a Name

IN A RUSTLING COCONUT GROVE *just west of town and on a beach of its own, the spacious Hotel Los Cocos is one of the fine lodging places in La Paz. There's a swimming pool, and a pier for private boats. You can watch the spectacular La Paz sunsets from the shaded tile terrace.*

PASTEL-COLORED, *gingerbread-trimmed post office is typical of many buildings in La Paz which are quaint and almost Victorian in appearance. Strolling is a pleasure on streets shaded by lovely old Indian laurel trees.*

CITY OF PEACE ✧ 179

REGION OF
Cerralvo

Final resting place of the roving vagabundos del mar—home of the golden grouper—Bahia Los Muertos, Bay of the Dead

The Region of Cerralvo lies almost due west of La Paz. It is dominated by the 16-mile long Isla Cerralvo, which in turn is dominated by domestic goats, wildcats, and cacti. The waters are rich with broadbill, marlin, sailfish, and other big gamesters. It's very possible that one day, when fresh water is available, imaginative developers will visit, explore, and survey this Region. They will plant gardens and build resorts. They will build roads and create easy access to fishing waters. They will open a land that, though barren, is blessed with a continuous springtime climate, almost constant daytime sunshine, balmy nights, little rainfall, and gentle breezes.

Some readers will say, "Let it alone — let it remain a deserted wilderness." I, too, believe in preserving large sections where there is an abundance of wild animals and natural vegetation, but the landside of this Region has little of either. I believe that if trees were planted and resorts were erected, these shores would be improved. Why should some of the world's richest water in terms of sea life be denied to the thousands who could find immense pleasure fishing and diving in it?

During periods when game fishing slows at La Paz, marlin cruisers take anglers out to spend the night in Puerto Los Muertos so they can fish the teeming waters out of Bahia de Los Muertos the next day.

It's obvious that the naming of this bay had nothing to do with its abundant sea life. Whether due to superstition or the Mexican's dislike of tragic memories, natives give the landside waterfront a wide berth. There

A FIGHTING MAD BLACK MARLIN.
He's alongside the boat, but getting him aboard
won't be easy. There are plenty of fish in the Sea,
and the marlin is only one of the challenges
that lure anglers back year after year.

are, at most, two or three ranch families who have settled and remained. Except for some cliffs, a stretch of beach around the cove that forms Puerto Los Muertos, and a large and flourishing farm area inland, there is little that is above the high-tide line about which to be lyrical. But below, there are plenty of wonders.

At Puerto Los Muertos there is a deserted wharf and the remains of a pier, built in 1925 by silver mining interests. Except for the elegant Rancho Las Cruces, a private club, 23 miles from La Paz, there is no hotel or public lodge between La Paz and Bahia de Palmas, a distance of 85 miles. Nevertheless, there is every reason for a popular-priced resort to be erected. Being close to the big-game fishing grounds off the southern tip of Isla Cerralvo, Puerto Los Muertos is especially suited as a port for a fishing fleet. Winter and summer shore fishing are excellent. There are many fine diving areas, a good beach, and a comfortable year-round climate with little humidity.

More ships and fish pass through the channel between the port and Isla Cerralvo than in any other similar area in the Cortez. In addition to the fishing boats, numerous yachts, and ships of commerce ply this sea lane to La Paz. In spite of all the traffic, it is the big-game fish on their migrations that really crowd the waters.

February is usually the end of the season for game fishes heading toward the tropics; but in Los Muertos and on around the south end of the Peninsula, many linger for another month or so because of the abounding forage. During warm-water years these migrating fish are overlapped by the advance scouts of the great northbound schools and the even greater numbers that stay on until the following January or February. Only the numerous California yellowtail vacate these warm waters in summer. Other species also thought to be absent in this season will rise to the surface when live bait is presented.

It is during the spring months that the water appears to be living. Fishes and all kinds and sizes of sea creatures come up from the depths to cavort on the surface of the bay in displays visible to the most casual observer. The water also pulsates with micro-organisms so thick that it is fitting to say that the Bay of the Dead is actually a bay of life.

THOUSAND-POUND BROADBILLS

The great amount of fresh water seepage from Los Planes' underground river has created a unique environment for sea life in Bahia Ventana. The back bay is quite shallow, but the southern stretch of the bay's L-shaped shore drops down to 100 fathoms a short distance out. This combination should provide a favorable habitat for a vast quantity of different species, but we must wait for more angling experiments and scientific collecting to estimate the numbers and kinds.

Broadbill swordfish (*Xiphius gladius*) are thought to be scarce in the Cortez. I have seen only three caught and no more than that number in the water, all of them in Bahia Ventana. I have heard reports of other catches made by native shark fishermen south of this bay but have met no western anglers who have seen many broadbill except in the Pacific.

CERRALVO is centered on Isla Cerralvo, the large island lying below La Paz.

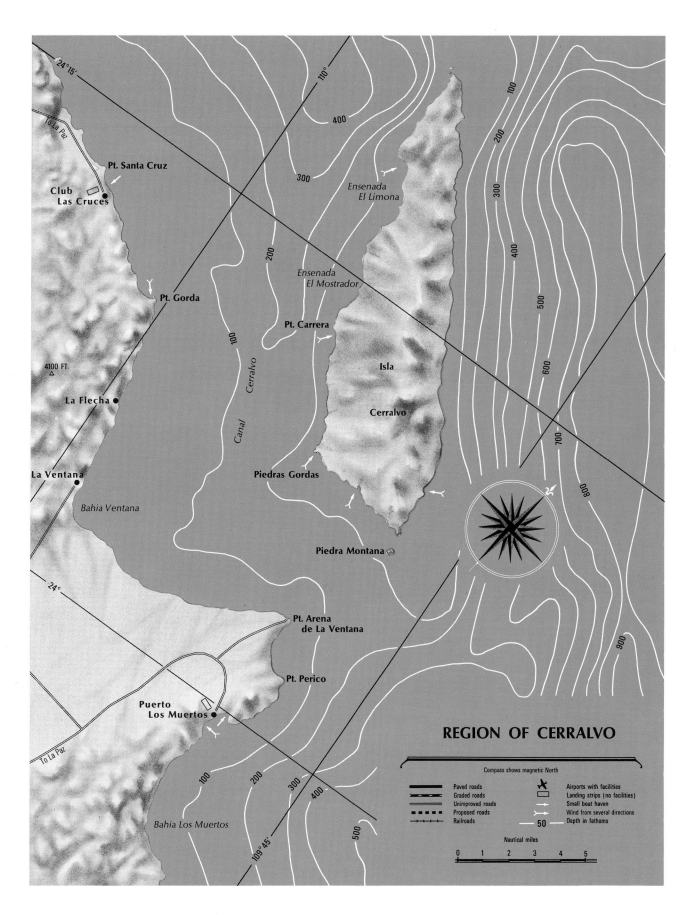

REGION OF CERRALVO

Compass shows magnetic North

▬▬▬ Paved roads	✈ Airports with facilities
▬ · ▬ · ▬ Graded roads	▭ Landing strips (no facilities)
▬▬▬ Unimproved roads	→ Small boat haven
▪▪▪▪ Proposed roads	⇝ Wind from several directions
┼┼┼┼ Railroads	——50—— Depth in fathoms

Nautical miles

0   1   2   3   4   5

Pt. Santa Cruz
Club Las Cruces
Pt. Gorda
4100 FT.
La Flecha
La Ventana
Bahia Ventana
Canal Cerralvo
Pt. Carrera
Isla Cerralvo
Ensenada El Limona
Ensenada El Mostrador
Piedras Gordas
Piedra Montana
Pt. Arena de La Ventana
Pt. Perico
Puerto Los Muertos
Bahia Los Muertos
To La Paz

In the water the broadbill is distinguished from other billfish by the curve of its tail dorsal fin. Out of the water the most marked feature is the flat, sword-like beak, unlike the roundish spear of the marlins and sailfish. A broadbill may achieve a weight of 1,000 pounds and require a number of hours to deck. A whole sierra, sizable barrilete, or mullet has proved attractive as bait when trolled slowly across in front of a basking broadbill.

I once saw a native in a small, oar-propelled dugout tow a couple of huge broadbill ashore in Ventana. How he managed to catch and subdue two such powerful fighting monsters is a mystery to me.

There is very little protection against storms in Ventana or anywhere up the coast, short of the coves at Las Cruces.

Rancho Las Cruces was formerly a pearling port with most of the work going on around Isla Cerralvo. The village was planted to tropical fruit trees in 1880, but the trees were abandoned soon after the drought set in — about 1912. When the pearling petered out in 1931, the settlement became a ghost town and remained so until 1950. Abelardo Rodriguez, son of a former President of Mexico, took over and started constructing the first major resort south of La Paz. The fruit trees, originally watered by a flowing stream, fortunately survived the drought through natural sub-irrigation. Surface irrigation developed by Rodriguez restored them to their original beauty and productivity.

The lodge at Las Cruces was later acquired by Bing Crosby and associates and turned into the Peninsula's finest exclusive club. Bing, an enthusiastic angler, built a spacious home at the site and has done much to encourage the building of resorts around the south end of the Peninsula.

A glance at the fathom lines on the map on page 183 will suggest the reason why many marlin cruisers from La Paz fish the north end of Isla Cerralvo. The dropoff to 300 fathoms within a mile of the tip of the island, and the continuous circle around to the great precipitous wall that plunges down to 800 fathoms off the east side, provide a terrain that is well suited for a big-game swimway.

Isla Cerralvo, a rugged, mountainous island, is the last island at the bottom of the Sea of Cortez. Most of its eastern shore line is rocky and faced with steep cliffs. The western coast is broken with intermittent bold headlands and arroyos, with beaches at the back of several of them. A lengthy beach and sandy point forms the southwest extremity.

THE STRANGE GOLDIE

Exploring the coast line and waters around Cerralvo has provided me with many strange and memorable experiences. The most exciting was the discovery of the fantastic behavior of the golden grouper (*Mycteroperca rosacea*), a gold-hued member of a less colorful species of bass generally called leopard grouper, which occupies almost every rocky sector of the Cortez. Mexican fishermen call the golden grouper la reina de la cabrilla or "queen of the basses." To the Seri Indians the golden grouper is known as mitano, "goddess of all the fishes."

When hatched, each fish is as plain as the rest of its brothers and sisters in the same spawn. The color of each is a drab brownish green with spots

BARREL CACTUS, a source of moisture when small chunks of it are chewed.

A FASCINATING CHANGELING, *this golden grouper started life in the same drab, brownish gray garb as his brothers and sisters, the leopard groupers. But he was destined to be a leader, and took on the beautiful fluorescent orange color of the golden grouper, now easily followed through the depths by the rest of the group.*

or blotches that change to camouflage against a rock background. There is no apparent difference until the fish become about 10 inches long. Then, as if by some internal, secret alchemy, three or four out of a spawn of several hundred take on a color like fluorescent gold.

According to Dr. Boyd Walker, who has made a study of the species, the change from green to gold in the chosen few is not albinistic but established by genetic processes.

Observing the apparent intelligence displayed by some "working" goldies in a cove at the south end of Cerralvo was the weirdest experience in all of my fishing years. I was bewildered by the instinctive brain power displayed as these fish appeared not only to make plans, but also to execute them with military precision.

It was a late afternoon when Hollywood photographer Ralph Poole and I landed on Isla Cerralvo. We were greeted by a hundred or more leopard grouper leaping up through the surface in unison and flailing down on a school of anchovy, an occurrence often seen wherever leopards hang out. We knew that the leopards wait half hidden against the rock bottom for forage fish to pass over them; then they attack and maim as many as possible for easy harvesting.

We grabbed our spinning outfits and dashed over to a 10-foot cliff overlooking the triangular inlet, expecting to catch an easy dinner. To avoid being seen, we crept to the edge, where we got our first close view of the crystal water.

EDIBLE SEEDS *are produced on low-growing pinon pine in arroyos of the Mainland and Baja.*

Vagabundos — the True Escapists

The name vagabundos is a title and a way of life that sea drifters apply to themselves. Their origin, according to one version, was with some Yaqui Indians around Bahia Adair in the north end of the Cortez who learned to use sailing canoes a century or so ago and deserted the land for a pleasanter life on the warm and abounding Sea. Happy-go-lucky Mexicans who disliked working for others and being subjected to rules and laws of the landside society imitated the Indians.

Since then they have been joined by an assortment of other men, from peons to college professors, who preferred complete freedom, breaking off land ties to follow a life without tensions or concerns.

These roaming vagabundos del mar, or sea gypsies, are not to be compared with vagrants, bindlestiffs, or drifters, for they ask favors of no man and of few women. Each has his own magic carpet — a weather-beaten canoe hewn from a single tree and propelled by a triangular sail or by oars that are seldom used. Usually, their only other earthly possessions are confined to heavy hand lines and hooks for fishing, an arpon for spearing sharks, turtles, and fish, a bucket, a couple of pots for cooking, a machete, wine bottles for water, a blanket, and a coil of rope.

Store foods are generally limited to small supplies of beans, tortilla meal, dried chili peppers, and salt. All major food-stuffs come from the sea and shoreside hills. Every few months, when additional supplies are needed, they take live turtles or salted shark meat to the nearest town for trading. Even in this contact they feel beholden only to the freely-giving sea. Their only conflicts are with the Sea's storms.

I had often seen a gang of leopards work over a hemmed-in ball of bait fish by blasting up through the surface en masse, but I never before had been able to observe how these carnage parties were organized or how little fish were corralled. In this instance I was baffled by the coincidence of the forage school appearing over this particular reef, when there was the whole Sea to swim in, and by what means the big groupers knew that the school would choose to move into this area.

Following the leopard's splashing avalanche, the arena became a free-for-all, and Poole and I were about to join in the action by casting white feather lures into it when we noticed a line of golden groupers emerge from the pileup, move into the shadow of our bluff, and proceed in single file just below us. We counted a dozen, the most we had ever seen at one time in a single area.

The maneuver was carried out as if a top sergeant were barking drill orders. At the perimeter of the cove the golden column made a sharp right turn, and the members continued until they were equally spaced across its mouth. Then a right-flank maneuver started them on an abreast approach to the reef.

Only then was the purpose of these tactics revealed. The forage fish that had escaped being eaten were scattered, and the goldies were frightening them again into a tight ball which they then forced right back over the reef. Panicked by the sight of the bright, orange devils, the anchovies forgot all about their hidden predators until they exploded up from the reef to repeat the crippling strategy. At this cue, the golden ranks broke and all plunged into the harvest.

We watched this peformance repeated eight times and were so awed that we forgot all about trying to catch one of the bass or getting photographs. As it got dark, as if a command to retire had been given, the leopards fell in and followed their golden leaders out toward deep water.

A COZY CAMPSITE

We clearly had seen something novel in fish behavior. We were convinced that the golden grouper performed special duties for the benefit of its colony, like the specialized warrior ant or nurse bee, and that the military-like precision and purpose required perception and exercise of a mentality. When I related my "bewildering" experience to Dr. Boyd Walker back in Los Angeles, his reply was, "If you tell that tale to anyone else, he'll think you're permanently bewildered." His second thought was to drop everything and go back with me to have a look.

We were fitted out for an expedition by our good friend, Col. Eugene Walters, the operator of Rancho Buena Vista resort, who gave us his largest boat as well as his two top skippers. When we got to Cerralvo, our skippers showed a lot of native intelligence and resourcefulness in making camp. We had brought nothing along for shade, and there was not a shrub with foliage. However, in a gulch the men found a couple of leafless bushes and trimmed off all of the lower limbs with their machetes, leaving the spreading top branches intact. These were covered with gunnysacks and pieces of canvas, producing two umbrella-shaped ramadas. We spread our sleeping bags under one and used the other for a kitchen.

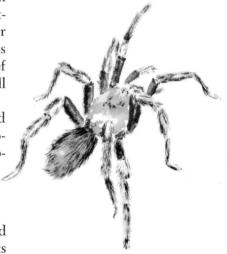

A VENOMOUS *reputation precedes the large, hairy tarantula whose bite may cause extreme illness.*

The kitchen was embellished with rocks, and we piled large chunks of dead coral for a windbreak. To our seafood menu we added oregano and other wild herbs, hearts of century plant, and various edible roots.

A thick barrel cactus was trimmed of its spines and sliced into disks, providing a dozen, clean white tables for dining and cooking. The smaller end slices were placed by our beds to serve as night stands, and we had a comfortable and convenient camp.

The golden grouper failed to perform for us, but since we were in the Cerralvo Region, Boyd Walker decided to do some collecting. We worked on a different cove each day and were able to gather hundreds of specimens, some of which were new and rare species. As a result, Boyd was delighted with the expedition but disappointed that his real mission to this area had not been fulfilled. (Before the trip was over, however, he did see the golden grouper working near Cabo San Lucas and was able to confirm the goldie's strange behavior.)

SEA DRIFTER'S BURIAL GROUNDS

Not far from our camp we came upon a graveyard with a couple of dozen crosses, some with candles freshly burned. Laborio, one of our Mexican skippers, who had spent several years as a sea rover, explained that this southernmost point of Cerralvo, the last island in the Cortez, was the only place the vagabundos ever congregated, and then only after they were dead. Laborio was unable to give us more than a sketchy history of the vagabundos and nothing more than a guess as to their numbers in the Cortez — which he estimated at somewhere between 100 and 300.

During the shark liver boom several years ago, their numbers increased. Every able-bodied man around the Cortez who could get a canoe or skiff joined in the vitamin gold rush. Fishermen sailed to distant islands and isolated shores for long periods, building little brush-covered shelters, some no larger than pup tents, at the back of almost every good cove. These deserted camps are occasionally occupied by vagabundos and also serve as landmarks for small boaters looking for a safe port. (Due to a scarcity of good crews in the Cerralvo Region, there are few camps there. South of Punta Pescadero, where there is less isolation, there are none.)

Many of the original shark liver fishermen, having enjoyed voyages to distant places and the freedom of it all, joined the vagabundo brotherhood. However, a few of them settled down to permanent residence and continued to fish for sharks as a market developed for salt shark meat.

In many personal contacts with the vagabundos, I have found this strange group eager to talk and always ready to be of service. On three occasions my companions and I have been saved from possible shipwreck by vagabundos, and at no time would they accept rewards. Our offers of cigarettes or wine were received socially as gifts but never as payment. The more I see and hear of these happy wanderers, the more I envy them.

PALMS, ADOBES, A HANDSOME CHURCH. For a brief time in its history, quiet little San Antonio competed with its neighbor, El Triunfo, in silver mining. It was soon outdistanced, however, and became the pastoral cattle ranching center it is today.

THIS FIGHTER HAS A HITCHHIKER. *A remora gets free transportation by attaching to a larger fish. If there isn't a fish at hand when he decides to take his trip, any boat that comes along will do as well. In this case the host is a fast-moving striped marlin.*

THE BIG BATTLE IS ON!   *OUT OF THE WATER...*   *...HIGH INTO THE AIR*

MUCH, MUCH LATER *a tired victor brings his fish to gaff. Striped marlins are the most plentiful of the billfish in the Cortez. They move into the Sea in early spring and remain there until after Christmas.*

Marlin are Plentiful, Wild, and Big

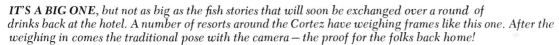

IT'S A BIG ONE, *but not as big as the fish stories that will soon be exchanged over a round of drinks back at the hotel. A number of resorts around the Cortez have weighing frames like this one. After the weighing in comes the traditional pose with the camera — the proof for the folks back home!*

REGION OF
Buena Vista

The greatest numbers of different game fish in the Cortez — ghost towns, abandoned mines, primitive settlements

The region between Punta Pescadero and Punta Los Frailes is named for Rancho Buena Vista, the first resort in this area. To say that this region has the best year-round, big-game fishing yet developed in the Cortez is only half the story. The other half has to do with a nearly perfect climate in a land of physical well-being. There are lofty mountains, varied landscapes, and long, inviting stretches of shore. Yet, it is the magnificence of this region's varicolored waters and its active sea life that gives it an enduring enchantment.

Of all the outlandish tales told about Baja California none bothered me more than the persistent one around La Paz about albacore being caught just south of Bahia Los Muertos. A mail truck driver offered to take an oath that he had seen albacora grande brought in on a shrimp boat at Rancho Buena Vista. He said that the albacore weighed about 100 kilos (200 pounds) each and were taken close to shore.

When all this was confirmed by a native who knew a lot about Cortez fishes, I really was rattled, for I knew that the largest albacore of scientific record weighed 96 pounds and that none had ever been reported closer to the Cortez than half-way up the Pacific side of the Peninsula, where they occur many miles at sea.

At the Rancho, all boat crews assured me there was mucha albacora, so I wasted little time getting out on the water. About 4½ miles above the lodge, my skipper, Fiole, revved the motors full bore toward a flock of

SUNRISE OVER THE SEA.
A gentle breeze ripples the quiet waters, and the beginning daylight adds a soft glow to the Sea's dark surface. Soon the sun will warm the morning and the boats will head out for a lively day in deeper waters.

193

pelicans diving close to shore. Thinking we were going in to catch some sierra for bait, I broke out spinning gear and let out a small jig.

A hundred yards from shore Fiole suddenly shouted, "Albacora aqui!" Just then a violent yank snapped my mono line. A second later I saw a small flyingfish take off 30 feet in front of the bow. Right on its tail the surface erupted, and a fish we estimated at 150 pounds vaulted through the air in a magnificent arch, hell-bent after the flier, which he tagged just as it hit the surface.

ALBACORA MEANS TUNA

I had seen the big fish quite clearly. In its shape and color it looked exactly like an albacore, but the long pectoral fin, by which the "core" is readily identified, was in use, and its length could not be estimated. In my startled condition I was doubting all scientific records and everything I had ever learned about the range and size of the albacore.

Before I could get mentally or physically adjusted, Fiole had shoved heavy tackle in my hands, with a large, white trolling feather already a hundred yards out. A minute later that feather was bombed with a running strike that zipped off another hundred yards so fast that the guides actually seeemed to smoke. I yelled "Hookup!" The fish headed down shore, the boat toward the open sea.

I tried to tell Fiole that the fish "went that-a-way," but my fingers were too occupied to point. By the time another hundred yards of line had peeled off, thinning the reserve down close to zero, I was being stretched on a rack. With the pull of the fish in one direction and that of the boat in the other, the point came to choose between being hauled overboard or easing up on the star drag. I chose the latter and helplessly watched the last few yards of line unspin. Fiole knew what he was doing, but I sure didn't.

With what seemed like no more than a single wrap left on the spool, the line came up in a great half-circle, slicing the water with a shrill hiss. The fish had altered course, as the skipper had anticipated, and as the loop narrowed, I saw a speeding wake like a movie shot of a racing torpedo come up off our starboard and zip on ahead, paralleling our exact direction.

I have been involved in many life-and-death situations in my time, but none provided such marrow-chilling suspense as the race between our boat and that fish, which continued for a full eighth of a mile. Finally, the extra work of pulling the bellying line caused the critter to start zigzagging. I was able to gain a few yards on the zigs, only to lose them on the zags.

Once I thought it was all for nothing when the fish made a run straight for the boat. I cranked the old 6/0 reel madly, then when I finally felt tension and had an opportunity to apply rhythm pumping, the fish became frantic, diving down, sideways, and up to the surface. After a long spell of more of the same, the critter was ready for the gaff and I was wild with anticipation.

On deck and checked thoroughly, Fiole's albacora proved to be an 86-pound yellowfin tuna! Only then did I realize that in Mexico, all large tuna are called albacora.

Although I knew yellowfin swarmed into the deep waters of the Cortez and were taken commercially in vast numbers, this was the first time I had

BUENA VISTA includes the resort area of the same name and town of Santiago.

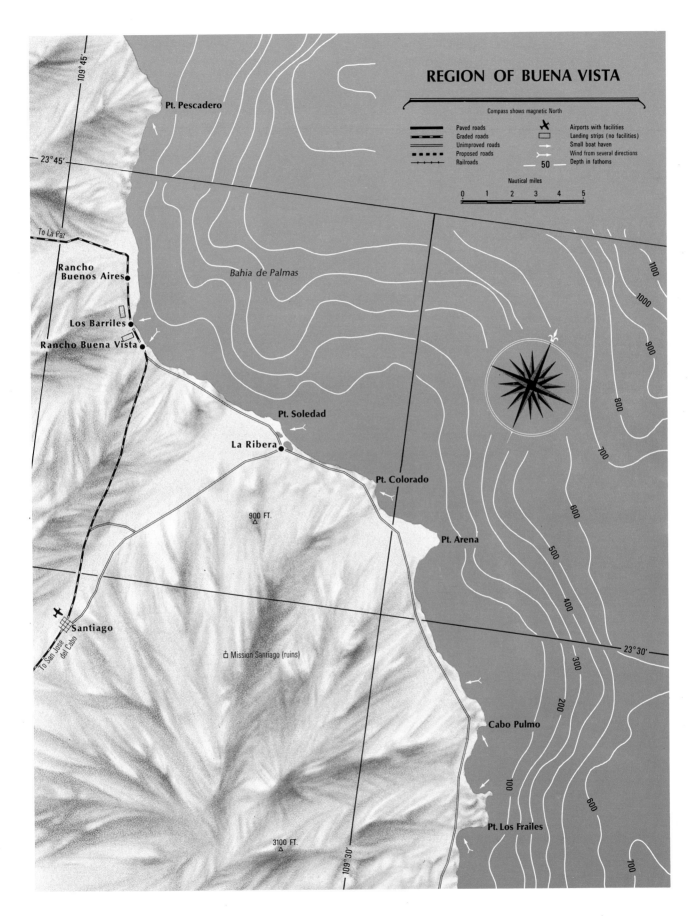

REGION OF BUENA VISTA

Compass shows magnetic North

Paved roads
Graded roads
Unimproved roads
Proposed roads
Railroads

Airports with facilities
Landing strips (no facilities)
Small boat haven
Wind from several directions
Depth in fathoms

50

Nautical miles

0   1   2   3   4   5

Pt. Pescadero

109°45'

23°45'

To La Paz

Rancho
Buenos Aires

Bahia de Palmas

Los Barriles

Rancho Buena Vista

Pt. Soledad

La Ribera

Pt. Colorado

Pt. Arena

900 FT.

1000

1000

900

800

700

600

500

400

300

200

100

500

700

Santiago

To San José
del Cabo

Mission Santiago (ruins)

23°30'

Cabo Pulmo

109°30'

3100 FT.

Pt. Los Frailes

ever heard of this species being caught so close to shore or in shallow water. Since that trip I have seen them only in two other near-shore, shallow places, both in the Region of Juanaloa. However, they do occur close up to several islands.

Try as I might since then, I have not been able to deck another yellow-fin above 80 pounds. Although I have hooked dozens of 100-pounders that busted tackle, straightened hooks, wrecked lures, or swiped gaffs, nary a one was got on board. As of this date, the largest yellowfin caught by angling in the Cortez was an 88-pounder taken by Harold Jewell of Los Angeles in March, 1960, at Buena Vista.

Having somewhat cleared up the mystery of the albacora, I thought our mission to Buena Vista was completed. But after an extra day, and another, and another, of the finest fishing for both big and small game, we knew that we were close to the biggest angling news scoop of half a century.

UNDERWATER CANYON AND TUNA

Throughout the year following that first visit to Buena Vista, I found yellowfin tuna running close up to shore in the same area where I had caught the first one. In addition to the permanent tuna population, this small area also had become crowded with numerous other big-game species. The mystery of why they chose this limited locality was solved when Laborio, our other skipper, and I lead-lined the bottom and discovered a steep-walled trench dropping from 50 fathoms a hundred yards off shore down to 200 fathoms to form a canyon that ran north-northeast to join a 600-fathom chasm 2 miles off Punta Pescadero. The depths greater than 100 fathoms were later surveyed and recorded by a group from Scripps Institute of Oceanography.

When we approached the area from the south, three sliced-off mountains were visible. The deep trench, referred to as Tuna Canyon, began at the foot of the first submerged mountain. The tuna in residence seemed larger than the migrating yellowfin that start entering the Cortez in May (some years as early as April) and spread up to the Midriff. The migrating schools appeared to be led by large pods of spinner dolphin, which remained close when the tuna halted to feed. The jumping and spinning habit of the mammals disclosed the schools to air spotters working with the purse-seining fleets. On one occasion in 1959, due to an overflow of Pacific mackerel off the mouth of the Cortez, the tuna piled up and remained to feed until June 10. When it was strung out northward, spotters estimated the continuous school to be a hundred miles long.

RANCHO BUENA VISTA LODGE

Herb Tansey, late owner of the Rancho Buena Vista Lodge, had created a happy, carefree atmosphere by his seeming total disregard for business-like methods. He assembled native crews and lodge personnel, taught them what to do, then let them run everything the way they liked. Every time a small group of guests arrived, the help would throw a fiesta. By the time

EXPOSED teeth and heavy digging claws mark the subterranean pocket gopher.

THE VIEW THROUGH THE WINDOW. Through a gap in the vegetation along the road near Cabo San Lucas you can enjoy this view of a peaceful little inland village. The natives call the viewpoint La Ventana, or The Window.

SCAVENGERS OF MEXICO, vultures aren't a pretty sight, but they do serve a purpose as a clean-up crew in the primitive areas. You'll often see them perched high atop a tree or waiting on a tall cactus.

a truckload of gay senoritas for dancing partners could be brought in from nearby Santiago, a roasted goat would be ready, and the skippers would have their guitars and other instruments tuned up for a rousing shindig.

Among the half-dozen other guests at the lodge on my first trip were a couple of Tansey's close friends and financial supporters who confided that for lack of paying customers the place was more than $10,000 in the red. I felt safe in assuring them that the little resort would be jammed within months. It was. A year later it could be called a success — then Tansey, who had been a professional aviator, crashed his small plane into a mountain top at El Triunfo. It was a profound tragedy to all who knew him.

The delightful atmosphere and native methods of running the place were taken over and maintained by Eugene Walters, a retired army colonel, who loved everything about the region. Walters directed the affairs of the lodge and enlarged the accommodations and fleet without changing any of the fine qualities of the now famed Rancho Buena Vista resort.

LA FIESTA MAGNIFICA

An example of the colonel's flair for arranging rollicking goings-on was shown when he held what started out to be a three-day fiesta. Advance notice of it had every room in the place occupied days ahead.

Accompanying the senoritas from Santiago was the town's spirited orchestra, which supplemented the resort's resident musicians. Whole kids were barbecued in a pit and covered to simmer all day. Along with the juicy meat there were wild fowl, fancy fish dishes, tropical fruits, fresh vegetables, and salads. The banquet was preceded and followed by a modest flow of special liquid concoctions.

Dancing lasted so late that boat crews and anglers went straight from the frolic to cruisers, and headed out for fishing. By the end of the third day the fun and excitement had built up to such a pitch that an angler who had just caught his first marlin announced that he would like to celebrate by buying the fiesta for an additional day. The idea caught on, and one guest after another found a reason, or invented one, to prolong the celebration, keeping the festivities rolling full-gear for two weeks.

There was quite a human pileup when guests with only three-day reservations refused to leave to make room for new arrivals. In the doubling up, beds and cots extended to the verandas. Weighed against the fun, privacy had little meaning. To accommodate everyone at mealtime, the length of the dining room table had to be doubled. This boarding-house arrangement became known as the "marlin table" and did much to create a unique social atmosphere. Anglers, divers, and hunters became acquainted at once, and before a meal was finished everybody was exchanging wild stories of their outdoor experiences.

THE PEOPLE OF BUENA VISTA

Because of the numerous species of fish and easy access to them, I spent much of my time working out of the Rancho all during the Tansey regime and the years that followed. Every possible facility for my studies was supplied by both Tansey and Walters.

Learning and developing techniques for catching more than 300 species could not have been done in a lifetime without the aid of divers to locate the fish, watch their reactions to baits, and figure out various methods of working them. Among the most proficient and enthusiastic was Bobby Van Wormer, who spent many months, year after year, working with me. He later started his own resort near Buena Vista.

A Trip into the Past

Primitive living is part of the scene in the Buena Vista back country. Many of the adobe hut dwellers still grind their corn by hand, and cook their food on rock stoves and in brick ovens. In some of the crude huts you can see wooden presses, hand hewn by early settlers, which still are being used to process cheese, squeeze grapes for wine, and press olives for oil.

Santiago, about 9 miles south of Rancho Buena Vista, is a hillside pueblo with an ancient sugar mill and several stores around a plaza. Another point of interest in the general area is a mountain which provides colorful flagstone for modern flooring. Nearby is a cave-like tunnel, its roof crowded with bats.

The little pueblo of Miraflores, 11 miles south of Santiago, is known throughout Mexico for its cheese and leathercraft, both of which you can buy in the village general stores. You also can buy locally made hammocks. If you are lucky, you may have a chance to see the last surviving maker of the unique Baja California vaquero (cowboy) hats at work shaping the heavy sombreros.

THE END OF A PERFECT FISHING DAY, *and a good-sized marlin is about to be weighed in at Rancho Buena Vista. The colorful raft in the foreground had nothing to do with the fishing expedition, but some children probably spent an exciting afternoon paddling around in the shallows.*

SMOKED MARLIN *is a delicacy prepared by the Mexicans for their own use from surplus marlin not needed for the lodge dining room.*

Much information was gained from native skippers, especially Laborio — so nicknamed because of his great ability to do the work of two or three men — whose real name is Cosio Cosio. When he was not running a boat, he kept busy setting tile, making bricks, thatching roofs, or doing whatever else there was to be done. Although resembling a Cromwell pirate, and he well may be a descendant of one of them, Laborio is a classic example of the gentleness mentioned in the old Spanish adage: "The gentle grass blade endures the violent hurricane." He seemed to like working with me from the first day out, probably because I insisted on going ashore to have lunch, which was followed by a two-hour siesta in a cooling cave, a stunt we made into a regular ritual.

Laborio's keen powers of observation and knowledge of the Cortez and everything in it were astonishing, not only to me but to Boyd Walker, who spent much time working with the two of us. Laborio's perception was so uncanny and accurate, Walker and I accused him of having a built-in sextant and telescopic eyes.

Many of the angling techniques mentioned in this volume, especially those that are unique, were worked out with Laborio. Among them were deep-fishing and working with live bait for billfish when they were not seen surfacing. He also was instrumental in developing the technique of circling a hooked fish, which is replacing the old style of backward and forward-running of the boat. It was in the Buena Vista Region that we expanded and refined the use of ski-bait (see Appendix), finding it not only more effective than frozen mullet and flying fish for billfish at times, but a killer for yellowfin tuna and numerous other species.

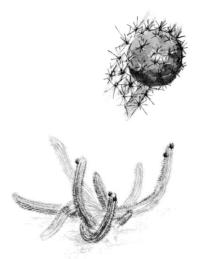

SOUR PITAHAYA *yields delicious edible fruit and a juice used to poison fish.*

CATCHING THE BIG NEEDLE

Ski-bait led us to one of the craziest discoveries made in the Cortez. Once while trolling for dolphinfish, our bait was being shredded, with nothing getting hooked. This baffled us until Laborio suggested a bait one-third smaller than the 8-inch ski we were using.

Almost as soon as we got the smaller strip out and skiing, I saw a splash a hundred feet off our port side. Then a living projectile, aimed at the ski-bait, came hurtling through space as if shot from a gun. Laborio yelled "Agujon grande!" as the animated missile skipped over the surface at spans of 12 to 15 feet. On its last bounce it hit the fast-moving target for a bull's-eye. The creature's long beak, set with bluish, saw-edged teeth, opened wide and clamped right down on the bait. But there wasn't enough flesh in the bony mouth to get the barb of the hook into.

On the second try, when another, even larger, spindle-shaped vaulter shot in and struck the bait, I gave free line and a long count, like fishing for marlin. When I slowly reeled in the slack I felt a strange vibration, but when I gave the rod a healthy heave it was as if I'd snagged a nerve in the Sea's intestines.

In the spray I watched the weirdest trampoline act I had ever witnessed. At the apex of each 10-foot leap the creature tried to flip the hook away from its snout with its tail. The contortions and gyrations had to be executed in the air, for in the water there would have been too much resistance.

After more than a dozen vertical leaps and a few side-swipes the jiver came in like a well-busted bronc.

Only after the 5-foot-long fish had been brought to gaff was I certain that agujon grande meant "big needle." I had often snagged many small needlefish, but had forgotten the scientific record of 6 feet for the giant needlefish, *Strongylura fodiator*. The strangest thing about this catch was that the fish had not been hooked at all but had taken advantage of the slackened line to revolve the way an alligator or eel does when trying to tear off a piece of meat. In spinning, the needlefish had wrapped the leader around its snout a dozen times and gotten itself caught with the snell.

Taking advantage of this twirling habit, I employed a technique like feeding yarn onto a spinning wheel, and was able to deck about one out of six. I improved on this method by adding a second No. 4 hook to the leader, forming a booby trap, a terminal gear I had developed years before for Pacific barracuda. Together, the points of the two hooks got a sort of ice-tong grab in the hard needlefish snout.

Anglers with patience enough to learn this offbeat technique are in for the most exciting spin fishing to be found, but they'll need a lot of 2-foot, 27-pound-test blue Sevalon leaders, since the leader gets coiled up like a spring with each snout wrapping.

Fishermen will discover that these big needlefish are among the best food fishes of all (give them a fast fry in a hot pan).

THE FINEST GAME FISH OF ALL

Although we had found ski-bait very good for several species, it was most effective for the common dolphinfish *(Coryphaena hippurus)*, and its smaller cousin, the pompano dolphinfish *(C. equisetis)*, both of which are called dorado by the Mexicans.

Dolphinfish have set up permanent housekeeping in a near-shore hole at Ensenada Palmas, just 2 miles north of Buena Vista. Here the Sea's most colorful creatures hold year-round open house.

If asked what was the most enthralling thing I have seen in the Cortez, I would have to sift through a thousand exciting incidents. But if I were

Dolphinfish — A Living Rainbow

Down through the ages, the dolphinfish has been an object of great praise and even a symbol of worship. Since man first sailed the seas, poets and writers have tried to describe the vivid but elusive colors of this living spectrum. The changing hues of a captured dolphinfish are just not equalled elsewhere. The changes begin the instant the fish is hooked, not after it starts dying. In nature there seldom can be seen a brighter saffron gold than on the belly of an airborne female. There also is an iridescent quality about her emerald-green dorsal and royal-blue fins.

Too often an average fisherman is so enthralled by the color radiance of the dolphinfish, he forgets that he is dealing with one of the most vicious creatures of the deep — a real satan that can tear tackle apart, shred baits, and take off in unbelievable leaps into the air.

A FIRST CATCH *is always a thrill no matter what size the fish. She has pulled in a medium-sized skipjack, and who knows, the next one may break a record! This one will be good eating at dinner, and the happy fisherwoman will have a man-sized appetite by then.*

to choose the one that stimulated the greatest number of head-to-heel emotions, I would select the time I saw a school of about a hundred dolphinfish rainbowing up in unison for a 50-foot-long leap. They formed a high continuous arch of much splendor. The last, sharp rays of a setting sun had caught the vaulters and intensified the brilliant colors.

There seems to be no satisfying the ravenous appetite of dolphinfish. I have seen them snatch baits just a few inches in front of the noses of big sharks and billfish. At first sight of a tobogganing bait, this voracious creature, like the needlefish, often takes off from a great distance and comes bounding through the air, or rips up the surface for a hundred yards to be first at a morsel. When hooked, it bounds as high as 15 feet. I know of no other 50 to 75-pound swimmer that will hit a lure trolled at 20 knots and pass the boat before the angler can feel the strike, then keep the fishing rod in the shape of a question mark for an hour and a half.

Add to this all the hocus-pocus tricks this protean showoff uses to flamboozle a fisherman: a hundred-yard peel-off straight away, then a sudden reversal right toward the boat; quick, unexpected slips under the craft, across its bow, then under and up near the outboard prop; twisting and gyrating jumps, never repeating a pattern or maneuver. Finally, if all else fails to dislodge the hook, the creature will possum until the over-confident angler relaxes the line, then spit the hook out right in front of the premature victor. It is no wonder that most salt water angling authorities say that no other fish of all the oceans can match the many qualities of el dorado, "the finest fish of them all."

El dorado will go for any bait that moves, including trolled lures, spoons, feathers, or plugs, and sometimes even a bare hook when it is jigged. If no live bait is handy, ski-bait is the second choice. A white feather is the third.

Dolphinfish roam the warm waters of all the open seas. They are often found under clumps of seaweed or anything else that floats, even under patches of foam where cool and warm waters converge.

IRONWOOD — a tough plant — has vicious thorns, very hard wood, leathery leaves.

If You Don't Fish . . . Hunt

In addition to fantastic fishing, the Buena Vista Region is noteworthy for its hunting. Game, especially dove, is plentiful. Quail and rabbits seem to be everywhere, and there are ducks and brant (dark-colored geese which migrate south in the fall) on some fresh water lagoons near the village of Ribera. Deer and mountain lion inhabit the higher reaches of mountains close to Buena Vista Rancho, and there are good populations of goats, pigs, and wild burros on mountain slopes.

Few but the natives can distinguish the wild from the domestic animals since the only actual difference is that the domestic stock go home at night. A hunter who mistakenly or otherwise shoots a tame animal is subject to a $5 fine. As a general rule, the animal's owner receives the money, the hide, and a quarter of the meat.

Hunting safaris for mountain lion can be organized at Rancho Buena Vista. Arrangements for fowling and other local shooting should be made a day ahead if you want to have guns, ammunition, a jeep, or the services of a guide.

Up to recent years, the name "dolphin," as applied to the dolphinfish, was terribly confusing. The true dolphin is a mammal and is a member of the whale order, while the dolphinfish is a true fish. Aristotle called the dolphinfish *Koruphaina*, from which its scientific name, *Coryphaena*, is derived. It is known universally by that name. The two species of dolphinfish are recognized by their tall dorsal fin which extends from the top of the head to the base of the tail, by their low-set eyes, and by their spectacular color. The pompano dolphinfish, *C. equisetis*, is distinguished from *C. hippurus* by having larger eyes, a less vertical head, and a shorter pectoral fin. The pompano is thought to achieve a length of 30 inches, but I have seen none over 22 inches. I have taken a great number of them on ¼-ounce white feathers. The rate of growth of the species *hippurus* is astonishing. A recent test showed a gain of about 50 pounds for the first year. According to native fishermen, 90-pounders are not uncommon in this region.

THE MIGHTY MARLIN

When I first hooked a marlin from a small skiff, I thought I'd caught the largest fish in the Sea. It latched onto a bait we were trolling for dolphinfish in a blind strike (without being seen by the angler). When it came up next to the boat, it looked as lethal as a Polaris missile. The fallout from the water that the great striper carried aloft not only drenched Laborio but forced him to bail bilge like mad. That fish showed no fear of the boat and did most of his jumping right alongside.

Keeping in mind that the monster was attached to the end of a 4-foot leader intended for el dorado and that the slightest touch of the taut line by the marlin's tail would snap it, we were forced to keep the line out on an angle, which meant running the boat away from the fish and circling broadly around it. By this method we were finally able to deck it. Although Laborio was disappointed when the fish was weighed in at only 158 pounds, the excitement created was far more soul-satisfying than the size.

Later, while from a cruiser, we employed the circling technique when billfish tried to sound, thus avoiding the straight-down leverage and the possibility of having the line touch the boat.

THE JAUNTY PLUMED heads and soft plumage of Gambel's quail blend with Mexican grasses.

Laborio became so proficient with the new method that I was able to work billfish off the stern portside with great ease. He also learned that by circling he could get more or less tension at will, so that even a frail woman or young child could catch a big marlin with little exertion. I found this easy-does-it style much more fitting to my own idea of pleasant angling. Other skippers at Buena Vista adopted the method and before long were getting a greater number of billfish to the boat.

TOWED TO SEA

I discovered so many advantages of fishing from a skiff that I advised all of my close friends to give it a try. The first to have a go at it was Herb Jenks, of Costa Mesa, California.

Herb took a skiff out, with Laborio at the outboard, and hooked a sizable striped marlin. It dashed no more than a hundred yards off starboard and jumped; then, in a definite attack, it made a savage drive straight at the little wooden boat. Laborio gunned the motor, and the attacker missed the boat by inches. A hundred yards off portside, the mad critter jumped again, turned, and made a second driving attack. This time, in true bullfighter fashion, Laborio swung the boat for a perfect valeriano, and the fish's flank actually scraped the side of the skiff.

Laborio stood poised with his iron arpon for the final estacado, but the furious marlin ran out about fifty yards, made a third jump, suddenly reversed, and caught the skipper with no time to maneuver. In that furious charge the hull was drilled amidship and below the water line. With a sweep of his machete, Laborio cut the impaled spear, and the fish took off again, leaving his bill stuck through the inside of the hull.

The de-beaked 165-pounder was finally gaffed and decked, but, as Jenks told it, Laborio appeared as defeated as a gored matador and expected to get a berating for the damage to the boat and for the delay in having to go back to port to exchange it for another one.

Returning to the same area an hour later in an even smaller skiff, Jenks tied into an enormous black marlin, estimated to weigh close to 800 pounds. Within 20 minutes it appeared to be pooped, and Laborio, whether by design or accident, muffed it again. Instead of hurling the arpon into a vital organ to kill the fish, he drove it just under the dorsal fin, with little injury to the big black. The marlin bolted. Laborio got to the bow and quickly threw a hitch around a post with his harpoon line, and the titan headed for Topolobampo as if dragging nothing more than a feather. It plowed up a wake almost as broad as a freeway. Laborio remained ready with his machete to cut the line if the fish decided to sound, for if it had, the skiff would have been pulled under like a waterlogged cork.

The afternoon wore on, and when the little skiff and its crew failed to show up by sundown, boats and planes were dispatched from the lodge to scour the bay and far beyond. Only after hours of pitch blackness did Jenks decide to break off the engagement and cut the fish free, and only then because there was barely enough gas to cover the many nautical miles that lay between them and port.

FROM SCABBARD TO SANDALS,
*if it's leather you want, you'll probably
find it (or can have it made) in Miraflores.
Even if you don't buy, it's interesting
to watch the craftsmen. Almost all
of the leather clothing worn by Baja's
vaqueros is made in Miraflores.*

Due to an overcast, no stars or landmarks could be seen. Yet, Laborio set a course directly into port. When he apologized profusely for giving Herb such a bad day's fishing, the answer was, "You'll never give an angler a better one."

BAG LIMITS AND LIVE BAIT

To date, not more than five per cent of the black marlins hooked are decked, principally because anglers are not mentally or mechanically prepared for either the battle or the remarkable endurance of this dynamic fish. When hooked in deep water, marlins usually sound to greater depths than those taken by other billfish, making a light-tackle catch a matter of luck. For the 1,000-pounders fished here and elsewhere, 130-pound-test line on a 10/0 reel is used with a live bait. The bait should weigh as much as 6 to 8 pounds and be caught in the same area. Heavy-weight leaders are often used and allowed for world record catches on minute lines. Thus, much of the fighting is done by the gloved deckhand after the fish has been eased up close enough for him to grasp the leader.

To encourage sportsmanship, advice is given to release all but one of each species of billfish. Some resorts have established this number as a bag limit. The fish is considered officially caught when the spear has been grasped. When releasing billfish, the leader is cut, with no attempt to remove the hook, which will soon be expelled or dissolved.

During the height of the season, any more than three billfish per boat would likely be wasted. That number can be made use of by nearby and distant native families, who send small boys over to load their burros with large slabs of the wholesome, take-home meat for barbecuing, smoking, or salting down.

The use of live bait has become a very important game fishing factor. It proved that roosterfish could be caught in July and that there was an almost continuous and permanent population of them stretching all the way from Buena Vista to Cabo Pulmo and on around into Los Frailes.

FISH ARE PLENTIFUL AT PULMO

Within a single square mile in the Buena Vista Region, the best year-round big-game fishing lies around the coral reef at Cabo Pulmo. I am sure that almost any other angler who gives it a thorough trial will agree. Although I had suspected this for several years, I was not so positive until I fished the Cabo on the live-bait expedition. Up to that trip, the fishing there during July and August had been so consistently slow, I had about decided that the big gamesters inhabiting this sector went elsewhere for their summer vacations. But using the live stuff, we started tying into enormous fishes, and before our three-day survey was completed we had caught most of the whole checklist. Some I had never seen taken in the area. One of these, a 40-pound black pompano, was perhaps an undescribed species.

My theory — that the vast abundances of migrators occurring northward in this season vacate Cabo Pulmo in summer — was wrong. Except for yellowtail, many of the species seemed even more plentiful, but only when live bait was offered. There are numerous reasons why the many species and great abundances congregate in, pass through, or take up permanent residence in the Pulmo-Los Frailes sector. Among the highly propitious conditions are: an abundant food supply, favorable water depths, convergence of cold Pacific and warm Cortez waters, and the geographical position of the two points. Being the most easterly landheads, they are a pivotal gateway into the Cortez.

The Pulmo Reef is the only extensive live coral bed in the Cortez. It is a veritable meadow, providing forage and habitat for great numbers of small fishes, which, in turn, attract enormous quantities of species up to the large marlins. But the basic food supply is the plankton, which is stimulated by fertilizing materials brought up from the depths of the Pacific with each shift of the tides. The south side of Punta Los Frailes receives the ocean wave action. Breakers recharge the water with extra oxygen, which adds another value to the marine environment, especially when incoming tides transport the charged waters northward.

The coral reef is half a mile off Pulmo and slants in, coming close to shore at one end. This is a popular spot for skin divers. In addition to the marine life, there are a couple of old sunken ships here. One of them, a mile off the north end of the reef, can be seen from the surface. Except for its exposure to chubascos and other strong south winds, the Pulmo sector has certain advantages over other areas for a resort site. There is a small lagoon just south of the foot of the cape that could be made into a tight little port.

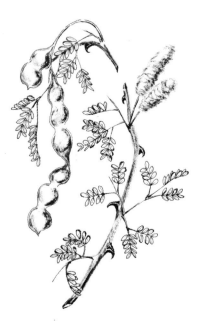

OPOPONAX, a perfume oil and medicine, was once made from cat claw (Acacia greggi) blooms.

A MAGNIFICENT SIGHT, *this is also an unusual one. A sailfish does not often spread his fin like this after he is hooked.*

Sailfish are Everywhere
in the Cortez

SHOWING OFF THE CATCH
at Rancho Buena Vista. These beauties are plentiful in this region during the summertime.

HERE'S THE PRIZE — *one of the finest food fishes of all, and one of the most challenging to catch. He gets up to 3½ feet long.*

Agujon Grande is an Aquatic Acrobat

NOT A CROCODILE, just a closeup of a giant needlefish. Blue lips and bluish green, widely spaced teeth add to his startling appearance. A smaller species has an orange mouth.

LOOKING LIKE A ROCKET (and almost as fast), a giant needlefish hurls himself high to shake the hook. It takes a special technique to catch this lively fish, and before he's landed he performs a fantastic aerial ballet.

FOR THE HUNTER, *there are plenty of game birds around the fresh-water lagoons south of Buena Vista. You can reach good hunting areas by jeep or by boat.*

Inland There are Ducks

A LITTLE PATIENCE *is sure to bring rewards. Occasionally a chubasco opens these lagoons to the sea, refreshing the water and sometimes rearranging the pattern.*

A GOOD EYE AND A STEADY HAND *are needed now. Great numbers of ducks (pintails, mallards, mergansers, and others) settle around the lagoons during the fall and winter months. Black brandts are plentiful, too, and there are doves and quail everywhere. A permit from the authorities is required to hunt in Mexico.*

THE SHOT WAS GOOD, *and here's the prize. The retriever this time is a deck hand from the boat, but there's usually a young boy around the lodge who is happy to go along and help out.*

REGION OF
Cabo San Lucas

The tip of Baja California, an area of deluxe resorts, where waters of the Pacific Ocean and the Sea of Cortez converge

The south end of Baja California provides a high-point for all who journey down the Cortez or the Peninsula. I have been lavish with my praise of each region of this land, but every mile southward seems to offer more than the preceding, and the Region of Cabo San Lucas—like each of the others—has certain features that are unique. The region's year-round big-game fishing has already attracted world-wide attention. Its deluxe resorts are unequalled anywhere around the Cortez. Its unspoiled back country is rich with small game. Its climate is subtropical but dry.

My first trip around the south end, with Frank Dufresne, noted sports writer, and Bill Escudero, started from Rancho Buena Vista in February. We had allowed ourselves a certain number of driving days for the journey, but the first hour after we left, our time schedule was shot since each kilometer revealed a new vista or something else worth stopping for. The wildlife ranged from rabbits to quail, from iguana to doves, any of which was an excuse to examine or photograph. There were scores of strange plants, unusual blossoms, and fruiting cacti. There was La Ventana (the window), a break in the bush at the top of a hill which gave a picture-frame view of a broad, verdant valley stretching westward to the magnificent, 6,000-foot Sierra de la Victoria. There were mule-mounted vaqueros, burro pack trains, and horse drawn carts. There were thatched-roof ranch houses and whole villages, unchanged for many life spans.

The longest stopover on the loop trip was divided between two areas, both of them noted for their fine resorts—San Jose del Cabo, and a few miles farther down the coast, Cabo San Lucas. In a fertile valley extending

LIKE A MOORISH PALACE ALONGSIDE THE SEA.
The luxury resort of Las Cruces Palmilla rises from a
patch of greenery on a barren point in the
sparkling sea. Wide-open porticos frame vistas of
the craggy shore and blue-water horizon.

CABO SAN LUCAS marks the cape region of Baja California where Cortez and Pacific meet.

up from San Jose del Cabo, we passed an increasing number of farm communities located in the midst of rich tropical growth. Closer to town, sugar cane appeared to be the main crop, but there were fields in tomatoes, other vegetables, bananas, and papayas, surrounded by orchards of mangoes, dates, and other tropical fruits. These flourished on into the town and down to the water's edge of a large lagoon. Bill explained that to avoid flooding the orchards and meadows, this lagoon was partially emptied at intervals by trenching the narrow sand barrier separating it from the ocean.

At the village of San Jose del Cabo, Frank and I had to adjust to an environment the like of which we had seen only in etchings and books of places long vanished. As we drove through the stone and dirt streets, history bounced up right in front of us. We passed dwellings, the mission, and inns that had been used and misused by famous and infamous characters since the time in 1709 when the Scot, Alexander Selkirk, said to be DeFoe's real-life Robinson Crusoe, stopped here after being picked up on Juan Fernandez Island.

Age had but added charm to the town's distinctive quality, despite its many ups and downs. Now it appeared that the beginning of truck transportation was about to lift the place from another recent low point, in which the population had dropped from 5,500, in 1938, to 200, in 1958.

We examined snook fishing at high tide when the sea poured through the man-made estero and were told that the largest, called robalo amarilla (yellow snook), grew to a length of 6 feet. We also heard that there was a species of goby weighing over 2 pounds in the lagoon.

On a later, mid-winter trip I found that the lagoon attracted several species of ducks and geese. Here, as elsewhere around this end of the Peninsula, whenever the shooting starts, small boys always show up to act as retrievers. However, the most proficient retriever at San Jose was a girl, named Ramona. She could dive and pull a maimed goose under before it suspected she was near. When retrieving land birds and animals, she could worm her way through cacti and thorn bushes that would have retired a dog permanently. Ramona continued her lucrative (25 cents per bird) art into her late teens.

Nowadays nimrods from nearby resorts enjoy the fowling at this lagoon. They have encouraged local residents to form their own hunting club. Its members conduct periodic turkey shoots, often substituting goats for turkeys, and throw a roast goat fiesta as a climax to the gala day.

CRYSTAL POOLS AT CHILENO

The shore fishing in the tide pools around Puerto Chileno had us wondering if we were still on this planet. At Chileno a series of circular, oblong, and angular tidal basins begin in a shelf that stretches for miles along the shore line. In some of these pools the water is 40 feet deep. In the first pool we tried, fishes that appeared to be all the colors of the rainbow floated up from a 5-fathom bottom, criss-crossed the 50-foot-wide pool, and glided in and out of small caves in the honeycombed wall. After I cast a lure down the full length and started to retrieve, a romping carnival of

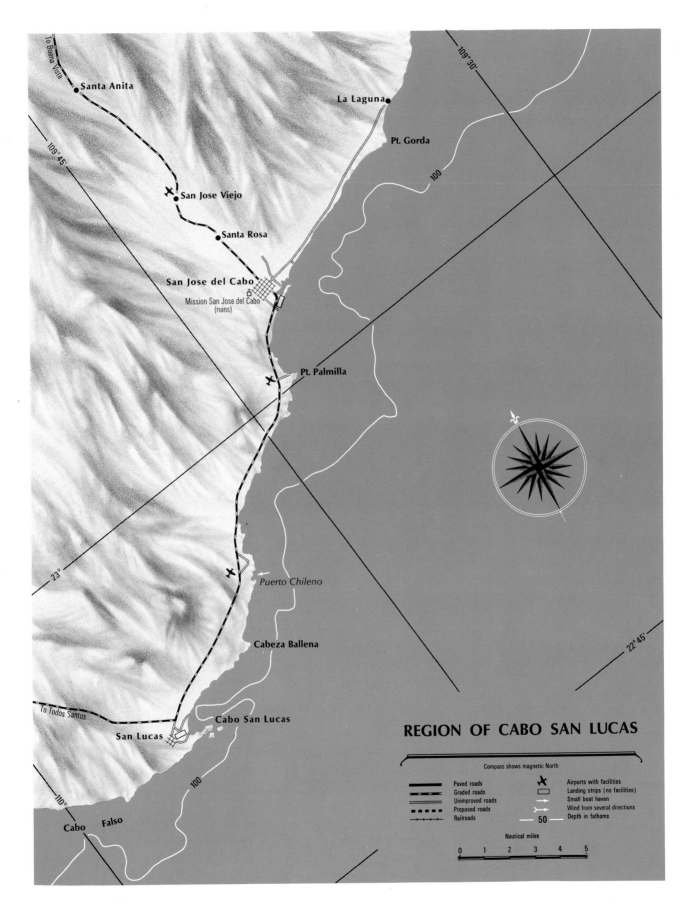

Santa Anita

La Laguna

Pt. Gorda

To Buena Vista

109°30'

109°45'

100

San Jose Viejo

Santa Rosa

San Jose del Cabo

Mission San Jose del Cabo
(ruins)

Pt. Palmilla

23°

22°45'

Puerto Chileno

Cabeza Ballena

To Todos Santos

Cabo San Lucas

San Lucas

100

110°

Cabo Falso

REGION OF CABO SAN LUCAS

Compass shows magnetic North

▬▬▬ Paved roads	✈ Airports with facilities
▭▭▭ Graded roads	▭ Landing strips (no facilities)
═══ Unimproved roads	→ Small boat haven
▪▪▪▪ Proposed roads	⇥ Wind from several directions
┼┼┼┼ Railroads	──50── Depth in fathoms

Nautical miles

0   1   2   3   4   5

multicolored fishes swarmed out in pursuit of the lure. It seemed that every large crevice, crag, and tunnel was jammed with marine life.

Out came yard-long blue crevalle, lineal striped blue-and-gold snapper, red Colorado snapper, the curious Chinese-design chino mero, yellow-striped goatfish, green and brown-spotted leopard grouper, brilliant golden grouper. There were orange-slashed triggerfish, turquoise-hued parrotfish, and a multitude of small wrasses glowing in unearthly radiance. In the words of Frank Dufresne, "It was like something swimming right out of a hophead's dream."

After an hour of crazy angling for big odd-balls, I switched to a dip net for the smaller ones. The first haul included an orange-and-blue striped wrasse, which had the unusual habit, when frightened, of diving down into the sand to a depth of 5 inches; a slender 2½-inch goby, which jabbed my fingers with a couple of needle-pointed teeth protruding from its lower jaw; and a 5-inch fringehead blenny, with hair-like tentacles on its forehead and above its eyes that gave the effect of a widow's peak, and eyelashes like one of Disney's cartoon fish. The most exciting find was a pair of quick-change artists belonging to the wrasse family, one of which turned out to be a new species. When first placed in a pail of water, its color was completely yellow. Within three seconds after it settled on the bottom, five bluish bars appeared encircling its body. As soon as it left the bottom, the bars disappeared. When it came up to some brown seaweed floating on the surface, it made a chameleon-like switch and changed to match the brown of the seaweed.

THE FISH WAIT IN LAYERS

After working the more fishable pools west of the big Ballena landhead, we journeyed on to the Cape. Here is where a mountain has been reduced by wave action after millions of years to a mile-long row of wedge-shaped rocks, the highest one 291 feet, the lowest about 8 feet above the surface. The Pacific's powerful waves continually pound against the outside of the Cape, which serves as a massive breakwater protecting calm Bahia San Lucas. The rock-walled side of the bay is separated from a fine beach, extending all along the back of the bay, by a pier that supports a sizable tuna cannery. As we approached the wharf we saw a crowd of small boys hauling in arm-long sierra, which they were catching on hand lines and single hooks baited with chunks of fish. The unusually large sierra were enough to attract us, but when Frank and I glanced down into the water from the pier, we saw more fish than either of us had ever seen in any one place. There must have been several tons of them within sight.

Just how so many fish could make a living in such a compact mass taxed our imaginations until we learned that they are chummed in and fattened on the blood and enormous amount of fish offal regularly discharged into the water from the cannery.

The milling fish, we discovered, occurred in layers, each species according to its preferred depth. The sandy bottom was completely obliterated by a silver plating of mullet; above them was a blanket of vast numbers of goatfish. These, in turn, were eclipsed by an almost solid layer of bigeye

SMOKY CLOUDS of blooms envelope the crown of the smoke tree (Dalea spinosa).

ACROSS PUERTO CHILENO, the luxurious Hotel Cabo San Lucas, hugging its site, occupies several levels on the point. Part of the hotel's fishing fleet rests at anchor offshore. From the left end of the hotel, a beautiful sweep of clean, sandy beach extends most of the way around the bay.

jack (ojo gordo). Young roosterfish and a couple of other distinct species occupied intermediate depths. All of them were about 10 inches long and perfect sizes for game fish baits. As we watched, we saw big, rampaging game fish streak through the ranks, sucking weaklings and stragglers into their gullets as swiftly as if they had vacuum cleaners.

SEVERAL OF THE BIG-GAME SPECIES that migrate in and out of the Cortez remain around the Cape during the winter. The general water temperature of the Cortez is much higher than that of the Pacific, and as the tides run out from the Cortez, the convergence line can often be identified by a low-hanging mist. As the tide rises, the line is seen to slowly shift back from the Cape area and around Punta Gorda. Natives and visiting anglers alike believe that fishing is better along this convergence, especially during the summer and fall runs of wahoo, sailfish, and black marlin. During the winter and early spring, other big-game fishes are usually too plentiful and scattered and don't seem to concentrate along the line.

Because of the year-round presence of striped marlin in summer and fall, lesser game fish were originally overlooked by the resort operators. Then they discovered that the exciting wahoo was plentiful and could be taken on live bait. This find led to the exploitation of other equally abounding species, especially dolphinfish, yellowfin tuna, roosterfish, amberjack, black-tip, mako and hammerhead sharks, and a long list of smaller game.

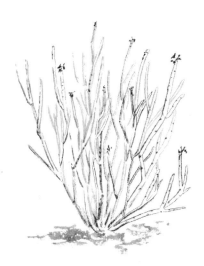

RED-TIPPED, *waxy white stems of candelilla contain milky juice, are burned for light.*

Driving the South End Loop Trip

Although Cabo San Lucas is easily reached by small plane and by boat, the motorist will find that the choice of roads to the southern tip of the Peninsula is limited. However, if you are a hardy traveler with a vehicle capable of surviving Baja California bumps, washouts, and sand, you can combine two major motor routes from La Paz to Cabo San Lucas and make a scenic loop trip around the south end of the Peninsula. From La Paz bear south and east to Rancho Buena Vista near Los Barriles. Then head inland, west to Santiago, turn south to San Jose del Cabo, and west to Cabo San Lucas. Return to La Paz by driving northwest along the Pacific Coast to Todos Santos, where you cut inland and head north to La Paz via San Pedro. Mostly narrow tracks, the 247-mile loop roads wind through scenic canyons, over vegetation-covered hills, across streams, and through villages.

This loop encircles a vast territory that was once called Tierras de Los Pericues (Land of the Pericues). It was inhabited by about 4,000 nomadic Pericue Indians when the Jesuits arrived. The Indians had no houses, scant raiments, no government, and few moral values. They lived in the woods and in the valley extending northward from San Jose del Cabo. The men did some hunting and fishing, but most of their time was spent reclining in "perpetual idleness in the shade of trees." Each man had many wives who served him by collecting wild roots and fruits. In 1730, Jesuit Father Tamaral, in charge of the San Jose del Cabo mission, recorded the conversion of 1,036 of the Pericues in a single year. At that time, the men are said to have willingly embraced monogamy and work along with Christianity.

STRONG BACKS AND WILLING HANDS *start crates of locally made cheeses on their way to market. They will be transferred from the skiff to the larger boat that waits offshore. Palo de arco is the sturdy wood that is used for the crates. A pliable wood when green, it has many uses and is often made into house walls and fences.*

"IS YOUR NAME WILLIAM TELL?"

The stretch of road extending over the mountains from the Cape and on toward Todos Santos was only slightly wider than the ancient carts that originally beat out the trail. It was several hours after we had been through the matted thicket that I developed a mad yen for a cup of coffee. Bill offered to produce one out of the wilderness, and disregarding our dubious comments, drove on for another hundred yards, then abruptly swung off on an almost obliterated trail. In a clearing he stopped the car, and we saw only a primitive cattle ranch. Several people came out to greet us. A boy of about sixteen, riding a mule with a rope attached to the saddle to draw water, waved to Bill.

We were introduced, and, according to custom, we all exchanged autobiographies. While the women were fixing coffee, Bill called our attention first to the boy, then to the father and his pack of dogs, and finally to a large bobcat skin nailed to a wall of the house. Knowing that a story was coming, we settled back, and Bill told of his first visit to the ranch.

He had ridden into the clearing and was quite startled to see, not far from the house, the boy leveling a rifle at the old man, who was standing under a tree, as still as if he had taken root. All around him the dogs were yelping and prancing.

Galloping toward the boy, Bill yelled, "Stop! Don't shoot that man!"

"But Senor," the boy answered, "he is my father, and he has el gato on his head."

Sure enough, there was a snarling, spitting bobcat on the father's head.

"Why is the cat on his head?" asked Bill.

"It won't come down because of the dogs, and every time he tries to knock it off, it gouges his head with its claws."

"But how did he get the cat on his head in the first place?"

"It was a mistake," said the boy.

It seemed that the dogs had treed the varmint, and when the old man shook a limb to dislodge it, the cat landed right on his head. The son got a stick to knock it off, but every time he came near, the cat would dig in with his claws. The old man was in tears from the pain, but he stood rock-still to keep the cat from joggling around.

"And that is why I got the gun to shoot," the boy concluded.

"Do you think you're that good a shot?" asked Bill. "What's your name — William Tell?"

"No, Senor, my name is Miguel Torres Orosco," replied the boy politely, and he proceeded to relate his family history.

Following social custom, Bill gave his name and antecedents. All through the long exchange, the old man stood with the cat on his head and the dogs barking at his feet.

Now that they had become friends, the boy handed the gun to Bill and asked him, "por favor," to shoot. As Bill squeezed the trigger, the cat sank its claws, the old man passed out, and the dogs made a mad scramble over both of them. Bill couldn't see which he had shot. It wasn't until they pried the cat loose from the old man and the dogs loose from the cat that they found the critter had been drilled right between the eyes.

As Bill ended the story, the father proudly showed us the scars on his scalp and the bullet hole in the bobcat's pelt.

LUXURY RESORTS OF THE CAPE

The modern Hacienda Cabo San Lucas is situated on a white sand beach where it gets cooling breezes from the Pacific as well as from the bay. The resort has flower-bedecked patios, a large swimming pool, and extensive tiled porticos and verandas. Bing Crosby and other celebrities often stay at the Hacienda when fishing for big game.

The Hacienda was the third of the resorts constructed in this area. The first, Hotel Las Cruces Palmilla, is even more elegant. Situated in a formal garden on Punta Palmilla, this resort commands a splendid view of the sea, the rocky shore line, and cozy little beaches. The main building has spacious dining and club rooms, a cocktail lounge, and guest rooms. Several annexes and a garden shrine have been added. Both this resort and the Hacienda were built by A. L. Rodriguez.

Hacienda Cabo San Lucas, close up to the Cape, should not be confused with the more elaborate *Hotel* Cabo San Lucas, which is at Puerto Chileno 7 miles eastward. In splendor, this hotel is unsurpassed by any other seashore resort in Mexico. It features baths in onyx, and split-level apartments with individual patios facing Puerto Chileno and the ocean. A dining veranda projects out over tide pools 50 feet below. From the adjoining dining room and an open lounge, stairs lead to a spacious cocktail room, then on past a man-made waterfall and swimming pool. The path continues through a tropical garden to clean little sand beaches separated from each other by bold rock headlands.

A TIMBER TREE, cape fan palm (Erythea brandegeei) trunks and fronds are used in building.

WAITING to be taken out to a freighter lying offshore. With no docking facilities at Punta Palmilla, the cattle will have to swim for it.

They Swim the Cattle Out and Hoist Them Aboard

ROPES KEEP THEM swimming close to the boat, and the crew keeps the boat afloat and the cattle moving, about eight at a time, out to deep water.

UP HE GOES! *What he'll do when he lands on deck is unpredictable, but he's fairly docile on the way. The foothills of the Cape Region mountains contain a number of small cattle ranches, and it is from these areas that the cattle are driven to several coastal loading points.*

REGION OF

Magdalena

Gigantic bay on the Pacific side of Baja, visited regularly by the gray whale — a fertile agricultural valley that feeds Mexico

Although a chapter dealing with the Pacific Coast of the Peninsula does not rightly belong in a volume on the Sea of Cortez, try as I might to drop it out, there are certain areas along the Pacific Coast that cannot be denied. One of these is the area around Bahia Magdalena. Despite the area's shortage of fresh water and limited supplies, the Region of Magdalena can be fascinating for anyone with an exploring spirit and a desire to see a new and different land. A 2-mile-wide channel and numerous islands shelter the greater part of the huge harbor from Pacific winds. Most of the bay's fishes are the same as those of the Cortez. It also has many turtles and other sea life. Its baylets and backwaters provide a natural preserve for game fowl. Other wildlife abounds here, but the human population of the region is small.

This Region (especially the southern extension of Bahia de Almejas just south of Magdalena), has the greatest potential for outdoorsmen of all areas along Baja's Pacific Coast. In the not-too-distant future we may see resorts in this area which will open up vast stretches of untouched shoreline to sportsmen.

Bahia Magdalena proper is only 17 miles long, but the connecting waters north and south from it extend for a total of about 175 miles. The shorelines of all the inlets around this inland sea probably would add up

A JACKPOT FOR HUNTERS AT MAGDALENA BAY.
Canada's game birds winter here, and at times the
sand bar in the distance is covered with them.
The magnificent land-locked bay is a breeding place
for the gray whale. Sea turtles are also plentiful.

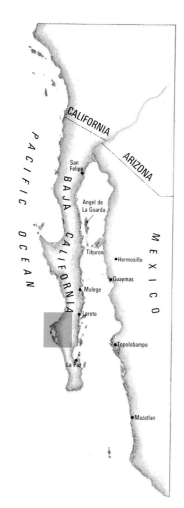

MAGDALENA *centers on Bahia Magdalena, located on the west side of Baja.*

to more than 700 miles. Most of the banks are overgrown with tree-size mangroves. Sparse desert vegetation extends back over a vast plain, which is bound by rich cultivated areas in the Santo Domingo Valley to the north and east.

On the loop trip of the south end (see the chapter on Cabo San Lucas) Frank Dufresne, Bill Escudero, and I drove to Magdalena from La Paz. At Puerto Chale, which is at the bottom of Bahia de Almejas, we pushed our way through a matted thicket of mangrove and got our first look across Almejas. Everywhere around us there was movement. Cranes and egrets were winging in and out of the mangroves. Curlew, snipe, plover, and other shore birds, some of which Frank (who is somewhat of an expert on wildfowl) couldn't even identify, were chasing crabs and shrimp over a tidal flat, where clams, scallops, and conches sought deeper places. Fish, sea fowls, and brant thrashed the deep water beyond. Ducks, arriving from long migrations to winter here, shuttled back and forth between the bay and the Santo Domingo grain fields. The land side was alive with jackrabbits. Even the ocean seemed less than pacific here, as its breakers climbed up and crashed over the outer sand bar.

A PROFUSION OF LIFE

For a short time we were spellbound by such a rich profusion of life but being subject to human appetites, we allowed them to take over. Bill broke out the guns, Frank rigged up fishing tackle, and I headed for the clam-crammed flats. In no time at all we had a large turtle shell filled with clams, a grand mess of fish, and enough wildfowl to feed an entire squad of hungry soldiers.

On the way from Santa Rita we had picked up a couple of men from a roadside ranch, and at Chale we were joined by an old turtle merchant called "Pantalones," who had a skiff and camp there. All joined in the preparation of a sumptuous meal of raw clams, clam broth, broiled snook, pompano, and roast goose and duck.

The place was not all roses, however. That night a cold wind brought in a Pacific fog almost thick enough to drown us. Our bedrolls and everything else that wasn't sealed got soaked. This harsh night atmosphere was nothing like the balmy, dry climate on the Cortez side of the Peninsula.

From Pantalones, the port's one-man population, we learned that Chale once had been a shark fishing camp. A fresh-water tank, and storage closets built of brick, were still standing.

AROUND A MAGNIFICENT BAY

The next day we moved to Puerto El Datil, less than 2 miles south. From the land side, El Datil is nothing more than another break in the mangrove groves, but its waters are visited by enormous schools of migrating fishes from the south, besides being a permanent habitat of many of the same fishes found in the Cortez. A new addition to the list was the boca dulce, or sweet mouth *(Ophioscion scierus),* a large croaker shaped somewhat like the yellowfin tuna but distinguished from it and other croakers by having

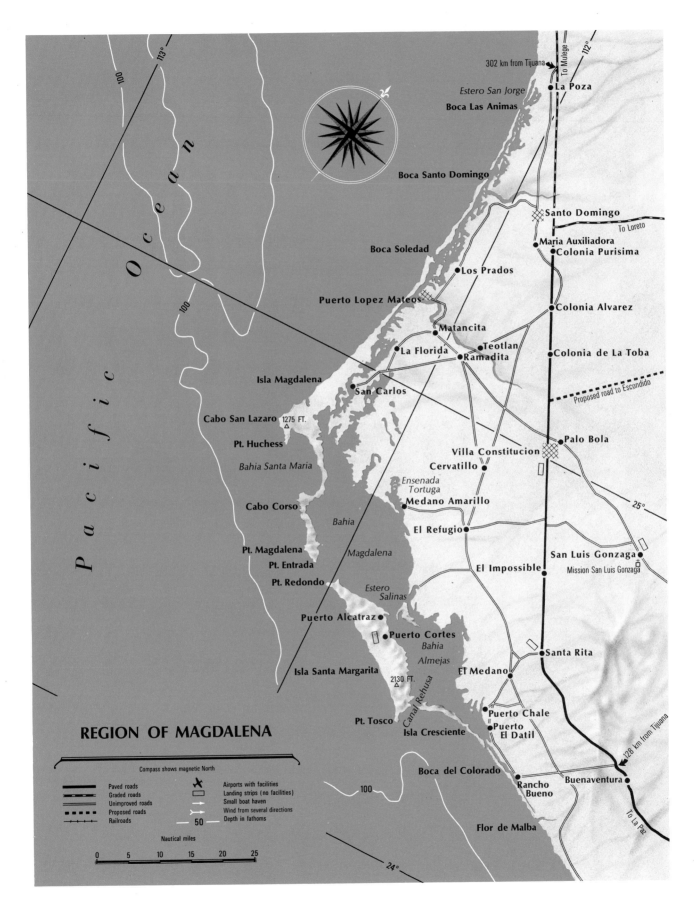

REGION OF MAGDALENA

Compass shows magnetic North

Paved roads	✈	Airports with facilities
Graded roads	▭	Landing strips (no facilities)
Unimproved roads	→	Small boat haven
Proposed roads	⇉	Wind from several directions
Railroads	—50—	Depth in fathoms

Nautical miles

0   5   10   15   20   25

Pacific Ocean

113°

112°

100

100

Estero San Jorge

302 km from Tijuana

To Mulege

La Poza

Boca Las Animas

Boca Santo Domingo

To Loreto

Santo Domingo

Maria Auxiliadora

Colonia Purisima

Boca Soledad

Los Prados

Colonia Alvarez

Puerto Lopez Mateos

Matancita

Colonia de La Toba

La Florida

Teotlan

Ramadita

Isla Magdalena

Proposed road to Escondido

San Carlos

Cabo San Lazaro   1275 FT.

Palo Bola

Pt. Huchess

Villa Constitucion

Bahia Santa Maria

Cervatillo

25°

Cabo Corso

Ensenada Tortuga

Medano Amarillo

Bahia

El Refugio

Pt. Magdalena

Magdalena

Pt. Entrada

El Impossible

San Luis Gonzaga

Pt. Redondo

Mission San Luis Gonzaga

Estero Salinas

Puerto Alcatraz

Puerto Cortes

Bahia Almejas

Santa Rita

Isla Santa Margarita

2130 FT.

El Medano

Pt. Tosco

Canal Rehusa

Puerto Chale

Isla Cresciente

Puerto El Datil

Boca del Colorado

Buenaventura

Rancho Bueno

128 km from Tijuana

100

To La Paz

Flor de Malba

24°

SOUTH FROM GABILAN PEAK

SIERRA DE LA GIGANTA

CAJON DE TECOMAJA

A SWEEPING SHOT OF BAJA taken from the
Gemini 5 space capsule, 100 miles up. It shows much of
the Peninsula from about Loreto southward to its
tip. The town of La Paz lies clearly on the
circle of Bahia de la Paz (top of the left curve
in this view looking down the Peninsula). The
island just left of La Paz is Cerralvo, and the
larger one below is Isla San Jose.

thick lips, a long, soft filament extending from the outer spine of the pelvic fin, and dark streaks running up and back from the lateral line.

While boca dulce are found all over Bahia de Almejas, they concentrate principally in deep holes in estuaries and up into narrow backwaters, where they feed during the run-out of the tide. They are taken on small, white feathers and other lures, and on 3-inch strip bait, near the bottom.

We also found the pompano-like yellow leatherjacket, snook, and a couple of species of corvina. Some of the deep holes are crowded with pinto cabrilla *(Epinephelus analogus)* and an occasional young jewfish.

There are more than two-dozen other species in or frequenting Almejas and Bahia Magdalena. An even greater number are found around the mountainous Isla Santa Margarita. These include bass, jewfish, marlin, dolphinfish, yellowtail, skipjack, sierra, and big broomtail.

Cabo San Lazaro, the westernmost land extremity in this region, is something of a boundary line between the many fish species that range north and south of it. There is some overlap, and there are a few fishes that ignore the boundary; but generally the southern forms are not inclined to venture into the somewhat cooler, upwelled waters north of this cape. Most of these fishes are also found in the Cortez.

NORTH ON BAJA'S WEST COAST

Back through history, since Ulloa visited the Bahia Magdalena Region in 1539 and was wounded there by Indians, there are accounts of a hundred enterprises and attempts at colonization that were started and failed. The last occurred in 1940, when irrigated farming was pioneered near the present village of Santo Domingo. Several old ranches did subsist, as have a couple of federal marine villages on Isla Santa Margarita. Two newly established fish canneries are doing well, especially the one at Puerto Lopez Mateos (across from the north end of Isla Santa Magdalena), where a small town has developed. A lack of fresh surface water has been the main reason for the area's tardy development.

There have been protracted discussions, but no action, on plans to construct a trans-peninsula highway which would connect the Magdalena area with the road that runs through Villa Constitucion (also known as El Crucero) to La Paz. The main purpose of this paved southern stretch, according to early plans, was to provide an overland route to La Paz for the farm products of Santo Domingo Valley.

The recent clearing of an old, 35-mile-long trail through a gap in the Sierra de la Giganta may soon result in the diversion of some shipping from the valley to Puerto Escondido, almost due east of Santo Domingo. Should this road be paved, it would help in opening the southern territory to overland travel.

Until a good coastal road connects the Magdalena Region with the highway from Ensenada that now terminates at El Rosario, some 500 miles north of Magdalena, there is little along the Pacific Coast between these points to attract outdoorsmen, except for yachtsmen. None of the bays or old deserted ports along this coast has anything to compare with Bahia Magdalena. Though the fishes are plentiful, they are the same species as those that are found off Alta California.

AGGRESSIVE SPINES of chollas don't really leap at human legs, but barbs are hard to remove.

A SUGAR MILL *at Todos Santos attracts many visitors. Sugar cane, delivered by cart, is crushed to produce a liquid, which simmers in great wooden vats, then hardens in hollowed-out forms.*

Sugar Production is a Hand Operation

CONE-SHAPED FORMS *hold the concentrate while it crystallizes into candy-like "panocha." When the racks are turned upside down and struck with a mallet, the cones fall out ready to be packed for shipment — or sampled on the spot.*

REGION OF
Guaymas

Lively old town on Mexico's west coast with a variety of resorts and a range of activities on the land and on the water

Though the Baja California Peninsula is just beginning to be opened by improved transportation, the Mainland coast of the Cortez was penetrated by all modes of travel several years ago. The first to attract U. S. tourists and anglers to Guaymas and Mazatlan was a railway line from Nogales, Arizona to Mexico City by the Southern Pacific and then later nationalized by the Mexican government. But it was the paved highway, completed a little over a decade ago, that brought a full measure of billfishing fame to the two Mexican cities and at the same time disclosed numerous points of interest to Norte Americanos.

The main highway (Mexican route 15) does not run right along the coast. It runs south from the border at Nogales, through Santa Ana and Hermosillo, then on down to Guaymas. It swings west to Empalme, then to Ciudad Obregon, Navojoa, Los Mochis, Culiacan, then once again goes to the shore at Mazatlan. From there it heads down to Guadalajara and then on to Mexico City.

Just below Guaymas, route 15 runs over a long fill and bridge across the entrance of the Laguna, then right into the sprawling city of Empalme, the railroad stop for bus connections to Guaymas. About 30 miles below Empalme there is a side road that runs shoreward to Bahia Yacicoris (Bahia del Yaqui on some maps). This bay is the home of some large corvina (up to 16 pounds). Here begins the series of bays and extensive backwaters that extend on down the coast beyond Mazatlan. Some of the waters are accessible by side roads from the main highway; others can be reached only by boat. The islands, peninsulas, and sand spits that separate

SPINY LOBSTERS ARE JUST A SAMPLE.
The clear, shallow waters of Bahia San Carlos near
Guaymas abound in fish and shellfish — scallops, clams,
spiny lobsters. You can gather your own supply for
a beachside barbecue, or buy them from a fisherman.

235

the rather shallow backwaters are mostly low, delta-like formations. Their inner banks and the banks of the Mainland are usually choked with mangrove thickets. Back of them are vast, inaccessible areas of tidal mud flats.

Another approach to Mexico's west coast is by way of a fully paved branch highway (route 2) which gets its start in Tijuana and runs east all the way across the top of the Peninsula through Mexicali and San Luis and the border town of Sonoyta. It joins route 15 at Santa Ana. Either of these roads is truly a pavement to pleasure. If you're old enough to remember, driving along one of them may bring back happy memories of long-gone, pastoral countrysides in the U.S. But the very first of the quaint, old villages or settlements brings a quick reminder that this is a foreign country where communication is in another language.

GUAYMAS includes the city of Guaymas and inland mountain country on the Mainland.

GUAYMAS–A STATE OF MIND

An old shipping and fishing port city, Guaymas has numerous historical landmarks and other wide-ranging points of interest. Although this side of the Cortez does not enjoy the dryness of the Peninsula, the Guaymas Region is far less humid than areas south of it, even during the hot and rainy months of July, August, and September.

Visitors can stop at the several good roadside auto courts along the highway approaching the town, or gather at one of the two most complete resorts around the whole Cortez — Bahia de San Carlos, or Bahia Bocochibampo, both north of town. By complete, I mean that the places are fairly jumping with all kinds of water sports and social goings-on, from skin diving to water skiing, from night club entertainment to extemporaneous mariachi bands. The two resorts have both moderate priced and deluxe accommodations for travelers whose tastes may vary from trailer park to plush hotel. It has been said that anyone from a gypsy to a king can find a place and amenities to fit his purse for a day or a month.

The smooth-water bays offer excellent boating and dockage, as well as water skiing and snorkeling. The International Skin Diving Derby and the Game Fish Tournament are two of the big annual events held in Guaymas.

The town of Guaymas itself is old, relaxed, and happy. It isn't much to look at, but there is a certain charm about the weary side streets and the ancient shipping dock, with its seaworn and creaky shrimp boats. In back of the imposing cathedral at the slopes of the Sierra de la Golandrina (Mountains of the Swallows), is a hillside area with a panoramic view that in most cities would be enjoyed only by mansion dwellers. In Guaymas, the view area is jammed with crib-size houses and appropriately called Zona Torida (Torrid Zone). Guaymas is reported to be so peaceful that no sounds of violence are ever heard below Zona Torido.

As a port, Guaymas has had its ups and downs. In early days great riches of gold and silver from all over Sonora were shipped through it to Spain. After the mines were depleted, the shipping dropped off, but from time to time farm and ranch products flourished, and the shipping tempo would revive. Then, the completion of the highway and the sudden expansion of trucking caused another drop in shipping. This was relieved for a

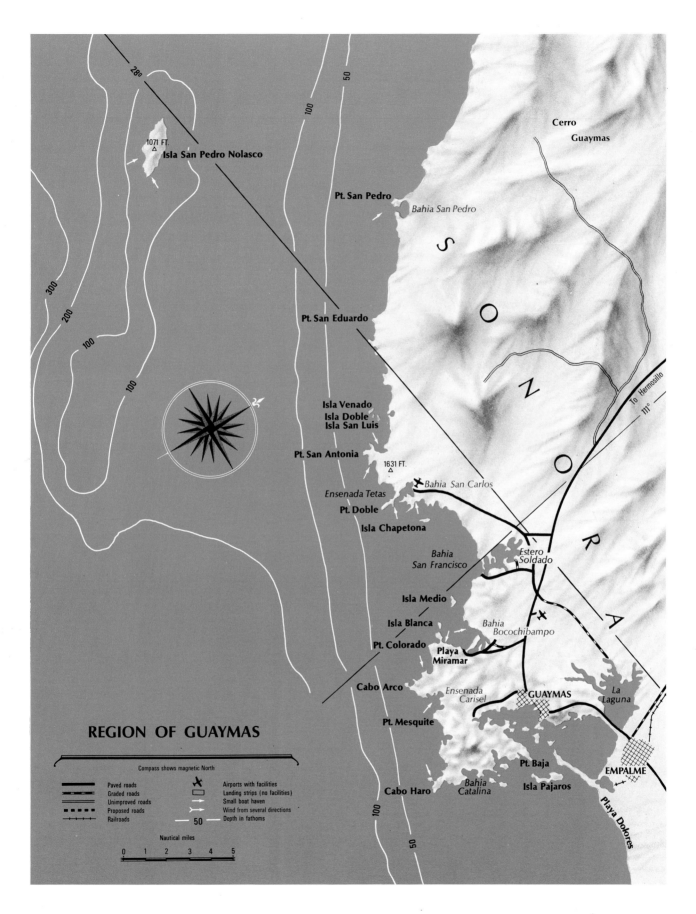

REGION OF GUAYMAS

Compass shows magnetic North

Paved roads		Airports with facilities	
Graded roads		Landing strips (no facilities)	
Unimproved roads		Small boat haven	
Proposed roads		Wind from several directions	
Railroads		Depth in fathoms	50

Nautical miles

0 1 2 3 4 5

1071 FT.
△ Isla San Pedro Nolasco

28°

50

100

300

200

100

100

Pt. San Pedro

Bahia San Pedro

S O N O R A

Cerro Guaymas

Pt. San Eduardo

Isla Venado
Isla Doble
Isla San Luis

Pt. San Antonia

1631 FT.
△

Ensenada Tetas

Pt. Doble

Isla Chapetona

Bahia San Carlos

To Hermosillo

111°

Bahia
San Francisco

Estero
Soldado

Isla Medio

Isla Blanca

Bahia
Bocochibampo

Pt. Colorado

Playa
Miramar

Cabo Arco

Ensenada
Carisel

GUAYMAS

La
Laguna

Pt. Mesquite

Pt. Baja

EMPALME

Cabo Haro

Bahia
Catalina

Isla Pajaros

Playa Dolores

100

50

time by the development of the shrimp industry and a small commercial fishery. Now with federal port improvements and a promise of grain and cotton products, and with the good possibility of tourist travel to and from Loreto and Mulege across the Sea, greater shipping than ever is likely.

Regardless of the few new structures and clap-trap novelty shops, little of the charm of the aging pueblo city has vanished. Nor can all of the progress for the next millennium destroy the beauty of the jade green bay contained in a setting of rugged mountains.

ON AND IN THE WATER

Sailfish, for which this region has long been noted, occur here from May through September, with a month added on either end according to the weather and perhaps food supply. Black marlin remain a few weeks after the sails have left. Striped marlin precede the sailfish by a few weeks, but remain a greater distance offshore.

During the slow season in this region — late winter and early spring — the most sought after and plentiful fish are the fighting ocean-whitefish and the delectable rose snapper. Both are native, non-migrating fish. With the development and greater use of live bait, several other species, including yellowtail, will likely become equally popular.

The fish commonly called red snapper *(Rabirubia inermis)* is abundant in moderately shallow water in this region. The Mexican name for red snapper throughout the Cortez is huachinango, but this name is also applied to other snappers. Since the color of the red snapper varies from light pink to bright rose, with a lighter pink to silver on its belly, the name "rose snapper" seems more appropriate.

This snapper is generally a tight-schooling fish and occupies a special and sharply defined type of habitat. Anglers fishing on the port side of a boat astride the edge of their feeding ground may not be catching any, while the fellows on the starboard side may be getting hookups as fast as baits reach the bottom. A strip of squid, sierra, or other fish appears to be the most attractive bait.

The ocean-whitefish *(Caulalotilus princeps)* is miscalled salmon in the region. It often is found associated with the rose snapper and is taken in fairly deep water on the same kind of baits, kept 10 to 15 feet above the bottom. Ocean-whitefish are also plentiful year-round in the Midriff and along both sides of the Baja California coast and up into Southern California, but nowhere are there as many as in the Guaymas Region.

Small sailfish have been taken about a mile offshore. Schools of 1 to 2-pounders have been seen for the past three years, suggesting that they had been spawned in the north end of the Cortez.

Since 1953, Guaymas has been the setting for an Annual Game Fish Tournament. The four-day contest draws anglers from all over the U.S. to have a go at taking a world record fish. The local businessmen and citizenry join with the resorts to stimulate a rousing spirit of fiesta that goes on for a whole week.

Although the resort operators and townspeople are quite friendly with amateur and scientific divers, some resentment developed a few years ago

OCOTILLO PRODUCES leaves after a rain and drops them as soon as ground becomes dry.

when a group of pros started a systematic slaughter of giant black sea bass and very large grouper, which they trucked back to the U.S. for sale. This was halted when a law was enacted providing that only fish may be speared that are eaten in the area, and that only one large fish per person, per trip, can be taken out of Mexico.

CRUISING IN AN OVERLAND YACHT

I have gone into Mexico by railroad, by auto down coastal highway 15 as soon as it was completed to Mazatlan, and by commercial and private plane. I have examined the coastline from boats of all sizes. But none of these modes of travel provided as much fun or comfort as an overland cruise I took aboard a camper. Driving down the Cortez highways and side roads in one of these rigs can be like cruising in an overland yacht.

Prior to this dry land voyage, camper manufacturers and writers had deliberately sought out and driven over the roughest roads they could find, to prove how well their road coaches could take the punishment. Our plans, however, were the opposite. We wanted to show how luxurious and convenient a long camper trip into wilderness areas, with stops at fine

BUSHY GROWTHS of Baja and Mainland oases attract the brown towhee (Pipilo fuscus).

What to Do in Sonora

There's a good deal to see and do in Sonora — for confirmed land-lubbers as well as for the serious salt-water fisherman. Here are some of the attractions of Mexico's second largest state:

Architecture. If buildings are your interest, you can find traces of Sonora's Spanish colonial heritage and handsome structures of more recent construction that follow the old Spanish design. Of particular note: the five Kino missions near Caborca; Hermosillo's plaza buildings; the colonial town of Alamos (a national monument).

The uncrowded shore. Almost anywhere along the shore are shell-strewn strands, clear water for swimming, a vast underwater aquarium to be explored, delectable clams and lobsters to be gathered for a grand beach barbecue.

Good Mexican food. Eating places in Sonora range from rustic outdoor sites featuring native foods to resort dining rooms serving "continental cuisine." Try the local specialties — especially the seafood — wherever you go. You can usually count on getting at least a satisfactory meal, if not an excellent one, at almost any Sonoran dining place that looks inviting. But beware of raw vegetables, milk, butter, and water at small village cafes.

The back country. From various points along the border, east of the Nogales-Guaymas stretch of Highway 15, or in the foothills outside Alamos, you can explore rural Sonora — the Mexico of open cattle range, real vaqueros, somnolent adobe villages, isolated haciendas, and a pervasive sense of manana.

Shopping. You'll find both European and Mexican goods in the border towns of Nogales and Agua Prieta. Farther down in Sonora, the best shops are in Hermosillo, Guaymas, Navajoa, and Alamos.

resits, could be. Also, we wanted to prove that even a fastidious family could thoroughly enjoy the fun of campering through a still-primitive land. We never hesitated to take off on cart trails, especially when they led toward the Sea.

Even though my companions were used to such travel, I felt a bit guilty at first, as if this method of roughing it were cheating. I always had believed that erecting a tent and making a camp were something of a must, if not a sacred way to the full enjoyment of outdooring. I still think this provides good training and stimulates natural initiative in the young, but I must admit that I soon learned to like the idea of quickly switching from the rugged outdoors to the comforts of luxury living. That first night aboard I felt ever so sneaky when I drew the big double bed that projects forward above the pickup's cabin, and even more so when I changed into pajamas and stretched out on a mattress. Although I am not finicky or adverse to roughing it, nor am I especially bothered by night creepers, crawlers, buzzing insects, or howling animals, I must admit that I prefer the convenience and comfort of a camper. The way our rig was fitted out, we could have remained away from civilization for months without missing any of it.

FROM PIRATES TO PLAYAS

Guaymas was named for a now extinct tribe of Indians known as the Guaymenas. The tribe's recorded history dates back to 1680, when it was first mentioned by Father Kino, the Jesuit mission builder of the State of Sonora. This was a century before the permanent pueblo, Villa de San Fernando de Guaymas, was established. Some of the finest of ancient stone implements, fashioned by the Guaymenas, are occasionally still found in this region.

The history of Guaymas could provide plots for a dozen comic operas, in which heroes and villains would alternate rapidly. Every time a stash of gold and silver from the nearby mines was brought to town and a ship pulled in for it, pirates would show up, capture the ore, scuttle the ship, and then sack the town.

In the plaza near the church stands a statue of one of the bravest of the Guaymas heroes, General Jose Maria Yanez. The outstanding deed of valor attributed to this "Defender of Guaymas" was his feat of outsmarting the pirate, Count Rousset de Bourbon, who, with 400 other cutthroats, descended on the town in 1854. The battle was a stand-off until the pirates saw a large company of cavalry charging down a distant hill, threatening to cut them off from their shore boats. The freebooters surrendered and, according to legend, the leaders, including de Bourbon, were hung without learning that the cavalry was in reality unarmed women dressed as men.

It was the custom in those days for pirates to bury their treasure, usually in sturdy chests. Count de Bourbon was different in that he always used barrels or casks, which could be easily rolled by a couple of men. This trademark is an indication that the Count was a success at his chosen trade, at least up until he had his neck stretched at Guaymas. His treasure barrels have been found in several places around the Cortez, and some are thought to be still hidden at Pichilinque near La Paz, and at Bahia Agua Verde.

EVER HUNGRY, *always alert, nothing escapes the eye of the turkey vulture, desert scavenger.*

NOT A RIPPLE *mars the still waters of Bahia San Carlos. Across the way the peaks called Tetas de Cabra, an area landmark, cast their dark reflection on the smooth surface. For underwater sightseeing with mask and snorkel, you can't find a quieter place than this.*

GUAYMAS AT SUNSET *does not look the active port it really is. Its natural harbor,*
spacious and sheltered, is the envy of the less-favored seaport cities. Mellow old buildings along the waterfront
are mixed with modern structures. The principal resort area is 3½ miles northwest of the town itself.

242

THE COLOR *of a Mexican waterfront is much in evidence at Guaymas. There's always something happening — here it is the hand-to-hand loading of cheeses.*

Guaymas is an Active Port and a Busy City

BACKPACKING BABIES, *an Indian family arrives in Guaymas for a day of marketing and sightseeing.*

REGION OF
Topolobampo

Area of great promise along the southeast boundary of the Sea of Cortez — Mainland terminus of the La Paz-Mazatlan ferry

Between Guaymas and the mouth of the Cortez, there are two other principal centers for the vacationist and outdoorsman — Bahia Topolobampo and Mazatlan. At Bahia Topolobampo, the wilderness glides down to the water's edge and the fish glide up to the beaches. It comprises an area destined to become one of the most popular outdooring stretches along Mexico's west coast. From the 8,000-foot peaks of the Sierra Madre Occidental that lie inland from Topolobampo to 800 fathoms below the surface of the Sea, there are animals and game fowl to hunt and fish to be fished for. The waters in and around the numerous bays and baylets abound in shallow-water shrimp, lobster, clams, scallops, and other shellfish.

Back in the Sierra Madre Occidental is Las Grandes Barrancas de la Tarahumara (The Grand Canyons of the Tarahumara), a geological wonder that rivals our own Grand Canyon in both size and beauty.

Between the mountains and the bay lies the million-acre El Fuerte Valley, a highly productive agricultural land, a portion of which is crossed by the paved Nogales-Guadalajara highway. In its center is the thriving, modern city of Los Mochis, surrounded by rice fields swarming with ducks, and cane fields thick with dove and quail. Not too long ago a dusty village, Los Mochis is rapidly becoming a major attraction for tourists and hunters driving down the Mainland.

The fuse to the Los Mochis boom already had been lit before the Ferrocarril de Chihuahua al Pacifico line was completed in 1961. An enormous power and irrigation complex began operating the previous year. It brought electricity to the city and fresh water to the sugar cane and grain fields throughout the broad El Fuerte Valley.

MEXICO HAS ITS OWN GRAND CANYON.
The dark, deep, inner gorge of the Barranca del
Divisadero on the Mainland is cut by
the Rio Urique. A Tarahumara Indian, at
right, acted as guide for the photographer.

A PLACE HOLDING ITS BREATH

The year I went with a group on a camper trip down the Mainland coast, we drove into Los Mochis and right into a gay, festive madhouse of excitement. The city was celebrating the most progressive period of its short history. And the fun of that day was only a prelude to the next, for it was then that Mexico's President Adolpho Mateos was due aboard the first train to run over the new line from El Paso, Texas. The visit of El Presidente was symbolic of the prosperity that was anticipated.

We had planned a stay of no more than a couple of days — to fish in Bahia Topolobampo — but after talking with Roberto Balderrama, manager of Hotel Santa Anita and organizer of the region's sports activities, we let ourselves get hooked on the place for a full and exciting week.

Warm and humid weather in August and September makes deep-sea fishing for billfish and other big migrators attractive, especially out at Isla Farallon and off Punta San Ignacio. A calendar needs to be developed on the dates of migrations of the marlins, sailfish, yellowfin tuna, wahoo, dolphinfish, and other warm-water forms. We already have knowledge of the great quantities of grouper, cabrilla, and other bottom fish there.

In some years, there are strong and persistent winds, especially in the afternoons. During such periods, anglers usually retreat to the mouth of Bahia Ohuira and the islands and shoreline just inside it. Coming and going on the shift of the tides are ladyfish, pompano, big orangemouth corvina, crevalle, snapper, small grouper, and sierra. Fishermen casting from the shoreline near Topolobampo's modern Yacht Hotel or from the opposite or south side of the bay can add roosterfish, yellowtail and other jacks, plus cabrilla, milkfish, and croaker to the species found in the back bay.

Had it not been for the mosquitoes, Topolobampo might have become a busy port city. The broad waterfront and land for miles around remained almost uninhabited until the malaria-bearing mosquito was wiped out completely. Malaria is no longer a danger here.

The old village of Topolobampo doesn't have much to offer in the way of tourist attractions. There is a working shrimp cannery and the Yacht Hotel nearby. Two little freighters, which run between Topolobampo and La Paz, worm their way carefully through a labyrinth of sand bars and a shifting entrance to get free of the bay. There has been talk for several years of dredging a deep channel for larger vessels. If this comes to pass, and a vehicle ferry is put into operation, the government will undoubtedly revive its plan to extend the railway from Los Mochis to the bay.

SOUTH TO MAZATLAN

The country along the lengthy stretch between Los Mochis and Mazatlan might well be termed the land of enduring spring. The vivid greens and multi-colored blossoms that blanket the mountains and slopes after the late summer rains appear as exaggerated as if they were painted there.

Whereas the underwater topography off Baja is precipitous and almost solid rock, this Mainland side is shallow and sandy. Starting at Punta San Ignacio off the north end of Isla Santa Maria above Bahia Topolobampo,

TOPOLOBAMPO is southernmost region in the Cortez, on the Mexican Mainland.

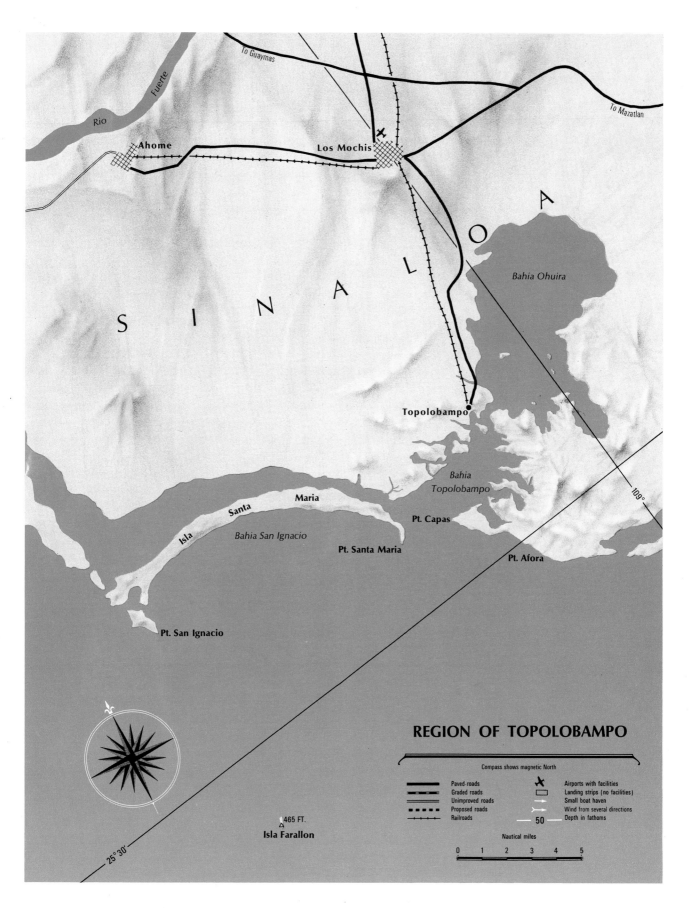

To Guaymas

Rio
Fuerte

Ahome

Los Mochis

To Mazatlan

S I N A L O A

Bahia Ohuira

Topolobampo

Maria

Santa

Isla

Bahia San Ignacio

Bahia
Topolobampo

Pt. Capas

Pt. Santa Maria

Pt. Afora

109°

Pt. San Ignacio

25° 30'

REGION OF TOPOLOBAMPO

Compass shows magnetic North

▬▬▬ Paved roads	✈	Airports with facilities
—·—·— Graded roads	▭	Landing strips (no facilities)
——— Unimproved roads	→	Small boat haven
■ ■ ■ Proposed roads	⤙	Wind from several directions
┼┼┼┼ Railroads	—50—	Depth in fathoms

465 FT.
△
Isla Farallon

Nautical miles

0   1   2   3   4   5

the 100-fathom line swings out from 3½ miles offshore to Isla Farallon; then it remains 15 to 25 miles out, on down past Mazatlan. This shallow shelf and the flat lands extending inland from the tidal basins have been filled by silt and sand transported down from the vast watershed of the Sierra Madre Occidental. As if to resist the intrusion, the on-shore sea winds have pushed back enough sand to form an almost unbroken series of narrow peninsulas and islands with enormous bays and channels back of them. Some of these landlocked waters are as much as 35 miles long.

Because of the mangrove thickets that spread over the tidal mud flats, there are very few shore places that can be reached from the highway. One road runs down from Guasave. From El Petrero, around a high mountain, to Bahia Santa Maria there is a good road out of the sprawling city of Culiacan to the port of Altata. There may be other possible trails to deep water, especially to the lower reaches of the three rivers, Elota, Piaxtla, and Quelite, but we passed them up in favor of the more accessible waters around and below Mazatlan.

A CLEAN, HAPPY CITY

Though Mazatlan lies just below the geographical mouth of the Cortez, it should be included in the story of the Sea. The fishes, climate, and almost everything else there are the same as in other Mainland stretches above. However, unlike areas above, marlin or sailfish occur here year-round, and double up in spring and fall months. There are only a few rare, unfavorable winter periods when marlin are absent.

Mazatlan is just below the Tropic of Cancer, where the sun's rays for one day (June 21) are perpendicular. But due to almost constant ocean breezes, the climate is moderate and delightfully balmy except during the rainy season (July through September) when it becomes quite humid. If the weather could be called "hot" during these months, the fishing is even hotter — for sailfish, black marlin, and most other big-game species, except striped marlin and yellowtail, which migrate northward in May.

As a city, modern Mazatlan has a short history, but as an up-and-down village and port it dates back to the time when the Cortez conquistadors thought it one of the fabled Seven Cities of Cibola. Its growth was restricted by hostile Indians and marauding pirates until about 1850, when a group of Germans established a permanent colony there.

DENSE GROWTHS *of cat claws screen streamways with thorny foliage. See page 208.*

There was a slow growth up to the 1940's. Then with the discovery of marlin angling, the completion of the coastal highway, and the introduction of marlin cruisers by the pioneering operator, Luis Patron, the big boom really got going. The nonfishing members of a family had enough to do to keep them jumping day and night, and the angling got so good that more than 5,000 billfish were caught annually (9,000 one year). This specializing in marlin and sails, to the neglect of other big and small game species, however, allowed the resorts on the Peninsula side of the Cortez to offer serious competition.

Mazatlan is a clean, happy place that is rich with bananas, papayas, mangoes, and flowers. There are several quiet, shaded plazas, restaurants par excellence, modern hotels, trailer parks, fishing fleets, and a good harbor with a modern dock for the ferry running across from La Paz. There is even a bullring, now used for baseball, and an international airport with commercial lines that provide service to many areas.

Emilio Aun, the city's enthusiastic shore-casting angler, has developed some fantastic backwater fishing a few miles below Mazatlan. He has caught 4-foot rainbow runners (a member of the jack family) on yellow feathers and live baits, in narrow openings to lagoons, but only when the tide was flowing in or out. He also has learned to catch milkfish on beef blood, black snook on live mullet, and big-eye snook on white feathers on incoming tides during summer rains. He catches ladyfish and barracuda from December through May, as well as several other species visiting backwaters, especially from October through June.

Next to the black snook, the largest fish occurring in these backwaters is the milkfish (*Chanos chanos*), which resembles an overgrown ladyfish. This 5½-footer is rarely caught by angling, and then only when the patient fisherman takes coagulated beef blood, attaches chunks of it on tiny, No. 4 hooks, drops the line to the bottom with a few other chunks for chum, then moves his boat a distance away. Milkfish are scattered the length of the Cortez and in many warm backwaters of the Pacific. In the Philippines and other Asian countries this species is prized as food and grown domestically in ponds.

A trailer camp and a fleet of outboard skiffs are now in operation on Laguna Caimanero, one of the area's most productive spots.

The long and narrow Isla Palmito de la Virgen, separating Laguna Caimanero from the ocean, provides some of the best wild fowl and small animal hunting along this whole coast. Among the game on this island are four species of ducks, two species of doves, quails, pheasants, rabbits, coyote, wild pigs, and ocelot. Hunting trips here and big-game safaris into the mountains for jaguar, mountain lion, and deer are well organized with expert guides, transportation (car and horses), camping outfits, and guns. Licenses are available at most of the Mazatlan hotels along Avenida Olas Atlas. The big-game season at present is December 15 to June 15. The fowling season varies, usually closing near the end of February.

MISSION *between Tepic and Mazatlan may have been founded by Father Kino.*

An Island for Picnics

Isla de Piedra (Stone Island) is the proper name of the little island just off the southeastern tip of the Mazatlan peninsula. But because of its tall groves of coconut palms, most visitors know it as Coconut Island. Only a 10-minute boat trip from the dock area of downtown Mazatlan, it offers no luxurious resorts or elegant facilities, but it does offer one of the most beautiful beaches on the entire west coast of Mexico. You can find someone at the Mazatlan docks who will take you across to the islands almost any time of day (agree on fare in advance). You won't need a guide on the island; just follow the one and only road past the daub-and-wattle houses of the islanders, through tall groves of coconut palms, and over to the beach. On weekends, families from Mazatlan frequently bring picnic lunches over to the island beach, spreading their meal across the rough picnic tables in the thatch-roofed pavilion, and sing and dance.

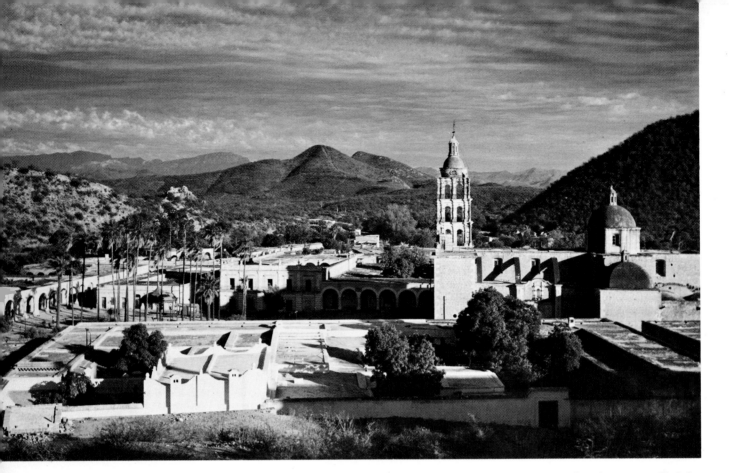

THE HEART OF ALAMOS, *viewed from the hilltop jail. You can see why this remnant of colonial Spain is called the "city of arches." The imposing church, which dominates the Plaza de Armas, dates from 1784. The tree-shaded patio in the left foreground belongs to Los Portales Hotel on the main plaza.*

Alamos is an Old City of Spanish Splendor

PALMS *and colorful flowers surround a tiny bandstand in plaza. At the left are the thick stone walls of the lovely old cathedral.*

SUNRISE ON ALAMOS, *seen from a hilltop southeast of town. As you climb the hill before dawn, the only sounds are your own footsteps, your breathing, roosters crowing, and burros braying. Alamos shows little change since its discovery by tourists, and as a national monument, it is now protected by law against undue "progress."*

A **LEISURELY WAY** to tour Mazatlan is by arana — a horse-drawn carriage that will clip-clop you all over town for a few pesos.

Mazatlan Can be Quiet or Lively

AN IMPROMPTU SERENADE by mariachis is not unusual in Mazatlan — or anywhere in Mexico. Sometimes a group like this is organized on the spot and includes any passerby who happens to have an instrument.

how to get there

About the first question asked by all who become interested in the Cortez and in Baja California is, "How about the road down the Peninsula?" The native will answer, "There is the grand Highway, but it exists only in the minds of a few prophets."

There is a kind of a road down Baja that can be traversed by hardy adventurers driving trucks, campers, or jeeps. This is the original cart trail called El Camino Real, which had the double meaning of the Highway Royal and Main Street. After trying a fleet of campers on it, a coach manufacturer called it the worst road in the world. Except at the north and south ends, very little improvements have been made in the centuries of its being, but workmen keep it reasonably passable, at least for its new mail-passenger bus service, a few freight trucks, and fewer campers. In its favor are statements by the hardiest of those who have driven it, such as "It was worth it," meaning the unique experience.

The fact of having a bad road and no railroad has brought on special developments in air travel in Baja. Every resort has an air strip for private planes, good gas, and other supplies. Most ranchers with enough cleared flat land have scraped out emergency landing strips for any pilot who wishes to set down and visit for a spell. Commercial airports have recently enlarged and modernized to accommodate the large jets of Aeronaves de Mexico Airlines. They also accommodate charter planes that shuttle passengers to all resorts and towns.

Up to the past couple of years most anglers and other visitors traveled to Baja mainly by commercial planes. Now the ferry boat that runs between Mazatlan and La Paz has made the Peninsula's south end accessible to cars and campers.

The Mainland side of the Sea is reached by all popular methods of transportation. There are up-to-date airlines, slightly less than up-to-date railroads, good airstrips, and fine yacht harbors. There is bus service over paved highways, and for camper or auto drivers there are gas stations at close intervals.

COMMERCIAL AIRLINE

Within the past few years the most distant places around the Cortez have been brought to within three or four hours of the border, and little more from anywhere else in the U.S. Dominating commercial air travel into and around the area is the big, government-owned airline, Aeronaves de Mexico. In addition to major hops from Toronto, Montreal, Detroit, New York, and Los Angeles to Mexico City and cities in between, Aeronaves has excellent local service around much of the Cortez. Flights go from Los Angeles, Tijuana, Tucson, and Nogales to Guaymas, Los Mochis, and Mazatlan, on the

Mainland, and to Santa Rosalia, Loreto, and La Paz, on the Peninsula.

Mexicana Airlines offers flights from Los Angeles to Mazatlan, Puerto Vallarta, Guadalajara, Mexico City.

Charter planes are available to South End resorts and other points, though at present, there is but one charter line in Baja. Servicio Aereo Baja has flights from Tijuana to Bahia de Los Angeles and Mulege, and to Puerto Vallarta on the Mainland.

For information on Aeronaves de Mexico, see a travel agent or write Carlos Gutierrez, Aeronaves de Mexico, 633 S. Hill St., Los Angeles, California. For Servicio Aereo Baja, write Francisco Munos, Servicio Aereo Baja, Suite 418, 510 W. Sixth St., Los Angeles, California.

The safety log of Mexican pilots is remarkable. Their discipline is rigid and sensible, and they are proud of their record. As of this date, not one of the Aeronaves (formerly Trans Mar de Cortez) planes has had an accident in 15 years of scheduled commercial flights down Baja. Since most travelers are American anglers and tourists, U.S. foods are featured, and the crew members speak English.

FLYING YOUR OWN AIRPLANE

Private plane owners have discovered that gliding down to resorts and out-of-the way places around the Sea of Cortez is now a breeze, whereas a few years ago it was thought to be extremely hazardous. It is still dangerous for the foolhardy who defy uncharted courses.

The boom in this mode of travel has spread down the whole Baja California Peninsula as well as along the Mainland side of the Cortez. Aware of the potential in this carriage trade business, resort owners, and Civic and Federal officials, have added new airstrips and lengthened and improved old ones. Additional radios have been installed, gas supplies and other facilities enlarged. Progress has been made to bring air-to-ground communications up to U.S. standards, especially along the Cortez coastal course.

Calexico is the major private plane entry to Baja California. Calexico airport officials will furnish weather information and file flight plans to La Paz.

The recommended air route down Baja starts at Calexico and follows the Peninsula's inner (eastern) coast line. This route has half-a-dozen distinct advantages over either an inland course or one along the Pacific Coast, both of which are characterized by fog, high mountains, and vast uninhabited areas. The paved road between the border and San Felipe carries little traffic, and could be used for an emergency landing if the need arose. From San Felipe south there are numerous landing spots, where gas and other supplies can be obtained.

The Mexican Mainland route down the Cortez follows the well-traveled north-south highway, which holds inland for the most part. Along it are several sizable airports with modern communication systems, as well as frequent small emergency strips.

There are several sources of detailed information on flying down to the Cortez and its surroundings. The book *Vacation Air Mexico*, by William and Edith Maddron (Vacation Air, Inc., Box 3382, Eugene, Oregon) gives notes on many Mainland airports. Flight safety in Baja is well treated in *Enjoy Flying over Baja California, Mexico*, a manual published by the San Diego Harbor Department and Flotilla 12-Air, U.S. Coast Guard Auxiliary. For a useful data card on flying in northwest Mexico and Baja, write to Calexico International Airport, Calexico, California. The U.S. Air Force World Aeronautical Charts do not show all of the many airstrips, but they are invaluable in flight planning and navigation.

To encourage private plane flights from the United States, Mexico has eliminated a lot of red tape. A few documents are essential: a tourist card (obtain from Mexican consulates or offices of the Mexican Government Tourist Department in the U.S.), a smallpox vaccination certificate (needed on re-entry into the U.S.), proof of ownership and registration of the plane, insurance that is valid in Mexico. Mexican papers will appear when you check in at a Mexican airport of entry. Even if you don't understand them, keep them until you leave Mexico—they may be requested.

Check with the Federal Aeronautics Agency, as well as with Mexican border airports, for weather information. Most control towers transmit and receive on 3023.5 kilocycles. The larger airports have VHF on 118.1 megacycles. Resorts use Unicom 122.8. If you don't make radio contact prior to approaching a resort, drop low and buzz the lodge before landing to have transportation ready at the airstrip.

PRIVATE PLANES

Aerial navigation down the Sea of Cortez is simple, since virtually all navigation is visual. For this reason, the first rule is: Don't fly at night. La Paz has the only lighted runways below the border, though a few of the bigger lodges will illuminate their strips if they can and if they know you're coming. Paved runways are as rare as lighted ones, so beware of bumps, dips, and rocks even on the hard-packed strips.

The following chart lists locations and facilities of most of the better airports on the Cortez side of the Baja Peninsula. All figures are approximate. The following abbreviations are used: All: All supplies available. EM: For emergency use only. ?: Conditions or facilities questionable.

FACILITIES FOR PRIVATE PLANES

Location	Degrees	Feet of Runway	Facilities
Mexicali (port of entry, paved)	90–270	5,000	All
San Felipe	40–220	3,000	Gas
Puertecito (diagonal)	150–330	2–3,000	Gas
Miramar Camp (mile from beach)	30–210	2,000	EM
Bahia Willard			
(1) 150 yards in	153–333	2,500	EM
(2) On sand spit	0–180	1,500	EM
Bahia de Los Angeles (by resort; if windy, use east-west strip 3 miles north.)	170–350	3,000	All Unicom (122.8)
Bahia San Francisquito (on flats south of inner bay)	30–210	2,000	EM
Rancho Barril (north of ranch houses)	8–188	2,000	Gas (?)
Santa Rosalia (on hillside south of town)	120–300	3,500	Gas
Ensenada San Lucas (two crossed strips near beach)	90–270	2,000	Gas (?)

Location	Degrees	Feet of Runway	Facilities
Mulege			
(1) Above resort (on beach north side of river mouth)	50–230	2,000	All
(2) Near resort (on bench north side of river mouth)	40–220	1,800	All
(3) South side of river	50–230	2,000	All
Bahia Concepcion (across bay from El Coyote)	20–200	1,500	EM
Loreto (northwest edge of town)	140–320	4,000	All Unicom (122.8)
Bahia Escondido (behind entrance of bay)	0–180	2,000	EM (?)
Bahia Tambobiche (just back of bay)	60–240	1,500	EM
San Jose salt works (on and near south end of Isla San Jose)	140–320	2,500	Gas
La Paz (port of entry)	160–340	5,000	All
Las Cruces (private club)	20–200	4,000	EM Unicom (122.8)

Location	Degrees	Feet of Runway	Facilities
Puerto Los Muertos (north side of cove and port)	15–195	1,800	EM
Los Plantos (center of valley in cultivated area)	160–340	4,000	Gas
Bahia de Palmas (next to lodge)	170–350	2,000	All Unicom (122.8)
Rancho Buena Vista (half mile northwest of large resort)	30–210	3,000	All Unicom (122.8)
Santiago (on bluff east of town)	30–310	3,500	Gas
San Jose del Cabo (near beach, south of town)	30–310	2,000	EM
Palmilla (1 mile north of resort)	170–350	4,000	All
Hotel Cabo San Lucas (1 mile northwest of resort)	180–360	4,000	All Unicom (122.8)
Hacienda Cabo San Lucas (north of town and resort)	0–180	4,000	All

DRIVING OVERLAND

Though paved roads down the Mainland are a pleasure to drive, a land journey down the Baja California Peninsula is, at present, a venturesome trip. The road is that rough and is likely to remain so for the next quarter of a century. This is a drive for the enthusiast of vast, lonely stretches. Most of the northern half of the Peninsula is naturally arid, and there has been a further reduction in vegetation and animal life, due to a 50-year drought. However, since it was broken in 1959, there are signs of a come-back in some areas. Cattle and other domestic animals have something more over their ribs than parched hides.

Below the border towns and after the paved roads run out, the traveler can expect to find good water at about half of the old ranches, a few gallons of gas at one out of five, and cold water, soda, and beer at a couple. Any other supplies are almost nonexistent, except in villages and towns. Away from the border there are no auto parts or machine shops, except in Santa Rosalia and La Paz.

Many of the roads swing around cliff edges too sharp for house trailers. Deep sand ruts must be prepared for. Ask road directions constantly. Some side roads may not be traveled for weeks or months and should be taken only with great caution.

Keep a Spanish dictionary handy, since hardly any of the interior residents speak English. Some have trouble counting U.S. money, so have a supply of pesos handy. Regardless of their poor appearance, the people have a dignity which must be respected, especially by foreigners. They may seem rowdy in a cantina or at a beer bust, but they are far more polite than we would imagine, and they expect the same of visitors.

Do not give money to native youngsters, even if they ask. Old but clean clothing, trinkets, and hard candy are appreciated. Adults will be grateful for almost anything from old tools to cigarettes.

TRAILERING A SMALL BOAT

To get papers exempting the boat and vehicle from import duty tax (required on the Mexican Mainland but not on Baja), stop at the customs office at Nogales or at Lukeville (one mile north of Sonoyta), no matter where you cross the border. This is an important *must*. A $1.00 tip is usually expected for this service. After leaving customs, keep all papers handy to show inspectors along the way, whose roadside offices are indicated by large ALTO (Halt) signs.

All trailer wiring should be waterproof and sturdy, since it will be soaked with salt water at launching and left in the open while you are at sea. A bow winch to get the boat properly cradled is advisable.

At regular launching places your car and trailer will be carefully watched and protected. Have the boat's name or number on it as well as the trailer so the launcher can easily find your trailer when you're ready to take the boat out of the water.

Launching facilities at ports are still on the crude side, except at Bahia San Carlos, Guaymas, and Mazatlan. But the Cortez is usually so calm and beaches are so firm that launching is simple most everywhere you can get a boat to the shore. It is still easier wherever there is a concrete slab, as at Puerto Penasco, Puerto Kino, San Felipe, and Puertecitos.

where to stay

Throughout the Cortez, especially during the spring months, and most especially around the southern half of the Peninsula, there is a great need for more accommodations. The total number of rooms in the entire Baja California Peninsula — an area of more than 50,000 square miles, roughly the size of the state of Florida — is less than that of a good-sized, modern hotel in the U.S. Because of shortages in both rooms and boats, reservations should be made and confirmed two or three months in advance, either through a reputable travel agent or directly. Several lodges have offices in the United States, listed under the name of the resort. Otherwise, a letter or wire addressed to the "Manager" of the place will serve. When wiring to Mexico, always include your address in the *body* of the telegram. If tagged onto the end, it will be cut off.

Since every lodge differs greatly from every other, there is no way of placing them in classes, as is common with U.S. accommodations, and the prices quoted do not always reflect the standard of quality or service. All rates given here include three meals. Local costs and conditions make it impossible to give exact, current prices, but the following key is used as a general guide to indicate the rate per day, for double occupancy.

Deluxe: $20.00 to $30.00
Popular: $12.00 to $17.50
Moderate: $10.00 to $20.00
Inexpensive: $7.00 to $9.00

SAN FELIPE

EL CORTEZ MOTEL, San Felipe, Baja California Norte, Mexico. *Inexpensive.* Near beach.
VILLA DEL MAR MOTEL, San Felipe, Baja California Norte, Mexico. *Moderate.* Near beach.
AUGIE'S RIVIERA MOTEL, San Felipe, Baja California Norte, Mexico. *Inexpensive.* Half-mile from beach.
DEL MAR MOTEL, San Felipe, Baja California Norte, Mexico. *Inexpensive.* Near beach.

PUERTECITOS

PUERTECITOS LODGE, Puertecitos, Baja California Norte, Mexico. Write: Rafael Orozco, Manager, San Felipe, Baja California Norte, Mexico. *Inexpensive.* Lodge; fleet of skiffs, charter boat; launching ramp; gas and boat supplies. On beach of baylet.

BAHIA DE LOS ANGELES

BAHIA LOS ANGELES LODGE, Bahia de Los Angeles, Baja California Norte, Mexico. Write: Antero Diaz, Manager, Box 579, Ensenada, Baja California Norte, Mexico. *Moderate.* Lodge; fleet of skiffs, cruisers, large charters. On beach, overlooking bay.

MULEGE

HOTEL MULEGE, Mulege, Baja California Sur, Mexico. U.S. address: Lurair, 4325 Sepulveda Blvd., Culver City, Calif. *Popular.* Lodge; fleet. North side of river.
SERENIDAD LODGE, Mulege, Baja California Sur, Mexico. U.S. address: Serenidad, 2850 Artesia Blvd., Redondo Beach, Calif. *Moderate.* Lodge; fleet. South side of river.
PLAYA DE MULEGE LODGE, Mulege, Baja California Sur, Mexico. U.S. address: Playa de Mulege, Box 478, Imperial Beach, Calif. *Inexpensive.* Lodge; fleet. On beach.
HOTEL LAS CASITAS, Mulege, Baja California Sur, Mexico. *Inexpensive.* Fleet. In town.
HACIENDA DE MULEGE, Mulege, Baja California Sur, Mexico. U.S. address: Hacienda de Mulege, Suite 418, 510 W. Sixth St., Los Angeles, Calif. *Moderate.* Fleet. In town.

LORETO

FLYING SPORTSMEN LODGE, Loreto, Baja California Sur, Mexico. U.S. address: Flying Sportsmen Lodge, Suite 618, 9465 Wilshire Blvd., Beverly Hills, Calif. *Moderate.* Resort; fleet. On beach, one mile south of town.
HOTEL OASIS, Loreto, Baja California Sur, Mexico. U.S. address: Oasis, 14646 Keswick St., Van Nuys, Calif. *Moderate.* Resort; fleet. On beach, below center of town.

LA PAZ

HOTEL LOS COCOS, La Paz, Baja California Sur, Mexico. *Popular.* Resort; fleet. On bay shore, two miles from center of town.
HOTEL LOS ARCOS, La Paz, Baja California Sur, Mexico. *Popular.* Lodge. On Malecon, quarter-mile from pier.
HOTEL PERLA, La Paz, Baja California Sur, Mexico. *Moderate.* Lodge. On Malecon, center of town.
HOTEL GUAYCURA, La Paz, Baja California Sur, Mexico. *Moderate.* Lodge. Two miles from center of town.

BUENA VISTA

RANCHO BUENA VISTA, Buena Vista, Baja California Sur, Mexico. U.S. address: Charles Walters, Box 486, Newport Beach, Calif. *Popular.* Resort; fleet of skiffs, marlin cruisers. On beach, half-mile south of airstrip.

LOS BARRILES

BAHIA DE PALMAS, Los Barriles, Baja California Sur, Mexico. U.S. address: Bahia de Palmas, 1116 W. Olympic Blvd., Los Angeles, Calif. *Popular.* Lodge; fleet of cruisers. On beach, two miles above Rancho Buena Vista.

(There are two other resorts under construction in the Buena Vista Region, one at Punta Colorado, another at Punta Pescadero; a third is planned at Cabo Pulmo.)

SAN JOSE DEL CABO

FISHER HOUSE, San Jose del Cabo, Baja California Sur, Mexico. *Inexpensive*. Hotel. In center of town.

PUNTA PALMILLA

HOTEL PALMILLA, Palmilla, Baja California Sur, Mexico. U.S. address: Hotel Palmilla, Box 1775, La Jolla, Calif. *Deluxe*. Resort; fleet of skiffs, marlin cruisers. On point, overlooking beach and sea.

PUERTO CHILENO

HOTEL CABO SAN LUCAS, Box 22, Cabo San Lucas, Baja California Sur, Mexico. U.S. address: Hotel Cabo San Lucas, 521 N. La Cienega, Los Angeles 48, Calif. *Deluxe*. Resort; fleet of skiffs, cruisers. On point, overlooking beaches and sea.

CABO SAN LUCAS

HACIENDA CABO SAN LUCAS, Cabo San Lucas, Baja California Sur, Mexico. U.S. address: Hacienda Cabo San Lucas, Box 1775, La Jolla, Calif. *Popular*. Resort; fleet of skiffs, cruisers. On beach, near Cabo Lucas pier.

EL GOLFO DE SANTA CLARA

EL GOLFO SPORTFISHING RESORT, El Golfo de Santa Clara, Sonora, Mexico. U.S. address: Juan Lopez, 2806 Jeffries Ave., Los Angeles 65, Calif. *Inexpensive*. Fleet of skiffs, charter. On beach, two miles east of town.

PUERTO PENASCO

HOTEL PLAYA HERMOSA, Puerto Penasco, Sonora, Mexico. *Moderate*. Lodge; fleet of skiffs, cruisers, charter. On beach, one mile above port.

BAHIA KINO

ISLANDIA MARINA, Bahia Kino, Sonora, Mexico. Write: Tiburcio Saucedo, Box 635, Hermosillo, Sonora, Mexico. *Inexpensive*. Lodge, trailer park. On beach.
MOTEL KINO BAY, Bahia Kino, Sonora, Mexico. Write: Hermosillo Mercanti, S.A., Box 104, Hermosillo, Sonora, Mexico. *Moderate*. Lodge. On beach.

BAHIA SAN CARLOS

HOTEL LA POSADA DE SAN CARLOS, Bahia San Carlos, Sonora, Mexico. Write: Hotel La Posada de San Carlos,

Box 57, Guaymas, Sonora, Mexico. *Deluxe*. On hill.
CASAS MOVILES APARTMENTS AND TRAILER PARK, Bahia San Carlos, Sonora, Mexico. Write: Casas Moviles de San Carlos, Box 212, Guaymas, Sonora, Mexico. *Inexpensive*. On beach.

MIRAMAR BEACH

HOTEL PLAYA DE CORTEZ, Guaymas, Sonora, Mexico. *Deluxe*. Resort. On beach of Bahia Bocochibampo near Guaymas.
HOTEL MIRAMAR BEACH, Guaymas, Sonora, Mexico. *Popular*. Resort. On beach.
FISHING FLEET, CHARTERS. Tom Jamison, Sport Fishing Director, Guaymas, Sonora, Mexico. Or, book at Hotels Playa de Cortez and Miramar Beach.

GUAYMAS

GUAYMAS MOTEL, Guaymas, Sonora, Mexico. *Inexpensive*. On highway approaching town.

LOS MOCHIS

HOTEL SANTA ANITA, Los Mochis, Sinaloa, Mexico. *Popular*. Hunting, fishing facilities, guides.

TOPOLOBAMPO

YACHT HOTEL, Box 209, Topolobampo, Sinaloa, Mexico. *Moderate*. Lodge; fleet of skiffs, cruisers, charter. On shore, overlooking bay.

MAZATLAN

HOTEL BELMAR, Mazatlan, Sinaloa, Mexico. *Popular*. On waterfront.
HOTEL LA SIESTA, Mazatlan, Sinaloa, Mexico. *Popular*. On waterfront.
HOTEL FREEMAN, Mazatlan, Sinaloa, Mexico. *Popular*. On waterfront.
HOTEL PLAYA, Mazatlan, Sinaloa, Mexico. *Popular*. On waterfront.
HOTEL ELDORADO, Mazatlan, Sinaloa, Mexico. *Popular*. On waterfront.
HOTEL CIMA, Mazatlan, Sinaloa, Mexico. *Popular*. On waterfront.

fishes of the cortez

In all games and sports the participants can enjoy themselves more when they know the objectives and the terms involved. In the game of angling, knowing the fishes, especially the families to which they belong, increases the pleasure of an already pleasurable sport. By being acquainted with the scientific and sometimes common names, an angler can learn of relationships between certain fishes — especially those in the Cortez — and those he may be familiar with elsewhere. For example, all croakers are in the family *Sciaenidae*, within which are those species in the genus *Cynoscion* — the weakfish and sea trout of the Atlantic, the white seabass of California, and the corvinas of the Cortez. Putting this knowledge to practical use, the informed angler will know that all these species have tender mouth membrane and must therefore be worked easily.

By rights, common names of the fishes of the Cortez should be those used by the Mexicans, but names for the same species vary from region to region, and trying to change old established names for the sake of common agreement would be futile. When there was agreement for fishes known only in the Cortez, Mexican names were used in this book: "cabrilla" for most basses, "pargo" for snappers, "roncador" for both grunts and croakers, "jurel" for several species of jacks.

SCIENTIFIC NAMES — A BASIS

Though common names are usually local, scientific names are recognized throughout the world. Scientific classification — called taxonomy — groups plants and animals according to their natural relationships. Classes are broken first into orders, then suborders, families, genera, and finally into species. Every attempt is made to keep the order of the arrangement in accordance with the natural evolution of living beings. Thus, the most primitive forms are listed first in this appendix.

It should be understood that fish with identical characters are placed in a species, but when there are some anatomical differences, the species are separated though still kept in the same genus. As the anatomical differences increase and become more pronounced, the genera are bunched into a family; with greater differences, into a larger aggregation, and so on up to classes.

The order and continuity followed in this volume are taken from the listing of the American Fisheries Society. The scientific notation, names, and abbreviated descriptions are from the checklist of Dr. Boyd Walker.

KEY TO THE DRAWINGS

To describe all or even most of the some 650 fish species in the waters of the Cortez would require a volume several times the size of this book. The following listing is therefore confined to those fishes which are likely to be of special interest to anglers.

Since a few of the popular big-game species are well described in the text, they do not appear in this appendix. Two are the dolphinfish and yellowfin tuna.

The dolphinfish, *Coryphaena hippurus* (family *Coryphaenidae*), can be readily identified by vivid and rapid color changes, long anal and dorsal fins, steep profile.

The yellowfin tuna, *Neothunnus macropterus* (family *Scombridae*), is easily recognized by the broad lateral stripe of bright yellow and finlets of the same color. (It should not be confused with the weaker, long-finned allisons tuna, miscalled "yellowfin tuna").

THE BEGINNER SHOULD keep in mind those locations of the various anatomical parts shown below in the drawing of a hypothetical fish. Remember that the pectoral and pelvic fins are paired, and refer back to this drawing when studying the fish descriptions that follow.

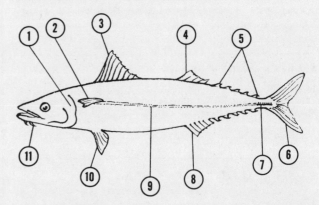

HYPOTHETICAL FISH. The identifying characters shown above and described here will apply to nearly every fish in the following pages. 1: Gill cover. 2: Pectoral fins. 3: First dorsal fin (spiny). 4: Second dorsal fin (soft rays). 5: Finlets. 6: Lower lobe of tail fin. 7: Keel. 8: Anal fin. 9: Lateral line. 10: Pelvic fins. 11: Barbles.

The drawings on the next pages are of those species that are prototypes representing the family shapes, in general. The descriptions and numbers of species listed in a given family apply only to the Cortez. Elsewhere in the world the same families may include many more species with different forms and shapes. When no family name appears with a drawing, it indicates that the species belongs in the same family as the fish preceding it.

The fish sizes given are the largest of scientific record, not world angler records. Length is measured from the tip of the snout to the fork of the tail fin.

Since most fish change color rapidly, color is used as an identifying character only when it is specified, and when the fish is freshly caught and is an adult specimen. In the young, the color (and shape) may differ greatly (see, for example, the drawings for the black seabass).

The small arrows indicate distinguishing characters.

■ Class CHONDRICHTHYES, Cartilaginous Fishes. Includes all sharks and rays. All edible. Several of the sharks are excellent fighters, some are jumpers. Will take whole or cut baits when chum of dried blood is used. An enormous unidentified species in the Midriff is yet to be caught.

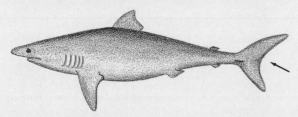

Family *Lamnidae*, mackerel sharks. 3 species. Bonito shark, *Isurus glaucus*. Alias mako, paloma. To 12'. Lunate tail and long keel on sides of tail. Takes large fresh baits. Will jump and fight like billfish.

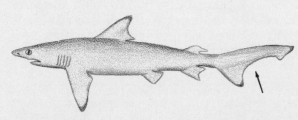

Family *Carcharhinidae*, requiem sharks. 10 species. Blacktip shark, *Carcharhinus limbatus*. Alias gambuso. To 7'. Only one of several black-tipped fin sharks entering very shallow water. Has special jumping and spinning ability. Favors live or fresh stripbait. Deserves top game rating.

Family *Sphyrnidae*. 5 species. Smooth hammerhead, *Spyhrna zygaena*. Alias cornuda. To 12', 1000 lbs. Flattened head extensions with eyes on ends. Will make unprovoked attacks on divers when blood is near. 3 narrow-headed species are called shovelhead.

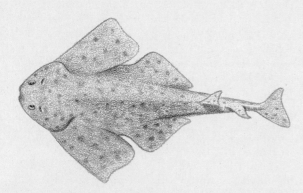

Family *Squatinidae*. Pacific angel shark, *Squatina californica*. To 5', 60 lbs. Large spreading pelvic and pectoral fins, flat head, skate-like tail. Fins and tail edible. Has strong and dangerous jaws. Takes fresh or live bait. Bears young.

■ In this Class there is another group or order called RAJIFORMES. In it only the sawfish and guitarfish are gamesters, but because some species are dangerous and often seen, they should be known. All have gill slits on bottom of body instead of sides, and most species have a poisonous spine on top of the long tail. A sting from it can be lethal. Treated by soaking injured part in very hot water.

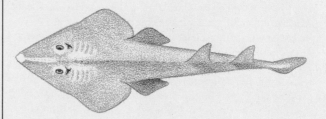

Family *Rhinobatidae*. 4 species. Guitarfish, *Rhinobatos sp*. Alias shovelnose shark, guitarra. To 4'. Long, pointed snout. Harmless, no poisonous spine on tail. Tail edible. All 4 species give birth to young.

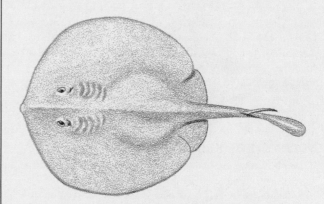

Family *Dasyatidae*. 10 species. Round stingrays, *Urolophus sp*. To 2'. Very dangerous because of their habit of remaining half covered in shallow sand or mud areas. Caught accidentally on a variety of baits.

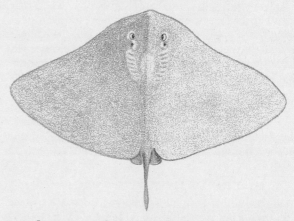

Butterfly stringray, *Gymnura marmorata*. To 3', 50 lbs. Not nearly as abundant or dangerous as the round rays—the tail is much shorter. Primitive peoples have used spines for spearheads.

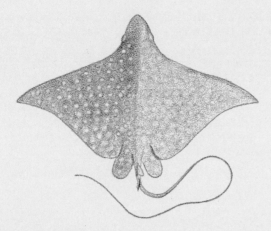

Family *Myliobatidae*. 3 species. Spotted eagle ray, *Aetobatus narinari*. Alias manta ray. To 5′. Slender spine-bearing tail 3½ times length of body and forward-projecting head, free of wings, identifies eagle rays. White spots over the back separates this species.

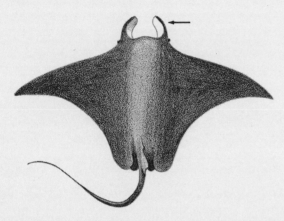

Family *Mobulidae*. 2 species. Pacific manta, *Manta hamiltoni*. Alias manta raya, devilray. Over 3500 lbs., 22′ across. Cephalic fins, horn-like extensions from the cheeks, used to flush foods into the cavernous mouth. The other species, a very small one, is a flapjacking jumper and assembles by hundreds for mass breeding.

■ Class OSTEICHTYHES Bony Fishes. The next 5 families are in an order of fishes (*Clupeiformes*) with soft rays. All have scales, a single, spineless dorsal fin, with the pelvic fins situated back on the belly. Only the first 3 species listed are game fish, the others are good bait and forage fishes.

Family *Elopidae*, tarpons. Ladyfish, *Elops affinis*. Alias machete, sabalo, tenpounder. To 3′. Small teeth on tongue, jaws, roof of mouth; a hard bone on throat. A jumper on small lures in murky shore water. Low on list of delectables.

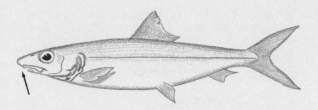

Family *Albulidae*. Bonefish, *Albula vulpes*. Alias sanducka, macabi. To 10 lbs. Large, ugly, bony head, projecting snout, and high-set eyes. Doesn't work flats. Taken on clams and strips of fish in most quiet bays. Great gamester in Atlantic, not so in Pacific.

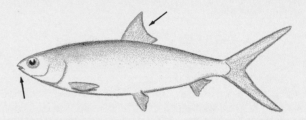

Family *Chanidae*. Milkfish, *Chanos chanos*. Alias sabalo, abuela. To 5½′. Heavy body, otherwise resembles ladyfish but has no teeth. Taken in backwaters on beef blood clots on minute hooks. Raised in ponds in south Asia. Prized food fish.

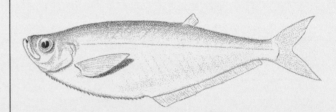

Family *Clupeidae*, herrings. 8 species. Drawing *Opisthopterus sp.* herring is prototype. Others called Pacific sardine, machete, sardina. Single dorsal fin but differ from anchovy by having projecting lower jaw. Superabundant in Midriff. Highly important as forage and bait fishes.

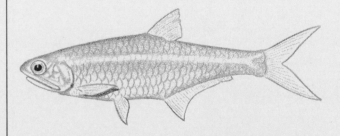

Family *Engraulididae*. 16 species. Anchovy, *Anchoa mudeoloides*. Alias anchovetta, sardina. Receding lower jaw, very short snout, long base of anal fin. Good bait but more vital as link in fish food chain. Species are difficult to separate.

Family *Ariidae*, catfishes. 12 species. Pacific gafftopsail catfish, *Bagre panamensis*. Alias pez gato. Typical salt-water catfish. All have barbles on chin and snout; bodies without scales, adipose fins. Abundant in mud bottom backwaters. Prefer clam. Some species carry eggs in mouth.

Family *Belonidae*. 5 species. Giant needlefish, *Strongylura fodiator*. Alias agujon grandes. To 6′. Blue lips, green teeth, green bones. Great game and food fish. Yellow-mouth needlefish, *S. pacifica*, has longer beak, and small teeth.

Family *Hemiramphidae*, halfbeaks. 5 species. To 2′. Upper jaw short, large pectoral fins. Young can fly short distances.

Family *Fistulariidae*, cornetfishes. 2 species. To 2½′. Skull much produced to form tube, on its end the mouth.

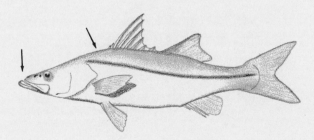

Family *Centropomidae*. 3 species. Black snook, *Centropomus nigrescens*. Alias robalo preito. To 6′. Lower jaw greatly projecting, small eyes, small anal fin. Great gamester. Takes live mullet. Robalito, *C. robalito*, has large anal spine. Shovel-snout, *C. pectinatus*, has concave profile.

■ Family *Serranidae*, true basses. 34 species. From ounces to 1000 lbs. The bass makes a good model fish form by which to compare others. Projecting lower jaw, large mouth, pointed teeth. All larger species excellent food. Found year-round in rocks, backwaters. Take stripbait, live bait, feathers, other lures.

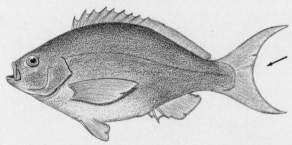

Pacific creole, *Paranthias colonus*. Alias rabirubia de lo alto. To 14″. Deep concave tail fin and bright red color distinguish the creole from all other basses. They mass along steep cliffs, are taken on small live and stripbait.

Rose coney, *Cephalopholis acanthistius*. Alias guativeres, Pacific coney. To 2′. Deeply notched high dorsal fin with only 9 spines and deep heavy body and rose color separate coney from other basses. Taken on live bait. Not abundant.

Enjambre, *Petrometopon panamensis*. Alias graysby, cabrilla ribera (Mexicans apply name "cabrilla" to most basses). Long projecting lower jaw, rounded anal and tail fins dark brown, numerous orange and blue spots on back and head. Taken on crustaceans and stripbait. Not abundant.

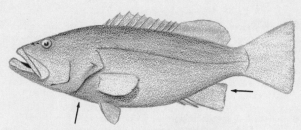

Baya grouper, *Mycteroperca jordani*. Alias garropa de astillero, gulf grouper. Over 200 lbs. 4 groupers in genus *Mycteroperca;* all have 11 soft rays in anal fins. Back edges of the anal and tail fins are squarish, not rounded as in cabrillas.

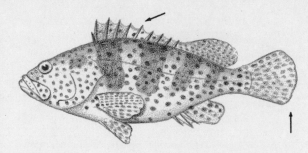

Pinta cabrilla, *Epinephelus analogus*. Alias spotted cabrilla, buchada. To 40 lbs. 4 species of cabrillas, all have rounded ends to anal, tail, and dorsal fins. True cabrilla covered with large reddish brown spots. Takes white jigs or feathers and fresh baits.

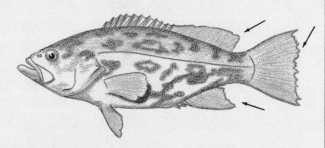

Leopard grouper, *M. rosacea*. Alias cabrilla pinto, golden grouper or calamaria in golden phase. To 3′. At 10″, a few make change from greenish brown, with very small reddish brown spots, to complete golden. The small spots separate the leopard from other groupers.

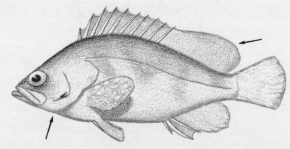

Flag cabrilla, *E, labriformis*. Alias cabrilla cualito. To 20″. Irregular white spots on reddish to green body. Inside of mouth red. Takes fresh bait in shallow rock areas. Two other plain brown species found at 50 fathoms.

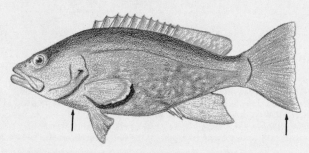

Broomtail grouper, *M. xenarcha*. Alias garropa jasplada. To 80 lbs. Mexicans believe there are 2 broomtail species. The one with a deeper scalloped tail is called garropa espiga (spiketail). Sawtoothed tail separates broomtail from all other fishes. Caught same as baya grouper.

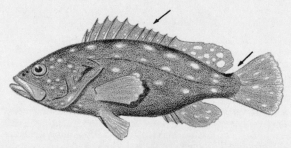

Pacific guaseta, *Alphestes sp*. Alias cabrilla clavel. To 14″. Differs from cabrillas by having 19-20 soft rays in dorsal, to their 16-17. Differs from other basses by having shorter snout and pink chin. Takes whitish lures and crustaceans.

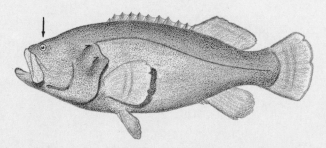

Southern jewfish, *Promicrops sp*. Alias guasa, mero. To 1000 lbs. Largest of Pacific coast basses. Differ from groupers and black sea bass by having rounded ends of dorsal, anal, and tail fins. Taken on 10-lb. baits. Young take feathers in backwaters.

Leatherfin bass, *Dermatolepis punctata*. Alias cabrilla de cuero, leather bass. To 3½′. Thick, leathery membrane in the fins, very compressed body. 18-20 soft rays in dorsal. Not abundant except around distant islands. Takes live baits but best lures unknown.

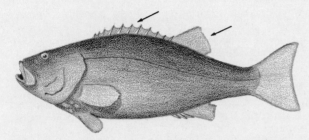

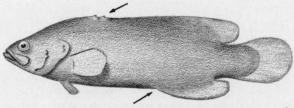

California black sea bass, *Stereolepis gigas*. Alias mero prieto, black jewfish. To 600 lbs. Body not compressed. Square ends to dorsal, anal, and tail fins, very small eye. Mature *gigas* habitate 40 fathoms in the Cortez. Rare below Mulege. Takes 1' long live bait.

Soapfish, *Rypticus sp*. Alias pez jabon. To 1'. 2 species. Only basses with 2-3 spines in dorsal and none in anal fins. Prefers live bait, stripbait, feathers. Seldom taken by anglers.

Juvenile black sea bass. Large fins, especially large pelvics. Young and adult have 10-11 soft rays in the dorsal; in jewfish 15-16; in groupers 11-12.

Family *Lobotidae*. Pacific tripletail, *Lobotes pacificus*. To 3'. Body deep, compressed; ends of anal and dorsal fins so long they appear like three tails. Otherwise closely resembles basses. Will take small live bait. Rare within our range.

■ Family *Lutjanidae*, true snappers, or pargo. 9 species. Bass-shaped but less divided dorsal fins; strong teeth in jaws, roof of mouth and on tongue; pelvic fins attached below base of pectorals. More abundant in backwaters than basses, less numerous in rocks. All take cut fish bait.

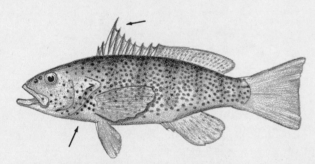

Spotted sand bass, *Paralabrax maculatofasciatus*. Alias cabrilla pintica. To 14", less than 12" in backwaters of the Cortez. Tall 3rd spine of dorsal and reddish brown spots on greenish gray background over fins and body. Takes stripbait or clams. Not a gamester.

Striped pargo, *Hoplopagrus guntheri*. Alias pargo mulato. To 2'. Deep, compressed body, front nostrils in tubes on upper lip; dark green and coppery color with darker stripes across back. Caught in 20' water on boulder bottom on chunk of fish.

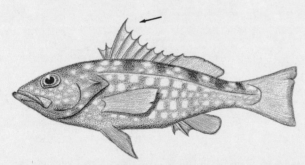

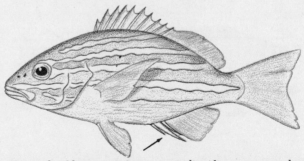

Gold spotted bass, *P. auroguttatus*. Alias cabrilla pintita. To 18". Gold spots over light brown on head, fins, and body. Taken on stripbait at 25 to 60 fathoms throughout Cortez. Excellent live bait and food fish.

Blue-and-gold snapper, *Lutjanus viridis*. Alias pargo rayado. To 1'. Blue stripes with dark border on greenish yellow background, red pin-lines on belly. Most snappers are red. Pargo colorado, *L. colorado*, has small teeth. Spotted snapper, *L. guttatus*, a dark spot on back.

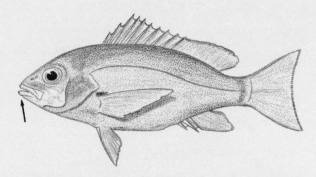

Ruby snapper, *L peru*. Alias pargo flamenco, huachinango, red snapper. To 3′. Separated by short head and snout and clear red to pink sides and white belly. In Midriff at 2 fathoms, at Guaymas 5-fathoms, in south end 40-fathoms. Takes stripbait. Among finest of foods.

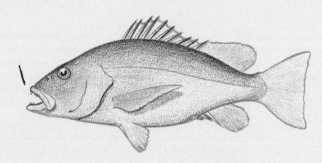

Dog snapper, *L. novemfasciatus*. Alias pargo mareno. To 85 lbs. Large canine teeth in both jaws, rounded ends of anal and dorsal fins. Color brownish red to dark green with darker fins. Young abundant in backwaters. Takes crabs, lures, or stripbait.

■ Pargo amarillo, *L. argentiventris*. Alias yellowtail snapper. Yellow on last half of body. Pargo raicero, *L. aratus*, has brown stripes along body. Small Pacific rabirubia, *Rabirubia enermis*, resembles a bass but with large eyes, rose color, forked tail, 10-11 soft rays in anal fin.

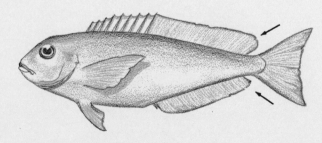

Family *Branchiostegidae*, blanquillos. Ocean-whitefish, *Caulolatilus princeps*. 2 species. Alias salmon. To 44″. Rays and most spines in undivided dorsal and anal fins same height, and small mouth. Taken on stripbait in deep water. Forehead of males bulge out during spawnings.

■ Family *Carangidae*, jacks. 28 species. Prototypes in next 7 drawings. Dorsal spines often without connecting membrane. Keels or bony shields on sides of small tail base in most species. Prefer live bait, will take stripbait or white jigs over feathers. Great gamesters. 3 species in genus *Seriola*. *S. dorsalis*, California yellowtail, has dark streak from snout through eye along lateral line to tail. *S. colburni*, amberjack, has streak from snout through eye to top of head. *S. mazatlan*, Mazatlan yellowtail, has deep, compressed body, with streak as in amberjack. All called "jurel." The roosterfish, *Nematistius pectoralis*, is recognized by the enormously high dorsal fin that resembles a cock's-tail.

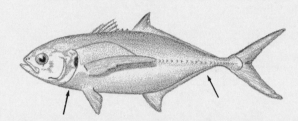

Green jack, *Caranx caballus*. Alias island jack, cocimero jurel. To 2′. Most slender and less compressed of all *Caranx* jacks; long pectoral fin, small scales on breast, anal, and soft dorsal fins. Caught from island shores. Drives bait schools onto beach.

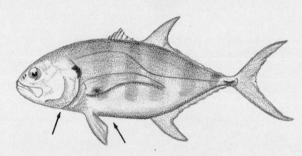

Jack crevalle, *C. caninus*. Alias toro. To 50 lbs. Pugnacious blunt head, scaleless throat; black spot on edge of pectoral and gill cover. Blue crevalle, *C. stellatus*, has black spots over head and back, bright blue on base of dorsal and anal fins. Caught from shore on white lures.

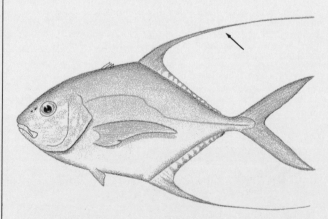

Threadfin pompano, *Citula otrynter*. Alias palometa de herbra. To 60 lbs. First one or two rays in soft dorsal and anal fins are greatly prolonged. Mouth telescopes out. (Another smaller species, the threadfish, *Alectis ciliaris*, has 6 long rays in dorsal and anal.) Will take white-and-blue lures.

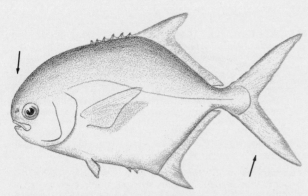

Pancake pomano, *Trachinotus kennedyi*. Alias palometa, pampaneras. To 2½'. Blunt, rounded snout and head, as in other true pompanos, but compressed, deeper body. Jumps high and flips when hooked, as does the 14″ paloma pompano, *T. paloma*. Both excellent food fish. Ski-bait best.

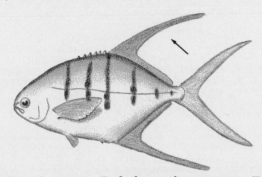

Gafftopsail pompano, *T. rhodopus*. Alias pampanito. To 1½'. First three or four rays of anal and soft dorsal fins extend almost to end of tail fin. Dark, vertical bars on sides. Efficient baits and techniques not developed but will take ski-bait and small live bait.

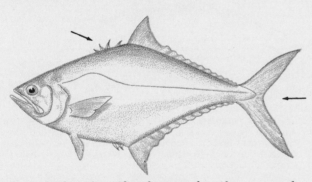

Bigjaw leatherjacket, *Oligoplites mundus*. Alias pez mundo. To 2'. Larger, deeper-notched tail fin than the yellowjacket, *O. saurus*, and littlejacket, *O. refulgens*, which only attain 1'. All have first one or two spines in dorsal pointing forward that are poisonous. All take ski-bait.

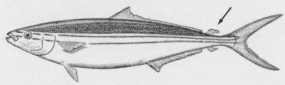

Rainbow runner, *Elagatis sp.* Alias jurel rayas. To 15 lbs. Rare. Finlet following dorsal and anal fins; body rounded, slender, with pointed head and snout like California yellowtail but with more than one lineal stripe. Both prefer live bait, or white lures over feathers.

■ Family *Pomadasyidae*, grunts or burritos. 22 species. Do not rate highly as food or game fish. Separated from snappers by having small mouth, small teeth, none on tongue or roof of mouth; profile steep, high shoulders, compressed body. California sargo, *Anisotremus davidsoni*, transplanted to Salton Sea.

Sargo burrito, *Anisotremus dovii*. Alias roncos, mojarrones. To 14″. Shoulders very deep and compressed. Profile straight; 5 black bars around body, cheek, and tail base. Will take crustaceans, clams, and bits of fish.

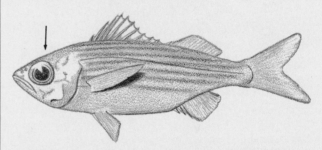

California salema, *Xenistius californiensis*. Alias bigeye, pajarillo, ojotones. To 1'. Small, oblique mouth, big eyes, 7 or more lateral dark stripes separates the salema from snappers and other grunts. This and the smaller-eyed *X. xanti*, excellent live baits. Very hardy when shoulder-hooked.

■ Family *Sciaenidae*, croakers. 35 species. Two or fewer spines in the anal fin, and lateral line that extends onto the tail fin. Snout usually projecting beyond lower jaw. Most use air bladder to make croaking sound. All but a few small species are good game and food fish.

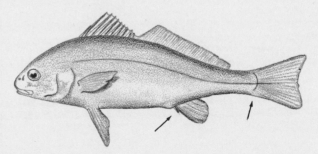

Berrugato croaker, *Umbrina sp.* Alias yellowfin croaker, gurrubatas. A genus of 4 species (under 16″) representing typical thick-rounded snout croakers. All have single, thick, short barble on tip of chin; 2nd spine in anal enlarged. Takes clams and crustaceans.

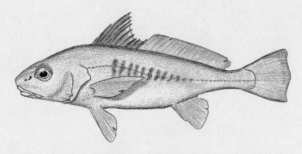

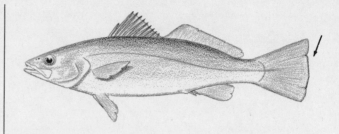

Boco dulce, *Micropogon ectenes*. To 2′. Two, hardy looking species in this genus. Resemble *Umbrina* but have several small barbles on chin instead of one. Adults have very thick lips. Superabundant in Bahia Almejas and similar backwaters. Takes live or various fresh baits.

Shortfin corvina, *C. parvipinnis*. Alias corvina pacifico. To 3′. Separated by S-shaped tail fin, straight profile (other corvinas slightly concave above eyes); the 3 or 4 canines in roof of mouth very large. Caught in surf at night on live or frozen shrimp, after chumming.

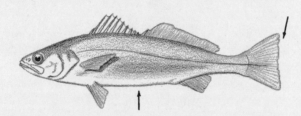

White seabass, *Cynoscion nobilis*. Alias corvina blanca, sea trout. To 80 lbs. Raised white cord along bottom of belly. *Cynoscions* have projecting lower jaw, in other croakers it recedes. Caught near Midriff and northward on live bait, stripbait, white feathers, and squid.

Orangemouth corvina, *C. xanthulus*. Alias corvina de aletas amarillas. Over 3′. Center rays in tail fin longer than others, forming a diamond shape, orange mouth (also in others). Favors live or fresh shrimp, mudsuckers, and lures.

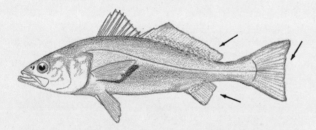

Scalyfin corvina, *C. othonopterus*. Alias gulf corvina, corvina azul. To 28″. Fins covered with scales, the base thickened by them. Tail fin edge straight. Darker than others. Corvinas look alike. Separating them is difficult. Taken in surf on live bait, shrimp, and light lures.

Totuava, *C. macdonaldi*. Alias white seabass. To 300 lbs. Tail diamond-shaped (middle rays longest); heavy, rounded (less compressed) body; dark color; no teeth in roof of mouth; no raised ridge on belly; small eyes. Native to north half of Cortez. Taken on foot-long live bait.

Striped corvina, *C. reticulatus*. Alias rayada corvina. To 2′. Separated by back and sides covered by wavy, irregular brown on black stripes, and long lower jaw. Taken by astute anglers working lures. Will also take clam and crabs in backwaters. Rates high as light-tackle gamester.

California corbina, *Menticirrhus undulatus*. Alias berrugato, chanos. To 20″. 4 species in this genus have single weak spine in anal; short, stout barble on tip of chin; slender body; no air bladder. In *undulatus*, upper rays of tail fin are longer. Taken on clam and crustaceans, shore casting.

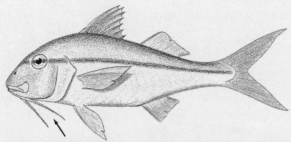

Family *Mullidae*. 4 species. Goatfish, *Pseudupeneus grandis-quamis*. Alias surmullet, chivallo. To 1½'. Two long barbles on chin. Yellow dominant color with broad stripes on greenish back, turning red soon after being caught. Very exciting bait fish. Will take minute baits.

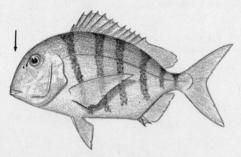

Family *Sparidae*, porgies. Tai, *Calamus taurinus*. Alias porgy, mojarron chino. Powerful heavy teeth in sides of jaw; body much compressed; head short, profile steep, almost vertical. Habitat deep water but enters estuaries. Prefers crustaceans but will take stripbait. Good food fish.

Family *Kyphosidae*, rudderfishes. 6 species. Chopa gris, *Kyphosus elegans*. To 4 lbs. Separated by deep, compressed body, short head, profile with bulge between eyes, prominent teeth. Gris and chopa salema, *K. analogus,* herbivorous, others nibble coral. No techniques nor baits as yet. Good food.

Family *Girellidae*, nibblers. 2 species. Cortez opaleye, *Girella simplicidens*. Alias ojo azul. To 5 lbs. Recognized by blue eyes and 2-3 white spots on each side of dorsal fin base. *G. nigricans* has one spot, rarely two. Generally vegetarians. Will take shellfish meat, sea moss.

Family *Ephippidae*. 2 species. Pacific spadefish, *Chaetodipterus zonatus*. Alias chambos. To 20″. Body very compressed; head blunt, short and deep; 6 dark bands around body. Good food fish. Taken on clams and crustaceans.

Family *Chaetodontidae*. 4 species. Butterflyfish, *Chaetodon humeralis*. Alias angel fish, muneca. Short, pointed snout projecting; large 2nd spine in anal fin; body greatly compressed, deep, almost circular; yellow with dark bands.

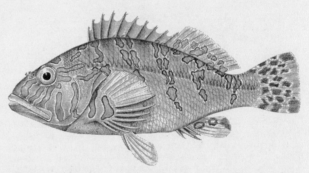

Family *Cirrhitidae*. 3 species. Chino mero, *Cirrhitus rivulatus*. To 1½'. Recognized by vertical dark bars with neon-blue edging, resembling written Chinese characters. Lower rays of pectorals very thick and used for walking. Excellent game and food fish. Taken near large rocks on lures and baits.

Family *Labridae*, wrasses. 14 species. *Halichoeres sp.* typical wrasse. Large scales, protruding, separated teeth (in parrot-fish teeth are coalesced to resemble a beak). All but a couple of wrasse species are small. Interesting because of vivid coloring and strange habits. Seen in tide pools.

Vieja (old lady), *Bodianus diplotaenia*. To 2½'. Large scales, long rays in dorsal, anal, and tail fins, pointed snout with projecting, separated teeth separate vieja from sheep-head and others. Brilliant red, yellow, blue, black trimmings. Male has bulging forehead.

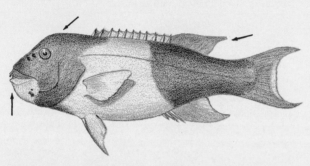

Sheep-head, *Pimelometopon pulchrum*. To 38 lbs. (Not Atlantic sheepshead, *Archosargus probatocephalus*.) Drawing of male. Fore and aft ends jet black. Females covered with red, with less bulging forehead. Both have white chins and bellies. Taken mostly in Midriff on crustaceans and stripbait.

Family *Scaridae*. 7 species. (Typical) parrotfish, *Scarus sp.* Alias escaro, perrico. To 30 lbs. Easily recognized by beak-like mouth in which teeth are coalescent, forming strong plates. Very large scales; deep tail base. Bodies of some species deep and compressed. The young take bait and lures.

Family *Acanthuridae*. 3 species. Surgeonfish, *Acanthurus xanthopterus*. To 18″. Sharp scalpel or jackknife blade which opens pointing forward from groove on sides of tail base. Will take small baits but are generally herbivorous. Colorful moorish idol in closely related family.

■ Family *Scombridae*, mackerels and tunas. A group of many species heretofore separated into several families. All have streamlined bodies for speed, power, and efficiency, the head and snout conical, slender tail base with keel on each side, widely forked fin, dorsal and anal fins followed by finlets. Excellent game fishes.

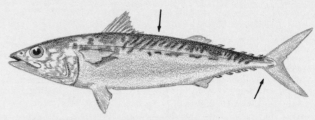

Pacific mackerel, *Scomber japonicus diego*. Alias macarela. To 25″. Body covered with scales; widely separated dorsal fins; back covered with wavy dark streaks (partially in others). Excellent for bait. Takes stripbait.

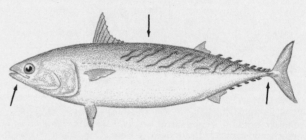

Frigate mackerel, *Auxis thazard*. Alias macarela, bullet mackerel. To 10″. Has even greater space between dorsal fins than Pacific mackerel; no scales except corselet around pectorals; 7-8 finlets following dorsal (Pacific has 5). Wavy streaks in small patch. Good bait. Takes ½-oz. white feather.

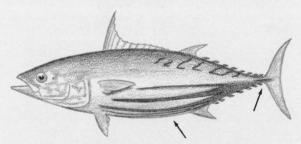

Ocean skipjack, *Euthynnus pelamis*. Alias barrilete blanca. To 43 lbs. 3-5 dark stripes on belly; no scales except a corselet around pectoral fins. Will take white feather but prefers ski-bait or live bait. Fine food fish. White meat.

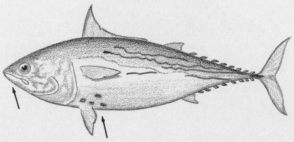

Barrilete skipjack, *Euthynnus lineatus*. Alias black skipjack, bonito. To 20 lbs. 3 or 4 dark spots below pectoral. Horizontal stripes on belly, which soon fade, and on back, which remain. Flesh dark, makes fine cibiche. Good live or cut baits. Takes white feather. Superabundant.

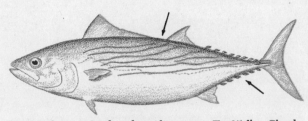

Mexican bonito, *Sarda velox*. Alias petos. To 25 lbs. Closely related to sierra, as shown by shape of dorsal fin, and which separates it from barrilete skipjack. Both have horizontal stripes (slanting on some) on back. Both take small white feathers, at fast troll.

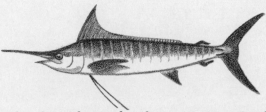

Striped marlin, *Makaira audax*. Alias agujon, pez puereo. To 425 lbs. Highest dorsal spine equals depth of body. Body and tail more compressed, and body more wedge-shaped than blue marlin. Abundant. Takes California flyingfish, mullet, ski-bait, or whole native baits skipped on surface.

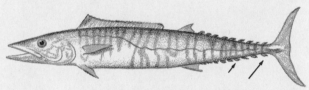

Sierra grande, *Scomberomorus sierra*. Alias sierra mackerel. To 14 lbs. 4-6 rows of orange or bluish spots on sides. Smaller sierra Monterey, occurring in northern half of Cortez, has the spots on about half their number. Light-tackle gamesters, on white feather.

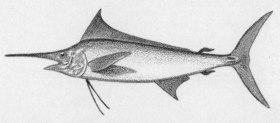

Blue marlin, *Makaira nigricans*. Alias marlin azul. To 2000 lbs. Largest of marlins. Has more cylindrical, less compressed body than others; lower dorsal fin and longer spines in anal than in striped marlin; lateral line has hexagon-shaped pattern. Live 10-lb. barrilete or large ski-bait best.

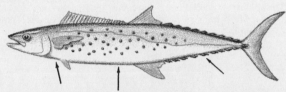

Wahoo, *Acanthocybium solandri*. Alias peto, sierra golfina. To 139 lbs. Separated by the slender body and shape of the dorsal fin, conical snout, numerous vertical bars, and absence of gill rakers. Abundant off south end. Fine food fish. Takes whitish lures, live bait, ski-bait.

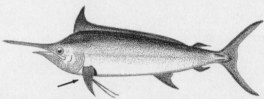

Black marlin, *Makaira endica*. Alias marlin negro, white marlin. To 1800 lbs. Can switch from dark blue to white. First spines of dorsal fin much less than depth of body; short pelvic fins and rigid pectorals which cannot fold against body. Taken same as blue marlin.

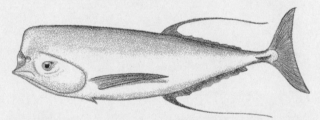

Family *Luvaridae*. Louvar, *Luvarus imperialis*. 1 rare species. To 6½'. Drawing good likeness but body coloring is delicate pink, the fins a staggering scarlet. Anus located equal to base of pectoral. Occurs in much of the world's warm waters, but rarely taken by anglers.

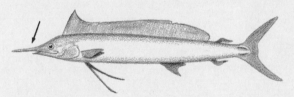

Shortbill spearfish, *Tetrapeurus angustrirostris*. To 120 lbs. Recognized by short snout, slender body, tall dorsal fin rays. Not plentiful near Cortez. Taken on live bait and ski-bait. May prove more plentiful with widespread use of live bait. Not highly rated as food.

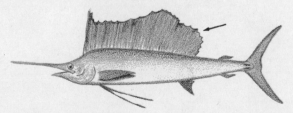

Family *Istiophoridae*, billfishes. 5 species. Pacific sailfish, *Istiophorus greyi*. Alias pez vela, spearfish. To 275 lbs. Distinguished by great bluish purple, sail-like dorsal fin, long spear. Abundant. Occurs to Punta Penasco, spring through fall. Taken same as striped marlin.

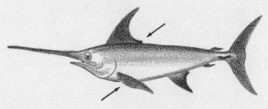

Family *Xiphiidae*. Broadbill swordfish, *Xiphius gladius*. Alias pez espada. To 1000 lbs. Flattish sword instead of a rounded spear of other billfish. No pelvic fins, no scales. Not plentiful in Cortez. Bait same as for marlin but is more reluctant. Has greater endurance. Favored as food.

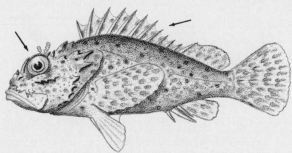

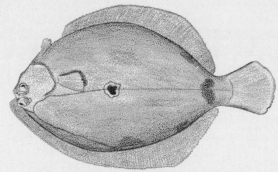

Family *Scorpaenidae*. 8 species. California scorpionfish, *Scorpaena guttata*. Alias pez alacran. To 1½'. Numerous cirri flaps and sharp spines over head and body identify all 4 species in this genus. A fin spine wound will cause agony. To treat soak in hot water, apply spirits of ammonia.

Family *Pleuronèctidae*, righteye flounders. Eyespot flounder, *Pleuronichthys ocellatus*. Alias turbot, lenguardos ojo. To 1½'. The right and left eye divisions are not always specific in any of the families.

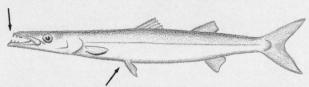

Family *Sphyraenidae*. 3 species. California barracuda, *Sphyraena argentea*. Alias buzo, picuda. To 4½'. Ranges Bahia Magdalena north. Darker Mexican barracuda, *S. enisis*, reaches only 14". Third species, a 5-footer, ranges south of Magdalena into Cortez. None dangerous. Takes lures, live, stripbait.

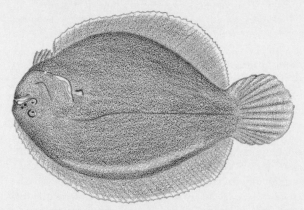

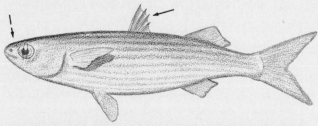

Family *Mugilidae*. 5 species. Striped mullet, *Mugil cephalus*. Alias lisa, macho. To 2½'. Snout and space between eyes very broad; large scales; eyes with adipose lids. Abundant in brackish water. Feeds by sifting mouthful of silt and sand. Fair food fish but is used for live or frozen bait.

Family *Achiridae*, soles. Mazatlan sole, *Achirus mazatlanus*. Alias righteye sole, tepalcate. Soles are small, seldom exceeding 1'. All have small mouths, small eyes bunched close together.

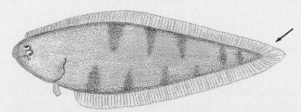

■ Flat fishes (29 species), a specialized series of fishes called *Pleuronectiformes*, which have both eyes on one side. There is much confusion in their common names. Not very gamey, therefore little technique is known. Larger species take live bait; others, bits of clam, shrimp, or stripbait. All are excellent food.

Family *Cynoglossidae*, tongue soles. Tropical tongue sole, *Symphurus atramentatus*. Alias rodaballos. To 8". Body wedge-shape; fin confluent, not separated around tail. Seven other small members in this genus.

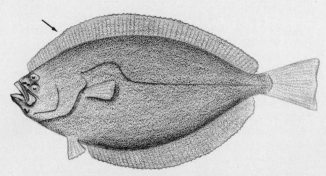

Family *Bothidae*, lefteye flounders. Cortez halibut, *Paralichthys aestuarius*. Alias alabato. To 25 lbs. *P. woolmani*, a larger species, to 30 lbs. Included in this family are the small (up to 2-lb, 12") sanddabs.

Family *Balistidae*. 3 species. (Typical) triggerfish, *Balistes sp*. Alias cochi, cochino. To 16 lbs. Large, rigid spine and two smaller spines in the dorsal; the third is the trigger. Strong and dangerous projecting teeth. Taken everywhere in rock areas on stripbait. Good food.

tackle and techniques

When primitive man first added meat to his vegetable diet, fish must have been the most promising. It was tender, the supply was bountiful, and it was easier to catch by bare hands than most land animals were. Somewhere along the line, the hook and line proved more productive than hands. Learning to make these devices may well have hastened civilization.

The Chinese were among the first people to develop fishing tackle. They have a legend which claims that their rapid advance was brought about by a monkey, for which the animal was deified. It seems that one inventive ancient substituted a dead monkey's hand, to avoid getting his own fingers nipped by sharks, and caught more fish than ever. This then was perhaps the first bit of fishing paraphernalia that could truly be called "fishing tackle."

Just about every kind of fishing tackle ever invented, including a monkey's hand, can be employed successfully in the Cortez. There is a place and a fish for everything, from the miniature fly rods to the big club-like devices used as mounts for 12/0 reels. Being a moderate in most things and concerned principally with efficiency and comfort in the very exciting art of angling, I will give only brief accounts of the extremes in tackle.

THE RIGHT HOOK FOR THE JOB

Fish hooks made from bones, thorns, and shells have been found among the most ancient of prehistoric tools throughout most of the world. Even before they made curved hooks, the Egyptians, American Indians, Polynesians, and Orientals stumbled onto a device for catching fish. It was made of bone and was about the size and shape of a toothpick. It was tied in the middle and was baited so that one end was flat against the line. When swallowed by a fish, a slight yank brought it crosswise inside the fish.

In 300 B.C., Chung Tei King, a Chinese prime minister, made history by leaving his post to go fishing with a straightened hook. He refused to use a bent one until all the crooks were kicked out of the government. He didn't catch many fish, but he won his point and made angling a revered sport throughout both China and Japan for evermore.

The heavy, short-shank hook with the curved-in, eagle claw point has proved far more effective for small game-fishes in the Cortez than long-shank, lighter wire, or offset hooks. This becomes more apparent when small baits are used. In fishing among rocks, the hook's shortness and slightly curved-in point make for less chance of it getting fouled. Hooks made from small-diameter wire tend to cut slits in the cheeks of a fish and are thus expelled easily.

With rapidly moving lures and baits, large hooks seem to be less noticeable. They are also overlooked by fish in a ravenous school, during competitive feeding binges, or when large baits are worked.

To my thinking, the perfect big-game hook is a hand-forged job made in Oslo, Norway, by O. Mustad and Son. Specifically a No. 8/0, it tapers from a diameter of 5 millimeters at the bend to 2½ millimeters just under the needle eye and to the long, slightly curved-in point.

It seems to be made of a tough nickel steel. The only problem is that it retails for about $3.00. If this type of hook were more economical, it would surely sweep the fishing tackle market.

Within the next few years, hooks in popular use will probably be half the size of those used today. It seems that the more a fish population is fished, the more hook-conscious it becomes; hence, smaller and smaller hooks become a necessity.

RODS FOR TROLLING AND CASTING

The efficiency and durability of glass rods and synthetic lines have more than compensated for the angler's loss of pride in his old Tonkin rods and Irish linen lines. However, many anglers still prefer the feel of their old tackle, as if it were a violin made by Stradivarius.

You don't have to be a purist or belong to a dry-fly cult to appreciate the charge that comes with seeing a violent fish slash at your skimming fly and then bend your fly rod into a circle. But before the full potential of fly fishing in the Cortez can be appreciated, years will need to be spent experimenting throughout all the dozen regions.

For shore fishing there are also numerous types and kinds of single-hand bait-casting rods on which an enclosed spinning reel or a conventional (revolving spool) reel is mounted on an offset or dropset reel-seat to provide a level wind. These outfits are principally for near-shore small game. They are far less popular than the lengthy two-handed rods.

Trolling rods as light as the large reels will allow provide comfort with little stress. And, in trolling, there is a lot more excitement in fishing from a belt with the gimbal nock seated in it, rather than planting the rod butt in the fighting chair.

The advent of spinning, with monofilament line on a spinning reel and the laminated tubular glass rod, brought additional pleasure and a high degree of satisfaction to the art of casting. Although none of this equipment has approached a state of perfection, it has come close to eliminating the old conventional tackle. Spinning equipment is entirely satisfactory for all casting. A 12-foot, one-piece rod is important in keeping the fish from encircling rocks and in adding fun to cast-

ing, but for traveling convenience, a broken and ferruled 10-footer is more practical. Here again, a rod with a rigid bottom half and a light, springy tip lets you cast a minute lure out a fair distance, while the sturdy base allows for retrieving a large fish.

An angler takes due pride and finds exhilarating delight in flipping a quarter-ounce lure for a distance with ease. But it is the sensitivity of the tackle in fighting a fish that gives the angler a grand feeling of the importance of the combat and of the eventual triumph.

Guides on a rod prevent bending stress in a single section and help to distribute strain along the rod. Roller guides have caught on and are now in use wherever salt water trolling is practiced. When a line is dragged through an ordinary eye-guide, there is considerable resistance caused by friction; with roller guides, line resistance is practically nil. This was brought home to me once when I hooked a large yellowfin tuna. During the first run, a whole spool of Dacron was dragged through the standard metal guides, and the line grooved every single one of them.

REELS FOR TROLLING AND CASTING

Nearly every reel manufacturer has an improved squidder-type reel that is geared for fast retrieve, that is corrosion resistant, and so on, but there was little improvement in the trolling reel until Penn came out with their No. 349. Very little thumbing is necessary to level wind the line. With the retrieve speed you can keep a taut line on a fish charging toward the boat. But, perhaps the best feature is the thinness of the reel. It lies flat against your wrist and doesn't flop from side to side when you are working a heavy fish; and you don't have to bend your wrist around it to grip the rod.

Far less thought has been applied to spinning reel design. An amateur fisherman can find a half-dozen bugs in almost any reel made. It's difficult to understand why a reel should be so poorly engineered as to allow a gaping tolerance between the spool and the

housing, which allows line or sand to get into the gears. It is also difficult to justify the clumsy, knuckle-busting bail, which gets bent, loosens, and clangs into gear like a Model-T Ford.

The greatest advance since the Scotch first made the flip-around, wooden spinning reel was the introduction of the automatic pickup finger replacing the bail. Several aggravating faults were eliminated by this device. It also reduced casting operations from five to two.

The closed-faced, spin-casting reel is fairly popular among fresh-water bait and plug casters, but because the line is subject to so much friction getting through the hook hole, casting distance is too limited to satisfy most salt-water spinning enthusiasts.

CHOOSING THE RIGHT LINE

Although a few angling organizations still hold to line thread number in calculating records, designation by pound-test now prevails. "Good old linen" is still preferred by some anglers, but the average fisherman will not take time to wash and dry a linen line. If linen line is left wet, it mildews or deteriorates. Synthetic materials won't do this but they will lose strength through over-exposure to sunlight. Synthetic lines are almost in complete use, owing to their superior strength and reduced diameters.

At present, monofilament is the most popular line for casting and Dacron the best for trolling. In trolling, especially when as much as 100 yards are played out, setting the hook is quite difficult if the line is elastic. Dacron has less stretch than any; however, some Dacron lines have been fabricated overly compact, which gives them a tendency to spring back once they are relaxed on the spool. This can cause a line to crisscross and tangle, especially after a heavy fish has been worked. The Gudebrod Brothers Silk Company has produced a soft Dacron which remains in place on the spool. It is a superior line in this respect and equal in other values to other Dacron lines on the market.

Monofilament lines are still being refined. Early mono lines were too hard and springy, and they ballooned up on the spool when tension was relaxed after retrieving. Then a limp line was produced, but it lacked sufficient spring to clear the spool flange and caused a retarding friction in casting.

This very spring action, however, is mono's greatest asset in spinning. Nevertheless, less elasticity is desirable, not only for setting the hook more effectively but also because stretching causes rapid deterioration. Commercial research will no doubt overcome these faults and produce a more ideal material for spinning.

READY AND HOME-MADE LEADERS

The Cortez has so many line-snipping, scissors-toothed sierra, needlefish, and small sharks, that fishing with a hook tied directly onto a monofilament line or using a mono leader can be wasted effort. Nevertheless, there are places and times that this skill can be practiced with much success.

There are several methods of attaching a hook to a mono line. Old-fashioned snelling works well for large hooks, but there are easier ways of making the tie. Folders illustrating these are given away with purchase of mono lines.

Single-wire leaders, which kink and snap off easily, were replaced by multiple-strand wire several years ago. Blue seems much more productive than other colors and has proved equally effective for fish ranging from 6-inch fringeheads to 500-pound black marlin. While a live bait is less encumbered and has more freedom to swim on mono, the flexible multiple-strand leaders allow greater movement over single-wire leaders.

If you prefer to make up your own leaders, you can order the material and a kit of clamp-on sleeves and crimper. Factory-made wire leaders have a single loop with the ends soldered. In homemade leaders, a double-strand loop is advisable. It can be kept spread out and the wire is less likely to pull free of the sleeve when made as follows.

First, make a loop at the top end of the leader (as if tying a simple knot):

Twist the short end of the wire around through the loop again:

Cinch up to desired size and run the end through once or twice more and cinch again. Then measure the end and clip it off so that it will barely be hidden when the sleeve is shoved up tightly to the loop and crimped:

A somewhat similar procedure is followed at the hook end of a leader. Run the end through the hook eye. Make the basic loop smaller in size:

Insert again through the hook eye. Cinch up and insert through the loop again:

Cinch up and follow the original procedure.

Sierra are especially attracted to swivels or other small bright objects and will often cut a line attached directly to them. To avoid this, divide the leaders into two sections and use a ball-bearing swivel or a McMahon sister snap to connect them. As a rule, ordinary brass snaps are too cumbersome and they weaken rapidly from salt water corrosion.

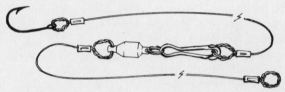

There are several advantages to this rig. The lower section can be snapped off and another snapped on quickly to save time in removing a hook. It is also handy when releasing a billfish or other big gamester.

SOME ANGLERS take pleasure in pouring their own sinkers—and there are number of good molds on the market. However, crescent sinkers used in trolling are difficult to make since they must be perfectly balanced so that they will not revolve in the water.

For bottom fishing with live bait, use any shape sinker with a hole, to allow the bait to pull line through it. Sinkers used as extra weight for casting should be the twist-on, rubber core variety. Oblong, cigar-shaped sinkers for fishing deep or among rocks seem as efficient as any. Any sinker should be the lightest that will serve the purpose—that is, hold against the current.

LURES AND BAITS

There are times and places when one kind of a lure will attract more fish, and, all too often, an angler will become so sold on that particular kind that he will be reluctant to try others that might be even more effective. For a short period, game fish will go for a lure similar in color and size to the forage fish they are feeding on, then suddenly start looking for a change. Because of this, it is risky to adopt any one lure until working it alongside other favorites and comparing its average and relative success.

Despite opinions to the contrary, fish are highly sensitive to color. But while one group of fish may pursue a red lure, another group may give it a wide berth. In or near the surface of the Cortez, white attracts more species in all months of the year than any other color or combination of colors. Grayish blue is also a good color; then come combinations of chrome and blue, white, and red. Yellow, favored by Pacific Coast fishes, appears to be the least attractive.

Lure action, or the lack of it, is often more effective than color, and great skill and art can be shown by an angler in working a lure. Plugs with erratic action are interesting to a few species, but less-active jigs and straight-line feathers seem to be more attractive to the great majority.

Every situation is a special case and calls for experimentation. Though there are hundreds of worthless diving lures, some are highly effective, especially for deep trolling. Erratic spoons and plugs will attract intermediate feeders. Surface trolling lures shaped like the century-old bone jig have a higher percentage catch record over many other shapes and kinds. They also do very well when cast out and retrieved from a drifting or anchored boat. There are conditions under which squid-like lures prove to be killers.

A lure with white feathers that slide up on the leader away from the teeth of the fish is a good, widely usable, artificial bait in the Cortez. It can be used for trolling for big and little game, as well as for casting. Many species will go for such feathers but will not touch other lures. On the other hand, several species will refuse feathers in favor of any of a dozen other baits. There are no workhorse lures that can be used for everything. Every situation is a special case and calls for experimentation. Finding the right lure for the right fish at the right time is half the fun.

I have seen about twenty Cortez species taken on flies. One of the most consistent everywhere along the Baja Peninsula south of the Midriff was the ladyfish, a fine jumper. A large white bucktail, nymph, or feather proved most desirable for this and several other species, but only when the water was not clear. Sierra, young roosterfish, and several small members of the jack, mackerel, and grunt families were among our catches.

HOOKING LIVE BAITS

Every fisherman has suffered through long periods when a species he is after will ignore anything he offers except a live bait or bait cut from fresh fish, such as ski-bait or stripbait. Game fish, when not overly hungry, show a decided preference for one or more of the hundreds of species of bait-sized forage fish. Many gamesters favor strong, oily baits in the herring and mackerel families, whereas others prefer to dine on the milder croakers and grunts. Again, it is often a matter of experimentation to find out what fish will take what bait and when.

Live and fresh baits will often be rejected or taken solely according to the way they are hooked. There are several good ways of hooking a bait so it will stay on

the hook, live longer, be more active, or at least appear less encumbered. Some of the tender-meated species should be hooked around certain strong bones, but hooking under the soft dorsal fin is generally better for baits expected to swim:

This method is employed for hardy bait fish, such as grunts, mackerels, and small jacks (anchovies are too tender). Baits hooked thus will more often swim away from the boat.

Casting a bait often stuns or injures it, making it less lively. For a casting bait, insert the hook just below the back part of the dorsal fin. The clavicle, or collar bone, of the otherwise delicate, weak-boned anchovy and some other herrings is strong enough to hold the bait fish without mortal injury. Insert the hook in the upper part of the gill opening, barely circling the bone; if the leader or line is kept light enough, the bait will swim with surprising strength:

Two of the herrings—the sardine and the round herring—have a tough bone structure back of the nose. If the size of the hook is kept small enough and is inserted crosswise through it, these baits will keep alert for 10 or 15 minutes; time spent beyond that is wasted anyway:

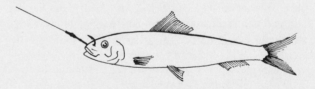

While large croaker baits, especially the hardy corvinas, are hooked under the dorsal fin, croakers less than 5 inches will stay attached longer and are more difficult for large fish to pull off when the hook is inserted around the pubic or breast bone, which projects forward from the pelvic fins:

Croakers are not overly active and should be given a very slight yank about every minute to keep them moving. Movements attract big fish from a far greater distance than any of the colors or qualities the bait may have.

When a live bait is to be cast out and retrieved at once, or when baits are trolled, no matter what species, send the hook up through both jaws, or crosswise under the eyes:

Retrieving a cast bait is more often done in pulls and halts of 3 or 4 feet each or more, according to the species sought.

The booby trap is mentioned in several places in the text as a special bait for large fish that habitually snap off the tail end of baits. This rig works for ski-bait as well as for live or fresh-dead baits. Some game fish cannot be taken on any other known baits with any degree of consistency. While the ordinary booby trap is easily applied, a lot of practice is necessary for working it with ski-bait and the like.

A booby trap is nothing more than two hooks, 2 or more inches apart, the top one hooked as for trolling, the lower one inserted near the tail end of the bait. Lead the hook up through both jaws; insert the bottom hook anywhere near the tail:

Most deep-bodied bait fish are hindered less when the hook is inserted just ahead of the first spines in the dorsal fin. Several of the game fishes will show less reluctance in taking and swallowing a shoulder-hooked bait than any other, especially the large jacks, such as amberjack, roosterfish, and yellowtail. For these and others without large cutting teeth, tie the hook directly onto the flexible monofilament line for less interference in the swimming of the bait. Hooked in this manner, the flied bait can pull like a yoked ox and can take out a lot of mono. If cast out, such a large bait will be stunned by the smack on the surface.

This method is especially good for enormous, 10-pound live bait for black marlin and other giants, since greater dimensions and ranges can be covered. With a gentle pull the bait can be reined up close to the surface when it sounds to undesirable depths.

When such a bait is on a hook that is tied directly onto monofilament, set the hook before the bait is swallowed, otherwise the line may get snapped off by the pharyngeal (throat) teeth.

HOW TO MAKE CUT BAITS

Styles for tailoring cut baits number in the thousands, and many of the strange shapes may attract some fish in some regions. The few simple strips shown here have proved most effective.

Not included are chunks and bits. Any of these, or strips, will be clobbered by the overabundant triggerfish in rock areas unless the bait is kept in rapid motion or is resting motionless on the bottom.

Oily fish are generally preferred for all cut baits. The herrings, needlefish, mackerels, Spanish mackerels, and tuna-shaped fishes are in the oily category: the basses, large croakers, and other white, watery fleshed fishes are not.

Some fish, especially bottom feeders, show a decided preference at times for a bait after one side has been cut away from it. The bait minus a side is sent down while the blood taste is fresh.

Stripbait is sliced and shaped to produce very little action, except that the cut away tapered end allows it to flap. Cut such a bait from a fresh-killed fish and retrieve or troll it slowly. Stripbait may be cut in lengths from 1 inch to more than a foot. Large sharks, jewfish, and black marlin will take a 10-pound slab. Regardless of the size, cut and hook the strip so it will not revolve:

A spinner bait is cut and hooked especially to revolve and is preceded by a crescent sinker and a swivel. Cut it the same as a stripbait, but insert the hook clear through the front end, pull it through, and insert it again half-way back. To avoid having the bait bunch up, lap the line around itself after the first insertion:

SKI-BAIT IS EFFECTIVE

The most effective cut bait so far developed in the Cortez is ski-bait. Once the technique of tailoring and using it is learned, the bait can be made rapidly. The main purpose in fashioning and hooking this bait is to get it to skip on the surface like a ski, without flipping over and over. When the proper trolling speed is achieved, the front of the bait throws up a couple of "roostertails," creating the illusion of a flyingfish about to take off.

Ski-bait can be made in all sizes, from a 1½-incher for pompano to a 1½-footer for black marlin. As with other baits, the oily fish are usually preferred and sierra and barrilete are favored.

First cut a slab from the side of a fish and level it off. Cut one end square and point the other, then slice each end to half thickness:

Now fold the head end up and put the hook through twice, making sure it is centered in the slab:

When trolled, the head end folds back, and the tail flips up and down slightly as the bait skiis over the surface:

PREPARING BILLFISH BAIT

The old involved method of sewing a semiconcealed hook in the belly of a bait for billfish is rarely used nowadays. A scientific approach suggests that the sharp hook tip should not point toward the gullet of the marlin or sailfish when the bait enters his mouth. Billfish usually swallow a bait headfirst so that the fin spines will be folded and it will go down easier. Anything resembling a spine—such as the tip of a hook—will cause a billfish to throw the bait.

The "Emmett Brooks halter" is the easiest to make up and is as good as, or better than, any other. It permits the bait to be taken, held, and turned without interference from the hook. Then when the bait is swallowed, the hook goes down easily and stays down.

First, insert a needle threaded with heavy doubled cord straight down through the top of the head, then cut the cord at the needle end:

Next, tie two of the four ends over each eye. Thread the needle with the two top ends and push it down through the snout and lower jaw. Cut the needle loose. Then thread it with the other two ends and push it back up through the snout:

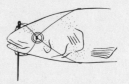

Cut the needle loose and tie all four ends in front of the snout (making sure they are of even length). Then tie them again a couple of inches ahead of the snout and make a loop for the hook. If you are using a flyingfish, use a separate single line to tie the pectoral fins snugly to the body:

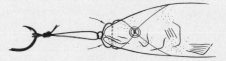

Striped marlin and sailfish in the Cortez show a slight preference for frozen California flyingfish over the frozen native mullet. On some occasions, fresh-dead baits caught in the vicinity are best. Live bait tops all.

OTHER BAITS

In spite of the popularity of live bait, not all fish are fish-eaters. The Cortez opaleye, chopa, and some others are vegetarians. Some few, such as old parrotfish, become vegetarians when they grow old. For these you can use sea moss, eel grass, canned peas, or other vegetation. There are a great many species that make a living grazing on loose ends of shellfish tentacles; others follow a strict diet of shrimp, squid, or sea worms. These appetites must be catered to if you expect to get these good gamesters that have hardly even been disturbed.

Then there are a great number of fish-eaters that show a decided preference for crabs. Snapper, for instance, will eat almost anything fresh, but they get so excited at the sight of crabs that they will grab them out of your hand. Hook live crabs and shrimp through the tail and remove the big claws. Some rarely taken rock dwelling fishes, such as the chino mero and the large wrasses, like all crustaceans and mollusks.

Many fish that inhabit calm, offshore areas, especially around rocky bottoms, can be attracted with chum made by crushing molluscs or crustaceans.

small-Boat cruising

San Felipe, being fairly near to the U. S. border, would seem the most logical starting port for cruising down the Cortez. However, between San Felipe and Bahia San Francisquito in the Midriff there are three potentially dangerous stretches of more than 50 miles each, without any kind of a haven. This route is subject also to ferocious winds and very swift currents, especially in most of the channels.

The recommended course is not a strict line but a flexible, point-hopping seaway with occasional alternatives. Visual navigation replaces instrument sailing, principally because of the strong and unpredictable currents. Charts and compass are used to pinpoint landmarks, then forgotten until the objective is reached. The process is then repeated for the next hop.

A marker sight placed on the bow directly in front of the helmsman's position at the wheel will take the guesswork out of visual navigation. It should always be kept directly on the selected landmark, regardless of currents that may be encountered.

Note: The distances in nautical miles given in the following courses are minimum straight lines and do not take into consideration current drift or wide berth taken when rounding points.

THE SAN FELIPE COURSE

If carefully planned by competent operators, boats above 20 feet can make the voyage down the Baja California coast from San Felipe, providing they are seaworthy, well-powered, and carry a quantity of gas.

Cruising from San Felipe down the Cortez requires experience in rough water and advance knowledge of the weather and tidal currents. If the rules are followed and no adverse winds or swift currents are encountered, several hours can be saved by a fast boat between San Felipe and Bahia San Francisquito. But luck should not be depended upon on this course.

There are two surfaced ramps at San Felipe with parking areas that are somewhat guarded. Gas, groceries, and bottled goods are in ample supply.

■ Hop No. 1 (52 miles): San Felipe to Puertecitos
Because of the 52-mile stretch with no coves or refuge, the boat should be given a few shakedown turns around the bay before setting out. The take-off should be timed at 30 minutes before high tide, and after a careful check of the weather. The Puertecitos Lodge at Puertecitos keeps gas and limited supplies.

■ Hop No. 2 (42 miles): Puertecitos–Bahia Willard
Between Puertecitos and Bahia Willard there are several good coves along the coast and as many lees around the Islas Encantadas. If an adverse tide is met outside of the islands, a counter-current, or less swiftness, can be found close to the Mainland shore.

Bahia Willard has three anchorages, each favored according to the direction of the wind. Gas is available at the north-side fish camp and at the back of the more open Bahia San Luis Gonzaga, separated from Willard by a sand spit and island. Bahia Gonzaga is subject to much wind, especially when Pacific storms hop over and hit it from the west. There is a landlocked cove that is completely hidden from the bay but which can be entered with safety by large boats. It is situated about midway on the cliffed southern side of Gonzaga.

■ Hop No. 3 (85 miles): Bahia Willard to Bahia de Los Angeles
The stretch from Bahia Willard to Bahia de Los Angeles is even more dangerous than the one below San Felipe, especially the 53 miles between Punta Final and Punta Remedios, where the coast is composed mostly of flat-faced cliffs without shelving. If current (very swift in the Canal de Las Ballenas and Canal Sal si Puedes) is favorable, the course keeps out from the coast below Punta Remedios and heads toward the west side of Isla Smith, recognized at a great distance by its high dome. From Isla Smith, small craft can favor the north side of Bahia de Los Angeles. After turning into it, the Los Angeles Bay Resort landmark can be seen. It is the northernmost of three domed peaks.

The resort is on the beach of a cove. It is separated from the bay by a lengthy sandbar which continues under water for a surprising distance (varying according to the 18-foot tide). Bahia de Los Angeles, like Gonzaga, is subject to winds. When the surface is too rough to beach, a skiff will be sent out as a shore boat. Gas is almost always available at this resort.

■ Hop No. 4 (58 miles): Bahia de Los Angeles to Bahia San Francisquito
Between the Bahia de Los Angeles resort and Bahia San Francisquito is the third hazardous stretch, which also has no haven except for a slight indentation called El Arco, recognized by a tall arched rock about midway between Bahia de Las Animas and Bahia de Las Mujeres. The small Bahia de Las Mujeres is sometimes mistaken for the close-by, one-mile-wide Bahia San Francisquito. The small inner bay (a completely protected port) is at the southwest corner of the larger San Francisquito.

MIDRIFF — FIRST COURSE

There are two recommended courses for cruising in the Midriff in small craft above 15 feet. The First Midriff Course, from Kino on the Mainland to Bahia San Francisquito on the Baja coast, is 70 nautical miles in island-hopping legs or 62 miles true course.

■ Hop No. 1 (29 miles): Kino to Bahia Las Cruces on Isla Tiburon

After leaving Kino and clearing the south end of Isla Alcatraz, get a bearing on Isla Turner, just below Tiburon. (Take note of the position of Bahia Perro, 6 miles north of Turner, and change course for it, in case of adverse wind.) Pass through the narrow channel between Turner and Tiburon on to Bahia Las Cruces. A dangerous rock, awash at low tide, is off the center of this bay. Enter it—and all other bays and coves—with caution. Select an anchorage after circling the area, remembering that the tide may drop as much as 18 feet.

■ Hop No. 2 (15 miles): Las Cruces to cove at southwest corner of Isla San Esteban

A ¾-mile-long natural jetty extending southwest from this corner provides fair protection from most prevailing winds, on one side or the other. If a strong south wind comes up after takeoff from Las Cruces, an alternate course is taken to the north end of Isla San Esteban.

■ Hop No. 3 (13 miles): Isla Esteban to southwest corner of Isla San Lorenzo

This course offers lee from prevailing north wind but is exposed to the south.

■ Hop No. 4 (13 miles): San Lorenzo to inner cove in Bahia San Francisquito

Get a precise bearing on Punta San Gabriel (or a high hill just back of it), which forms the southern side of outer Bahia San Francisquito. The hidden entrance to the inner port is in the southwest corner of the bay. Beware of motor-choking weeds in summer near the beach in this cove and other sheltered waters. Also, if boats are left anchored too close to this beach they will be grounded by receding tide, which drops as much as 18 feet here during extreme highs. If no gas is available in this port, some may be found at Rancho Barril, 7½ miles south.

MIDRIFF — SECOND COURSE

The Second Midriff Course, from Kino to Bahia de Los Angeles via the islands, is 110 nautical miles.

■ Hop No. 1 (29 miles): Kino to Las Cruces on Isla Tiburon (Same as First Midriff Course.)

■ Hop No. 2 (14 miles): Las Cruces to north end of Isla San Esteban

Three coves on the north end of San Esteban provide shelter except from north winds.

■ Hop No. 3 (22 miles): San Esteban to Isla Sal si Puedes, off northwest end of San Lorenzo

The channel separating Isla Sal si Puedes from San Lorenzo is over a mile wide but reefs extend out from both, making caution necessary for passage at low tide. There are snug baylets on either side of Sal si Puedes. The best protected is on the southwest side. Many rocks project up from a broad reef extending westward from this bay and on past the west end of the island.

■ Hop No. 4 (5 miles): Isla Sal si Puedes–Isla Raza

This low island is not visible from a great distance. Its sides provide fairly good lees from prevailing winds.

■ Hop No. 5 (5 miles): Isla Raza to Isla Partida

A baylet on the north side is open to north winds only. A cove on the south side provides protection from north winds. A rock 75-feet high is connected with the larger section of the island by a reef.

■ Hop No. 6 (10 miles): Isla Partida to southern tip of Isla Angel de La Guarda

A good anchorage and the nearest protection from south winds is found above Isla Estanque, 5½ miles up the east side from this tip. A reef, exposed at high tide, connects this island to Isla Angel de La Guarda. Below Isla Estanque the coast recedes, providing a lee against north or west winds.

There are few sheltered places to recommend along either side of La Guarda during November through May, when northwest winds prevail for as long as three or more days. During other months, when south winds are more likely to prevail, protection can be found up the whole east side of Punta Rocosa, 14 miles above Isla Estanque.

■ Hop No. 7 (25 miles): Southern tip of Isla Angel de La Guarda to Bahia de Los Angeles

The visual landmark is the 3,423-foot round-top peak directly back of Los Angeles Bay Resort (not to be confused with two equally tall peaks farther south). The port is situated behind the end of a low sandspit which continues submerged and shallow for a half mile southward. Storm winds hit this bay with considerable force.

THE MAIN COURSE DOWN THE CORTEZ

The recommended course for cruising down the Cortez follows the First Midriff Course from Bahia Kino to Bahia San Francisquito. From there it continues as a visual, point-hopping course southward.

Hop No. 1 (83 miles): Bahia San Francisquito, via Cabo Miguel and Cabo Virgenes to Santa Rosalia

A towering smokestack from the copper smelter at Santa Rosalia can usually be seen shortly after passing Cabo Virgenes, and it serves as a landmark for the port. In its well-protected harbor tie up to tall piling across the south side. Hire a taxi to go uptown to arrange for gasoline and supplies. Small boys are always around to get a cab if none is handy.

Hop No. 2 (40 miles): Santa Rosalia, via Isla San Marcos, Punta Chivato, Punta Santa Inez, Mulege

There is a choice between two courses. If the current and winds are favorable, the best deep and clear course is outside of Isla San Marcos. However, the inside course can be very interesting, especially if time permits visits to the very shallow Ensenada San Lucas and its estuary, and to the shore village and airport near it. Take a look at the gypsum works on San Marcos or dock alongside its pier for the night. Emergency medical and other services and supplies are available at this port.

A word of caution: The channel between the south end of Isla San Marcos and the coast is shallow, with many dangerous rocks. Though the running is shallow, there is a passage starting a half mile off the end of the pier, heading straight toward Cabo Chivato. A large resort with small-craft facilities is planned on Chivato.

After rounding Cabo Chivato and Punta Santa Inez, consult navigational charts for directions to the dome-shaped Roca Sombrerito, the landmark at the estuary of Rio Mulege. Do not attempt to enter the river until taking aboard a pilot from the Playa de Mulege Lodge, situated in a cove a quarter mile below the river. Someone comes out to meet boats there. There are several resorts in Mulege. Complete supplies are available, plus a machine shop.

There are no navigational problems in taking a side trip back into Bahia Concepcion to Laguna Santispac and Bahia Coyote (site of a planned yacht club), but some coves beyond have cobblestone bottoms and should be watched.

Hop No. 3 (76 miles): Mulege, via Punta Concepcion, Isla Ildefonso, Punta Pulpito, Isla Coronados, to Loreto

Along the stretch below Punta Concepcion are several rocks that should be given a wide berth. There is a farmhouse with good water at the back of Bahia San Nicolas, and three good anchorages in the Punta Pulpito area.

Between Pulpito and Isla Coronados there is good shelter at the back of Bahia San Basilio, which is below Punta Mangles.

In the channel inside Isla Coronados there is a broad reef that extends from the island to the Baja shore. Crossing it at low tide is risky. There is one less-shallow passage 100 yards offshore; the deeper, recommended one is out close to a small satellite rock west of Coronados. A lookout on the bow is required to run them. After passing through, there is still a sandbar to watch, extending southward from Coronados.

The southmost grove of palms along the beach is the landmark for the Flying Sportsmen Lodge and pier. The nearer, massive grove is Loreto proper, with the Hotel Oasis about midway on the beach. A harbor is under construction at Loreto at present. If not completed, gas and complete supplies can be taken on at either of the resorts.

Boat operators going on to La Paz or planning a long stay in the adjoining Juanaloa Region should stock up at Loreto, as it is the last port for supplies, at present, short of La Paz.

Hop No. 4 (138 miles): Loreto, via Juanaloa, Islas San Jose and Espiritu Santc, to La Paz

The first cove below Loreto is Bahia Chuenque (northwest corner of Juanaloa Region). The perfect Bahia Escondido is barely separated from Chuenque, but the narrow and deep entrance to Escondido is on around and below Punta Coyote. There is a good cove on either side of Isla Danzante.

Here again there is a choice of two courses, both immensely interesting. The longer course, east and outside, starts from the north end of Isla Danzante, runs 3 miles north of Islas Las Galeras, satellites of Isla Monserrate, and follows heading to Jeffries Cove, 1 mile below the north end of Isla Catalan. There are several good coves on the west side of this island, one on the south end, and good lees on either side of a peninsula on the east side. From Catalan this course continues past Isla Santa Cruz and Isla San Diego to Bahia Amortajada at the south end of the 17½-mile-long Isla San Jose and to the salt works at the west end of the bay. Here it meets with the inside, or west, course.

The shorter west course (starting from the north end of Isla Danzante) stays between Danzante and a coastline of many coves and several islands to Bahia Agua Verde. The landmark to the entrance of this bay is the 115-foot-high Roca Solitaria, which is usually white with guano. Agua Verde is generally calm, but during winds refuge may be taken in coves at either end of it. Some emergency gas is usually available at Agua Verde.

After leaving Bahia Agua Verde and rounding Punta San Marcial, care must be taken to avoid rocks awash at low tide. From San Marcial the distance to Punta San Telmo is 13 miles. Above and north of San Telmo is Puerto Gatos, with a good cove at the north end.

A mile below Punta San Telmo the coast recedes to form the open Bahia Tambobiche, at the back of which a small quantity of gas is maintained by the Rancho Tambobiche. The large and interesting Laguna Benziger lies between this bay and Puerto Gatos.

There is a fairly good cove 1½ miles below Punta Nopolo (5 miles south of Rancho Dolores). Farther south (6¾ miles) there is good protection from all directions on the north or south sides of Punta San Evaristo (on Isla San Jose), which projects out mushroom-shaped, ¾ mile from the shore line. At a small nearby salt operation there may be some emergency gas but it is not to be depended upon.

There is very little shelter between Punta San Evaristo and La Paz along the coast. Small craft cross over the channel to Isla San Jose and down to Bahia Amortajada, where the two courses converge. Warning: During lunar high-tide periods, Canal San Jose develops a very strong current, and a heavily loaded boat trying to head into it will make little headway and will consume a lot of fuel.

Adjoining Bahia Amortajada are an estuary and lagoon that can be entered by small boats. Puerto Salinas on the south side of Punta Salinas has a small salt works, and there are a dozen workers living near the beach. Gasoline can usually be bought there in an emergency. There is a small airstrip at this port.

There is considerable vegetation in the canyons of Isla San Jose, and fairly good hunting for mule deer, rabbits, and domestic goats gone wild. The big-gamefish

swimway swings to within 5 miles of the southeast corner of San Jose, and swings in again off its northern top. This 400-fathom trench encircles Islas San Diego and Santa Cruz.

From Bahia Amortajada the course runs to Isla Partida (22 miles) via the east side of Isla San Francisco, which is just off the foot of Isla San Jose. This island has fairly good coves at either end and a deep indentation at the south end.

At the north end of Isla Partida, make a choice according to the direction of the wind. If favorable, take the west (Bahia La Paz) side because of the numerous coves and baylets which extend to the southern tip of Isla Espiritu Santo. From there, good havens continue on along the Baja coast for 13 miles to the Pemex oil tanks, landmark and outer perimeter of inner Bahia La Paz. Small-boat operators should have U.S. Geodetic Chart No. 2103 to navigate this inner bay.

The inner bay between El Magote, which is a low sandy peninsula, and the approach to La Paz has a shallow center. The navigable troughs run close up to either side. Follow the Magote trough, which is poorly marked, to opposite the city pier. The better, inside depression is well marked from the Pemex pier. This 4-mile course follows very close to shore to within a half mile of the city pier. Then it angles out to deep water around it and on back into the back bay, called Ensenada Los Aripes. There is a small-boat dock on the inside of the La Paz pier and another at the Hotel Los Cocos pier. All supplies, machine shops, and big-port facilities are available in La Paz.

■ Hop No. 5 (78 miles): La Paz, via Punta Coyote, Isla Cerralvo, Bahia Los Muertos, Punta Pescadero, to Rancho Buena Vista

The small-craft sailor venturing down beyond Bahia La Paz, especially below Punta Coyote, should remember that coves and lees are far apart and that there is practically no protection against north winds short of the south end of Isla Cerralvo and at Punta de Los Muertos, where there is a good harbor with coves protected from all directions. Punta Pescadero shields against north winds; and at Rancho Buena Vista small craft up to 30 feet can easily be taken ashore if winds become violent. All supplies and facilities are available at Buena Vista.

Cruising on south of Rancho Buena Vista becomes increasingly hazardous. There is a lee from north winds below Punta Los Frailes, but there is no refuge from there to the Palmilla cove and Hotel Palmilla resort. The next is at Puerto Chilena, where the elegant Hotel Cabo San Lucas is located; the next, with a protected pier, is at Cabo San Lucas. The Hacienda Cabo San Lucas resort is situated nearby, and that is the end of the line for wise small-craft sailors.

The whole front below Punta Los Frailes and around the south end is subject to almost constant ocean shore breakers, making beaching very difficult, even for experienced sailors.

BIBLIOGRAPhy

BOOKS

Automobile Club of Southern California. *Log of Baja California*. 1962. Guidebook to Baja's main roads, resort information.

Baegert, Johann Jakob. *Observations in Lower California*. (Trans. by M. M. Brandenburg and C. L. Baumann.) University of California Press, Berkeley and Los Angeles, California, 1952. Descriptions and disillusions of a Jesuit missionary in Baja in 1751.

Bancroft, Hubert Howe. *History of California, Volume I*. The History Company, Publishers, San Francisco, 1886.

—— *History of Mexico, Volumes I and II*. The History Company, Publishers, San Francisco, 1886.

Blaisdell, Lowell L. *The Desert Revolution: Baja California, 1911*. University of Wisconsin Press, Madison, Wisconsin, 1962. Details 1911 military campaign in Baja California led by Magon, a Mexican anarchist, to overthrow Porfiro Diaz.

Blanco, Antonio de Fierro (Walter Nordhoff). *The Journey of the Flame*. Houghton Mifflin Co., Boston, 1955. Novel about early Baja California.

Castillo, Bernal Diaz del. *The Discovery and Conquest of Mexico*. Farrar, Straus, New York. A foot soldier with Cortez, Castillo wrote this account during his later life.

Chapman, Charles E. *A History of California, The Spanish Period*. The Macmillan Co., New York, 1921.

Clavigero, Francisco Javier. *The History of [Lower] California*. (Trans. by Sara E. Lake and A. A. Gray.) Stanford Press, Palo Alto, California, 1937.

Cleland, Robert Glass. *California Pageant: The Story of Four Centuries*. Alfred A. Knopf, New York, 1955.

Cortes, Hernan. *Letters of Cortes*. (Francis Augustus MacNutt, ed.) G. P. Putnam's Sons, New York, 1908.

Cowan, Robert Ernest and Robert Grannis Cowan. *Bibliography of the History of California, 1510–1930*, 3 volumes. John Henry Nash, San Francisco, 1933.

Crow, John. *Mexico Today*. Harper and Row, New York, 1957. Personal description of current trends in art, architecture, industry, education, agriculture, and politics, plus history.

Davidson, Winifred. *Where California Began*. McIntyre Publishing Co., San Diego, California, 1929.

Dunne, Peter Masten. *Black Robes in Lower California*. University of California Press, Berkeley and Los Angeles, California, 1952.

Eldredge, Zoeth Skinner, ed. *History of California, Volume I*. Century History Co., New York, ca. 1915.

Engelhardt, Zephyrin. *The Missions and Missionaries of California, Volume I*. Mission Santa Barbara, Santa Barbara, California, 1929. Covers the Jesuit, Franciscan, and Dominican mission period.

Gardner, Erle Stanley. *The Hidden Heart of Baja*. William Morrow and Co., New York, 1962. Baja description and travel, cave drawings.

——. *Hovering Over Baja*. William Morrow and Co., New York, 1961. Description and travel in Baja by helicopter.

——. *Hunting the Desert Whale*. William Morrow and Co., New York, 1960. Personal adventures investigating the breeding grounds of the gray whale.

Gerhard, Peter and Howard Gulick. *Lower California Guidebook*. Arthur H. Clark Co., Glendale, California, 1964. Guidebook, with detailed mileages of all Baja California roads.

Holmes, Brig. Gen. Maurice G., USMC, ret. *Spanish Nautical Explorations Along the Coast of the Californias*. University of Southern California, 1959. Thesis for PhD.

Krutch, Joseph Wood. *The Forgotten Peninsula: A Naturalist in Baja California*. William Morrow and Co., New York, 1961. Pictures Baja today.

Leopold, Aldo Starker. *Wildlife of Mexico*. University of California Press, Berkeley, California, 1959. Illustrated book on mammals and game fish, from the point of view of a zoologist and sportsman.

MacNutt, Francis Augustus. *Hernando Cortes and the Conquest of Mexico*. G. P. Putnam's Sons, New York, 1909.

Mardariaga, Salvador de. *Hernan Cortes: The Conqueror of Mexico*. The Macmillan Company, New York, 1941.

Martinez, Pablo L. *A History of Lower California*. Mexico, D.F., 1960. Available through Heinman Imported Books, New York. General history of Baja.

Mateo Manje, Juan. *Luz de Tierra Incognita, 1693–1701: The Journal of Captain Juan Mateo Manje*. (Trans. by Harry J. Karns.) Arizona Silhouettes, Tucson, Arizona, 1954. Diary of a captain who accompanied Father Kino on major explorations in the New World.

McHenry, J. Patrick. *A Short History of Mexico*. Doubleday and Co., Garden City, New York. Mexican history.

Miller, Max. *Land Where Time Stands Still*. Dodd, Mead and Co., New York, 1943. A 1400-mile travel record of a driving trip from San Diego to Baja's Cabo San Lucas.

Morrison, Roy F. *Trailering in Mexico*. Trail-R-Club of America, Beverly Hills, California, 1961. Formalities, tips, and adventures relating to trailering around Baja and the Mainland.

Murray, Spencer, *Cruising the Sea of Cortez*. Desert Southwest, Inc., Palm Desert, California, 1963. A personal narrative of a trip into the Cortez in a cabin cruiser; maps, charts, tables, photos.

National Auto Club. *About Baja California*. Guidebook.

Norman, James. *Terry's Guide to Mexico*. Doubleday and Co., Garden City, New York, 1965. Detailed guidebook.

Parkes, Henry Bamford. *A History of Mexico*. Houghton Mifflin Co., Boston, 1960.

Pesman, M. Walter. *Meet Flora Mexicana*. Dale S. King, Publisher, Globe, Arizona, 1962. Descriptions and drawings of Baja and Mainland plants.

Pourade, Richard F. *The History of San Diego, Volume I: The Explorers*. Union-Tribune Publishing Company, San Diego, California, 1960. Discovery of New World and California by first explorers.

Prescott, William H. *Conquest of Mexico* and *Conquest of Peru*. Modern Library, New York. History of conquest of Mexico and Peru by Cortez and Pizarro.

Rush, Philip S. *History of the Californias*. Philip S. Rush, San Diego, California, 1958.

Shreve, Forrest and Ira L. Wiggins. *Vegetation and Flora of the Sonoran Desert*, 2 volumes. Stanford University Press, Stanford, California, 1964. Plant life of Mexico's State of Sonora.

Steinbeck, John. *The Log from the Sea of Cortez*. Viking Press, New York, 1964. A narrative portion of the Sea of Cortez (now out of print), the report of the Steinbeck-Ricketts marine biology expedition in the Gulf of California.

...BOOKS

Sunset Books and Sunset Magazine Editors. *The California Missions*. Lane Magazine and Book Co., Menlo Park, California, 1964. A pictorial history of the California Missions.

——. *Mexico*. Lane Magazine and Book Co., Menlo Park, California, 1966.

Toor, Frances. *New Guide to Mexico Including Lower California*. Crown Publishers, Inc., New York (rev. ed. by Frederica Martin), 1965. Up-to-date guide; data on air travel, highways, hotels, restaurants, amusement, foods, fiestas, arts, markets, and customs.

——. *A Treasury of Mexican Folkways*. Crown Publishers, Inc., New York. Customs, myths, folklore, traditions, beliefs, fiestas, dances, and songs; illustrations and photographs.

Venegas, Miguel (and Andres Marcos Burriel). *Noticia de la California y de su Conquista temporal y espiritual hasta el tiempo presente. Sacada de la historia manuscrita, formada en Mexico ano de 1739 por el Padre Miguel Venegas de la Compania de Jesus; y de otras Noticias y Relaciones antiguas y modernas*. Madrid, 1757. Information on California and its secular and spiritual conquest taken from the historical manuscript of Father Miguel and other ancient and modern records.

Verissimo, Erico. *Mexico*. Orion Press, New York, 1960. Personal account of a Brazilian novelist.

Violette, Paul E. *Shelling in the Sea of Cortez*. Dale Stuart King, Publisher, Tucson, Arizona, 1964. Hunting shells on Cortez beaches.

JOURNALS, MAGAZINES, PAMPHLETS

Grafica de Mexico, Publishers. *Mexico This Month*, Atenas 42, Mexico, D.F.

Kroeber, Alfred L. "The Seri," *Southwest Museum Papers*, VI, Southwest Museum, Los Angeles, 1931.

Loftin, Grace, Publisher. *Mexico's West Coast Magazine*, 301 Sycamore Road, San Ysidro, California.

Massey, William C. "Tribes and Languages of Baja California," *Southwestern Journal of Anthropology*, V (Autumn, 1949), pp. 272–307.

——. "Brief Report on Archaeological Investigations in Baja California," *Southwestern Journal of Anthropology*, III (Winter, 1947), pp. 344–359.

McGee, W. J. "The Seri Indians," *Bureau of American Ethnology, Annual Report, 1895–1896*, No. 17, Washington, 1898.

Nelson, Edward N. "Lower California and Its Natural Resources," *Memoirs of the National Academy of Sciences*, XVI, Government Printing Office, Washington, D.C., 1921.

Ocaranza, Fernando. "Cronicas y Relaciones del Occidente de Mexico," *Biblioteca Historica Mexicana de Obras Ineditas*, V, Mexico City, 1937, I 113–123.

Roden, Gunnar I. "Oceanographic and Meteorological Aspects of the Gulf of California," *Pacific Science*, XII (1958), pp. 21–45.

Wagner, Henry Raup. *Baja California, Yearbook for Las Californias, Baja y Alta*, 301 Sycamore Road, San Ysidro, California.

——. "The Discovery of California," *The California Historical Society Quarterly*, I (1922), pp. 36–56.

Glossary

Throughout much of the Cortez, especially around the popular resort areas both in Baja and on the Mainland, English is spoken and understood. However, even in those areas where English is used, many Spanish words and expressions are still part of the regular vocabulary and do not change their form. Thus the language is somewhat of a mixture of both. The most common expressions that retain the Spanish are geographical terms, such as roca, estero, bahia.

A number of such words that are most likely to be encountered around the Cortez or on maps, and which are used frequently in this book, are listed below.

Agua: Water, stream
Amigo: Friend
Arpon: Harpoon
Arroyo: Wash
Bahia: Bay
Barranca: Gorge, cliff
Barrill: Barrel
Boca: Mouth
Cabeza: Head
Cabo: Cape
Cabra: Goat
Canal: Channel
Capitan: Captain
Cerro: Hill
Cerveza: Beer

Chubasco: Hurricane
Ciudad: City
Conquistador: Conqueror
Encantada: Enchanted
Ensenada: Cove
Escondido: Under cover
Estado de Baja California Norte: State of Northern Baja California
Estero: Estuary
Fiesta: Celebration
Fuerte: Fort
Gato: (bob)cat
Golfo: Gulf
Hacienda: Estate

Hombre: Man
Isla: Island
Javelina: Wild pig
Jefe: Mayor, chief
Laguna: Lagoon
Mar: Sea
Mestizo: Half-breed
Neustra Senora: Our lady
Occidental: Western
Piedra: Stone
Playa: Beach
Prieta: Dark
Pueblo: Town
Puerto: Port
Punta: Point

Rancho: Ranch
Refugio: Shelter
Rio: River
Roca: Rock
Santo: Saint
Sierra: Mountain
Simpatico: Agreeable
Sombrero: Hat
Territorio de sur de Baja of California: Territory Southern Baja California
Tierra: Land
Todos Santos: All Saints
Trabajo: Work, travail
Vaquero: Cowboy

acknowledgements

I am deeply indebted to Carla Laemmle, who, from the very beginning, joined in making this work a full-time job year in and year out. She called herself secretary, but her function was that of partner.

Much is owed to ichthyologist Dr. Boyd Walker, head of fisheries studies at the University of California, Los Angeles. He was my teacher, adviser, and co-worker on the scientific aspects of this volume, and my mentor before I started the Sea of Cortez explorations.

Enduring appreciation also goes to teacher - adviser, Dr. Carl L. Hubbs, Scripps Institute of Oceanography, foremost ichthyologist.

I am indebted to engineer William J. Burke for the great amount of time and concentration he gave translating my rough outline sketches into the fine regional maps, and to artist and marine biologist Mike Fahay of the U.S. Fish and Wildlife Service for his splendid drawings of the fishes and his efforts at reproducing the topography for the twelve regional maps.

I am deeply grateful to my early sponsors, Trans Mar de Cortez Airlines — its president Mayo Obregon, vice-president Luis Coppola, and public relations director Guillermo Escudero; to the more-recent Aeronaves de Mexico Airlines, their western regional manager Carlos M. Gutierrez; and also to travel agent Enrique Ortega. I am similarly grateful for the early and continuing support of resort operators Bud Parr, Rod Rodriguez, Eugene Walters, and his son Charles Walters, Bobby Van Wormer, Carlos Riva Palacio, Ed Tabor, Bill and Gloria Benziger, Luis Federico and Don Johnson, Bill Lloyd, Rafael T. Caballero, Roberto Balderrama, and the late Herb Tansey and Octavio Salazar. I also owe a debt of gratitude for the help of fleet operators: Rudy Valez, the Ruffo brothers, Bill Callahan, and Tom Jamison; and charter boat operators Charles Rucker and Andy Chersin.

I am greatly indebted to boat builder Mike Ryan of Gardena, California, for organizing, financing, and working with me on the four small-boat surveying and charting expeditions, and to the other small-craft owners who headed up my 32 other expeditions and voyages into the Cortez, most of whose names are mentioned elsewhere in the text; also to Mrs. Jerry Swenson for her detailed logs of Midriff expeditions, and to camper manufacturers Don and Everett Hamel.

Among the many scientists who happily gave advice and assistance are Dr. Kenneth S. Norris, University of California at Los Angeles; Dr. George Barlow, University of California at Berkeley; Dr. Lionel A. Walford and Dr. Elbert H. Ahlstrom, U.S. Fish and Wildlife Service; Dr. Julio Berdegue, Guaymas Marine Laboratory; Drs. John Isaacs, J. R. Curray, and Tj. van Andel, Scripps Institute of Oceanography; Dr. R. C. Miller, California Academy of Sciences; John Fitch, California Department of Fish and Game; and Dr. Raymond Gilmore, California Western University, Point Loma, California.

Then there is another list of people who contributed much in so many ways: publisher Burt Twilegar, Bob Jurgens, Dr. Sterling G. Pollock and his son Rick, Jose Andres Jiminez, Emmett F. Brooks, Martha Haggar, Grace Loftin, Howard Gulick, Peter Gerhard, and my brother, the late M. L. Cannon.

Ray Cannon

PHOTOGRAPHERS

WILLIAM APLIN: 42; 81 upper; 152 upper; 250 upper. MRS. KENNETH BECHTEL: 14; 15 upper, and center; 25 upper; 28; 128; 157; 163 upper. JESS BRAVO: 27. RAY CANNON: 37 upper; 59 upper; 89; 105 lower; 173; 185; 211 upper, and lower; 226. ANNETTA CARTER: 25 lower left, center, and right; 95 lower left, center, and right; 137 lower; 152 lower; 231 upper, center, and lower. CLYDE CHILDRESS: 70. GLENN CHRISTIANSEN: 80. RON CHURCH: 34; 45. FRANCES COLEBERD: 57; 149; 179 lower; 214; 233 upper, and lower; 244; 252 upper, and lower. DICK DAWSON: 93; 164; 234; 241; 243 upper, and lower. BILL EICHLER: 46. GERALD FRENCH: 73. MARTIN LITTON: 8; 37 lower; 38; 62; 75; 76 upper, and lower; 79 upper, and lower; 81 lower; 82; 99 upper; 109 upper, and lower; 110 upper, and lower; 111; 122; 127 lower; 129 upper, and lower; 130; 134; 158; 165 upper, and lower: 176; 178; 179 upper; 219; 242; 250 lower; 251. JACK McDOWELL: 141 upper, and lower; 142 upper, and lower; 143; 161; 168; 200 upper, and lower; 203; 207. HARRY MERRICK: 16 upper, and lower; 18; 22; 54; 90; 95 upper; 99 lower 101; 138; 140; 144; 150; 162 lower left, center, and right; 163 lower; 166 upper, and lower; 167 upper, and lower; 188; 192; 197; 198; 209 upper, and lower; 212 upper, and lower; 213 upper, and lower; 222. NATIONAL AERONAUTICS AND SPACE ADMINISTRATION: 230. ROBERT T. ORR: 41; 61 lower; MARION PATTERSON: 32 lower; 33 lower. RALPH POOLE: 31 lower; 60 lower; 61 upper; 102; 112 upper; 113 upper; 114; 127 upper. GERHARD P. SCHUMACHER: 112 lower; 113 lower. AL TETZLAFF: 39; 59 lower; 60 upper; 105 upper; 162 upper; 180; 190 upper, lower left, center, and right; 191 upper, and lower; 221. WESTERN WAYS: 31 upper; 32 upper; 33 upper; 58; 67; 86 upper, and lower; 96; 108; 137 upper; 224 upper and lower; 225. ROBERT WHITAKER: 104. LOUISE WERNER: 17. DONALD WOBBER: 15 lower; 48 upper, lower left, center, and right.

index